The Toolbox Bo

The Toolbox Book

Jim Tolpin

The Taunton Press

Cover: *Andy Rae's tool cabinet features dovetailed drawers (see pp. 96-97). Photo by John Hamel.*

Back cover: *Sanford Buchalter's tool chest (see p. 66). Photo by Jonathan Binzen.*

Front flap: *Sean O'Rourke's drawer box features unique handles (see p. 60).*

Back flap: *Inlay detail inside lid of Dowling chest (see p. 11). Photo courtesy of Birmingham Museum of Science and Industry, Birmingham, England.*

Taunton
BOOKS & VIDEOS
for fellow enthusiasts

Printed in the United States of America
10 9 8 7 6 5 4 3 2

The Toolbox Book was originally published in hardcover
©1995 by The Taunton Press, Inc.

The Taunton Press, Inc., 63 South Main Street, P.O. Box 5506
Newtown, CT 06470-5506
e-mail: tp@taunton.com

Distributed by Publishers Group West

Library of Congress Cataloging-in-Publication Data
Tolpin, Jim, 1947-
        The toolbox book / Jim Tolpin.
            p.   cm.
        Includes index.
        ISBN 1-56158-272-7
        1. Toolboxes.   2. Cabinetwork.   3. Woodworking tools.
        I. Title.
TT197.5.T65T65   1995   95-15048
684'.08 — dc20   CIP

I dedicate this book to the memory of my mother and father

Fanny and Alvin Tolpin

ACKNOWLEDGMENTS

This book owes its existence to the contributions of many talented craftspeople, museum curators, tool collectors and editors. Indeed, I could not have written it without their help. My thanks to them all.

TOOLBOX CONTRIBUTORS

Kit Africa, Stephen Alexander, Bill Baird, Joe Barbeau, Peter Bartell, David Bevan, Sanford Buchalter, Peter Cabot, William Clayton, Martha Collins, James Delsman, Frances Diemoz, Michael Doiron, Eric Englander, Reinhold Faeth, J. Fischer, Linden Frederick, Stephen Freund, Garrett Hack, Judith Hanson, Beth Ann Harrington, Michael Hayes, Jerry Hillenburg, Todd Hobday, Kevin Ireton, Tim Kimack, Tony Konovaloff, Steve Johnson, Leonard Langevin, Tom Law, Wayne Law, Bertram Levy, Adam Manes, Mark Nels, George Nesbitt, Inger Olsen, Jeff Olson, Sean O'Rourke, Mario Rubio Ospina, Sheldon Perry, J. Francis Pfrank, Charles Platt, Louis Plourd, David Powell, Ray Prince, Harold Purcell, Greg Radley, Andy Rae, Rodger Reid, Karen Robertson, Sam Robinson, Ellis Rowe, David Sellery, Tetsuo Shibata, Kevin Skurpski, Bill Slaby, Eric Smith, George Snyder, Stern Spirt, Tom Sulvalskas, Jane Swanson, Bill Tinney, Chris Wanlass, Doug Warren, Donald Wing, David Winter and William Tandy Young.

CONSULTANTS

David Baumer, the Mariner's Museum, Newport News, Virginia; Dave Borgatti; Dale Butterworth; Mike Dunbar; Merri Ferrell, The Museums at Stony Brook, Stony Brook, New York; Jay Gaynor, Colonial Williamsburg, Virginia; Steve Habersetzer; Jim Hoffman; Charles Landau, TimberCraft Homes, Port Townsend, Washington; Alexander Lebeaux; Norman Muller; Francis Natali; Debbie Padgett, Jamestown Settlement, Jamestown, Virginia; Emil Pollack, The Astragal Press, Mendham, New Jersey; Daniel Semel; David Shayt, The Smithsonian Institution, Washington, D.C.; Roger Smith; Phil Stanley; and Philip Walker.

AT THE TAUNTON PRESS

Helen Albert, Amy L. Bernard, Jim Chiavelli, Jodie Delohery, Ruth Dobsevage, Barbara Hudson, Kevin Ireton, Vincent Laurence, John Lively, Chuck Miller, Charley Robinson and Alec Waters.

I would also like to thank the photographer, Craig Wester, and the illustrator, Michael Gellatly, for their work in creating the graphics for the book. Special thanks to Audrey Jean for logistic support. And, of course, thanks once again to my indefatigable editor, Laura Tringali.

CONTENTS

INTRODUCTION

Well before the first colonists set their toolboxes down on the eastern shores of this vast "new" world, indigenous craftsmen of the Pacific Northwest were safeguarding their chisels, knives and gouges in cleverly made bentwood boxes. Eons before them, at the dawn of woodworking, people made, used and stored tools. Imagining myself seated at the hearth of an elderly ancestor, I watch as he gathers up his precious bone and obsidian cutting tools. With great care, he wraps each tool in a scrap of oiled sealskin and places it gently into an elegantly made satchel of hardened leather. As he turns the box-like bag in his hands, light from the cooking fire glistens off the intricate ornamentations formed from shells and teeth. As much a tool as the implements it contains, the satchel protects and organizes the fragile extensions of his gifted hands. And more: I imagine this primordial toolbox as a totem—a symbol of the ancient craftsman's stature as a creator of life-giving tools and weapons for his people.

Back to the present. I am invited to the shop of a fine furniture maker to see a desk she has made, yet my eye is drawn more to her exquisitely made standing tool cabinet. The cabinet is at once a thing of unabashed beauty and of ultimate practicality. Placed just a step

"There are many [tools] which a cabinetmaker soon collects... which take up room and need their proper places, and to provide them is a task which becomes a pleasure to a craftsman interested in his tools."

— from Modern Cabinet Work by Percy Wells and John Hooper (London: Batsford, 1909).

away from the vise end of her workbench, the hand-joined hardwood box with its bookmatched panel doors contains nearly all of her most commonly used bench tools. As she shows me how she made the high-style dovetails on one of the drawers, I find myself watching with growing fascination as one tool after another flows out from the cabinet, down to the work, and then back again to its resting place.

Suddenly I make a connection: Like the ornamented leather satchel of the Stone Age toolmaker, this furniture maker's toolbox is also a totem—a symbol of her commitment to a trade and an expression of the best of her art and skill. And I realize that the toolboxes that hold our tools are, like it or not, a highly visible testament to ourselves as woodworkers, a measure of the care and skill we instill in the objects that we create and offer to the world.

In writing this book I hope to pay homage to these containers that cradle our tools, and also to encourage you to build a toolbox of your own. The book begins with a look at tool chests from the golden years of the last two centuries, highlighting the cabinetmaker's tool chest. These chests richly document the highly evolved technical skill and artistry that flowed from the hands of master craftsmen. Following that is a gallery of tool chests built by the students of North Bennet Street School in Boston. The rest of the book explores contemporary toolboxes, both those designed for use in the shop (chapters 5, 6 and 7) and those meant to travel to the job site (chapters 9, 10, 11 and 12).

To help you choose the box best suited to your needs, there are discussions of fundamental design considerations for both types of boxes: in-shop tool storage in Chapter 4, and site boxes in Chapter 8. These more theoretical chapters will help you design your own tool-storage system by analyzing how and where your toolbox will be used and what tools to store in it. Knowing these things will allow you to develop the outside proportions and the layout of interior compartments and tool holders. There is also discussion of materials, joinery and finishing.

Perhaps you already have a mystical, irresistible desire to build your own toolbox (or should I say totem?). If not, here are some down-to-earth reasons for doing so. The first is that there are surprisingly few commercially made toolboxes for woodworkers—most ready-made boxes are designed to contain mechanic's and machinist's tools. The layout of the drawers and other compartments—and the fact that many of these boxes are made from metal (which is notoriously unfriendly to cutting tools)—makes them generally unsuitable for the woodworking trade.

The second reason for building your own toolbox is to gain the opportunity to design and construct a storage system that perfectly accommodates your specific tools and your own working situation. Finally, it's a pleasure to own a carefully planned, well-built toolbox where every tool has its own well-protected, easily accessible niche. In a box you make yourself, your hands know where to find each tool, and your eyes tell you in an instant if one is missing. A toolbox is the kind of project that makes you wonder not only why you waited so long to undertake it, but also how you ever got along without it.

Most of the projects and techniques described in the book are well within the reach of a woodworker familiar with basic woodshop skills. There is nothing particularly tricky, for example, in the building of my hanging wall cabinet (pp. 83-91), my rolling tool cart (pp. 114-123) or my toolbox for carving chisels (pp. 160-167). To be sure, some of the toolbox projects contributed by other professional woodworkers are considerably more complex. But illustrated step-by-step construction notes should ease you through some of the fussier procedures and specialized techniques. You may also be pleased to discover that many of the projects—especially the smaller ones—can be built from scrap stock, costing you next to nothing.

Consider the building of your own toolboxes as a challenge to push your skills. Use these projects as an opportunity to try out new joinery techniques, to work with woods you haven't touched before, and to apply previously untried finishes. At the worst, you'll end up with a good place to put your tools. But at the best, you'll have built for yourself an object of lasting pride, utility and beauty—a symbol of your joy in woodworking both for yourself and for those around you.

ABOUT YOUR SAFETY

Working wood is inherently dangerous. Using hand or power tools improperly or ignoring standard safety practices can lead to permanent injury or even death. Don't try to perform operations you learn about here (or elsewhere) unless you're certain they are safe for you. If something about an operation doesn't feel right, don't do it. Look for another way. We want you to enjoy the craft, so please keep safety foremost in your mind whenever you're in the shop.

1

TOOLBOXES AND THE
BUILDING OF A NATION

In the early 1600s, English adventurers and would-be colonists
sailed into the Chesapeake Bay area of the New World to settle what
would soon become Jamestown, Virginia. Even during the earliest
landings, it's a good bet that wooden boxes full of building tools were
among the first items to be set down upon these fresh, exciting
shores. (We know from the ship's manifests of some of these early
voyages that "tool boxes" were listed as cargo.) With the tools carried
within these boxes, the settlers would create one of the first
European toeholds in this vast, and largely unknown, continent.

Though it will never be known for sure what those first toolboxes
may have looked like, Jamestown's historians feel they probably were
similar to the ship's storage boxes found preserved on the *Mary Rose*,
a late 1500s British warship recently raised from its mud-encased
grave near Portsmouth, England. Though these boxes were simply

In Jamestown, ship's storage boxes like
this reproduction were probably pressed into
service as carpenter's tool chests. Photo
courtesy of Jamestown-Yorktown Foundation,
Williamsburg, Va.

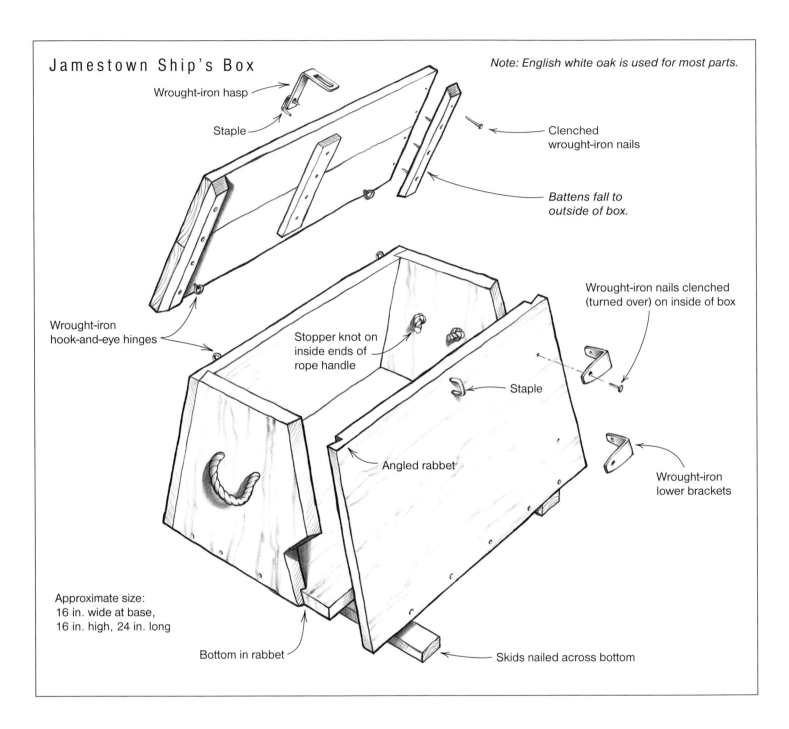

Jamestown Ship's Box

Note: English white oak is used for most parts.

Wrought-iron hasp

Staple

Clenched wrought-iron nails

Battens fall to outside of box.

Wrought-iron hook-and-eye hinges

Stopper knot on inside ends of rope handle

Wrought-iron nails clenched (turned over) on inside of box

Staple

Angled rabbet

Wrought-iron lower brackets

Approximate size:
16 in. wide at base,
16 in. high, 24 in. long

Bottom in rabbet

Skids nailed across bottom

and economically built of oak planks with a minimum of joinery, there is much cleverness in their design and construction. The end planks, for example, were locked in place by a full-length angled rabbet joint. In addition, the box's front and back were canted inward, forming a trapezoid, probably to allow the boxes to fit tightly up against the curved hull of the ship, thereby making the most of the limited cargo space. Another speculation is that the canted sides made the boxes more stable in shipment. The shape is inherently bottom-heavy, and it also tends to compact the contents toward the lowest regions of the box.

Carpenter's Boxes

While ship's-type boxes probably served the settlers well enough during their first years, by the mid- to late 1700s many carpenters had substituted a box modeled after the type of household chest used to contain blankets and other domestic goods. At the time, there were few roads and vehicles, and itinerant carpenters who had to carry their

Carpenter's Box of the Late 1700s

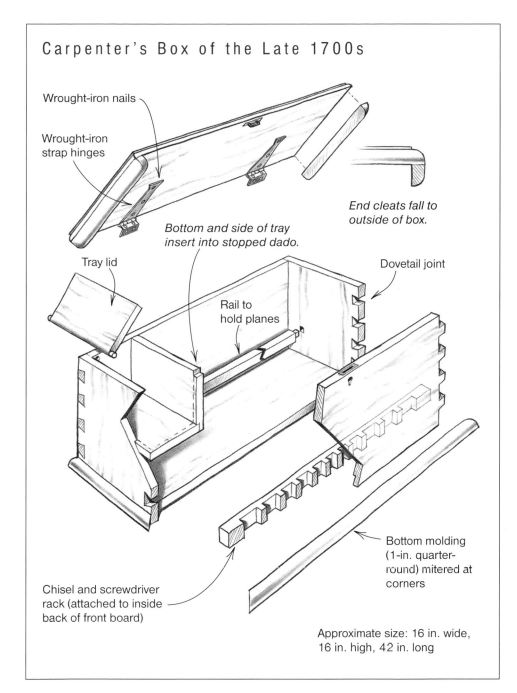

Wrought-iron nails

Wrought-iron strap hinges

End cleats fall to outside of box.

Tray lid

Bottom and side of tray insert into stopped dado.

Rail to hold planes

Dovetail joint

Chisel and screwdriver rack (attached to inside back of front board)

Bottom molding (1-in. quarter-round) mitered at corners

Approximate size: 16 in. wide, 16 in. high, 42 in. long

This toolbox, thought to be from Pepperell, Mass., is typical in size and construction of a colonial carpenter's box of the late 1700s. Photo courtesy of the New York State Historical Association and the Farmers' Museum, Inc., Cooperstown.

toolboxes on their shoulder or slung to one side from a leather strap had good reason to keep them as small and light as possible. When fitted out with notched tool perches and lidded trays, these boxes could hold an array of tools sufficient for a variety of tasks, from building a simple piece of furniture to cutting the timber-frame joints for an entire building. These chest-type boxes had greater storage area than the old ship's boxes with canted

sides, and they allowed easier access to the tools stored within.

Though these boxes were simply built and plain in appearance, they were not uncraftsmanlike in construction. The corners were usually dovetailed, and the interior tool braces were mortised into the end panels. The side and bottom of the tray compartment were often dadoed into the box's side walls. In some boxes, such as the one shown in the

photo above, the tray lid was cleverly hinged by extending rounded tenons into holes on either side of the box. Countless carpenters carried these rather crude but eminently practical toolboxes throughout the colonies, hammering together the foundation of their new nation.

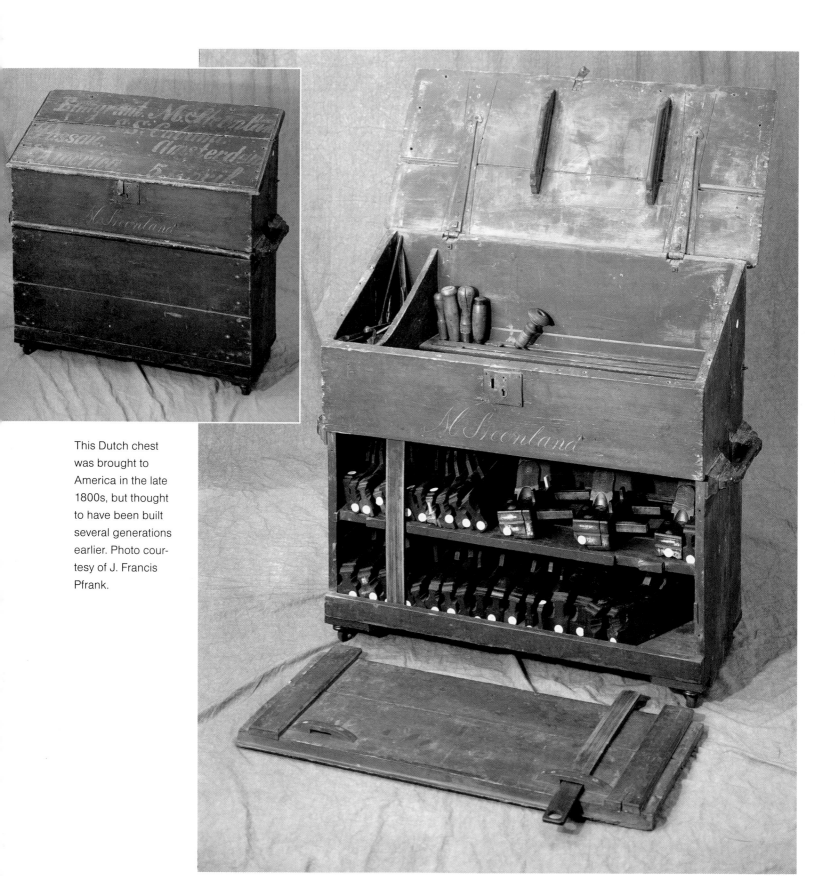

This Dutch chest was brought to America in the late 1800s, but thought to have been built several generations earlier. Photo courtesy of J. Francis Pfrank.

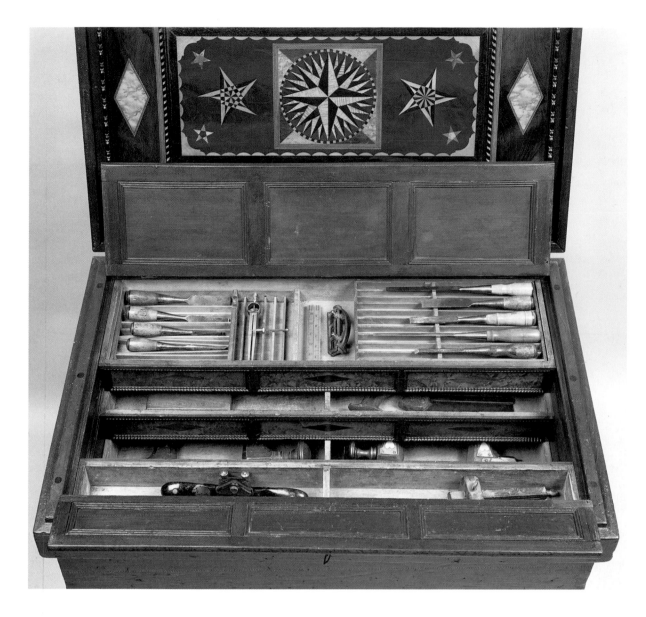

Enter the Golden Age: The Cabinetmaker's Chest

Eventually, many craftsmen settled down in and around the burgeoning townships and cities of the colonies. With the rapid expansion of the well-to-do merchant class came a market for specialized workmanship of the highest order. Woodworkers no longer had to be jacks-of-all-trades, and many tradesmen began to specialize in cabinetmaking: the building of fine English and European style furniture. By the mid-1700s,

increasing numbers of experienced cabinetmakers were emigrating from England and elsewhere to set up shops. Workmen offloading a heavy, trunk-like chest from the back of a wagon and trundling it into a new woodworking shop was a common sight along the bustling boardwalks.

Unlike the ship's boxes of the early woodworkers or the chests of the itinerant carpenters, the toolboxes of specialized cabinetmakers were so large and heavy that it took at least two men to carry them. Luckily, they weren't moved often. The toolbox normally sat next to the workbench, unless the craftsman

moved on to another shop. If he had to take some tools to a work site, he would generally place them in a bag or basket, looping the carry strap over an ax handle or a stick specifically cut and shaped for this purpose.

These stoutly built cabinetmaker's chests looked plain, hiding humbly under many coats of dark paint. Inside, however, there was often a glorious display of meticulously polished exotic woods, ivory knobs, inlays, stringing and highly figured veneers mimicking the most impressive and expensive furniture of this era. Unless the underside of the lid was used to store saws, tools were nowhere to be seen—you would need to pull open one of the many drawers or lift the lid of a tray to see what treasures might lie within.

Why were these toolboxes so large and heavy? Why were they built in the shape of a chest? And why did craftsmen go to such extraordinary lengths to make their chests masterpieces of woodworking?

The first question is relatively easy to answer: 18th-century cabinetmakers built big chests because they had a lot of tools to store. They had a lot of tools because they were being asked to build furniture featuring fine joinery, extensive inlay and stringing, exotic veneers and complex moldings. Which came first, the demand for a style or the tools needed to create it, is anyone's guess. But we do know that by the mid-1700s the tools needed to apply veneers, create inlays and run moldings were being mass-produced in numerous factories throughout England and Europe. Possessing a chest full of these tools was a sure sign that you were an up-to-date master craftsman who was capable of building the high-style furniture of the time.

But why did these skilled cabinetmakers build their toolboxes in the form of a humble chest instead of a chest-on-frame? With some minor modifications, these furniture pieces would have offered a great deal of highly efficient tool storage. Cost was definitely a factor. First, a low chest would have been considerably cheaper to build in labor and materials) than almost any other type of furniture offering equivalent volume. The cost of overseas shipping, which was figured on the volume of an object, not its weight, was also a consideration. To save money, 18th-century craftsmen had to fit their tools into the smallest amount of space possible, and not much beats an unadorned cube.

The low-chest configuration was also functional. This style of toolbox would fit easily under the end of a workbench yet still offer relatively easy access. (As long as you could open the lid, you could probably get at everything within the box.) By contrast, a box built in a vertical orientation would necessarily take up precious wall space and, in the invariably small, poorly lit shops of this era, might get in the way or block a window.

There may, however, be yet another explanation for the low-chest style: adherence to tradition. You built what your master taught you to build, which is what his master taught him to build, and so on back into antiquity. There were few books, and certainly no magazines, to spark fresh ideas.

It seems quite likely, then, that the cabinetmaker's chest was a direct descendant of the medieval coffer—a common, versatile piece of furniture found throughout Europe and the British Isles. While often used as a seat or table, the coffer also served another, perhaps more important, function: the safekeeping of valuable household goods. In the event of fire or attack (two rather common annoyances of those dark days), two people could easily hoist this furniture up and cart it away to safety. I surmise that the 18th-century craftsman learned early on in his apprenticeship the techniques of building a coffer. That being the case, it's not surprising that a cabinetmaker would house and protect his valuable collection of hand tools in a coffer-style chest.

One question still remains: Why did craftsmen lavish such fine artistry and technique upon their utilitarian toolboxes? One popular theory is that the building of a tool chest was a requirement of apprenticeship or a rite of passage to journeyman status. It might follow, then, that to dazzle the master and ensure passage, young apprentices would put all they had into the project.

Is this theory borne out by the facts? It's not clear. We do know from some 18th-century apprenticeship contracts that many apprentices received tools from their masters upon completion of indenture. It seems obvious that these young men would have been expected to provide a place to keep their tools. Indeed, the making of a chest would

A Typical European Coffer

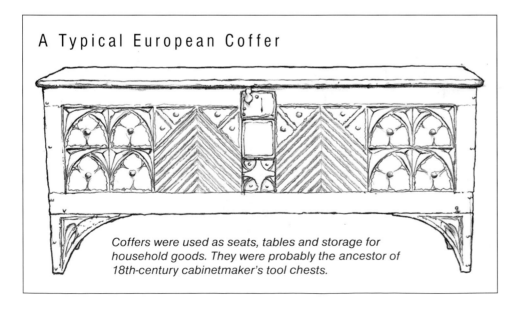

Coffers were used as seats, tables and storage for household goods. They were probably the ancestor of 18th-century cabinetmaker's tool chests.

In addition to intricate inlay work, some chests exhibit extensive banding and relief carving. This example appears in the interior of an early 19th-century American chest. Toolbox courtesy of Donald Wing; photo by Vincent Laurence.

have been an excellent and practical exercise. But there doesn't seem to be any hard evidence that there existed, at least in the New World, any formal rite of passage concerning the building of tool chests. In fact, the institution of the apprenticeship itself was a far more informal affair in the colonies than it was in Europe.

It seems more likely that masterpiece-quality tool chests were the products of master craftsmen rather than some singular expression of youthful exuberance. And perhaps for these masters, their chests were not particularly extraordinary at all. Instead, these toolboxes simply represented the level of skill the craftsmen expected of themselves and were offering to the world. (If the work were only for show, you would not find—as I did under a loose piece of molding—exquisitely made dovetails hidden under overlying moldings or veneers.) This fine work was probably done in the spirit of pleasing oneself and one's comrades rather than in some vain attempt to impress the

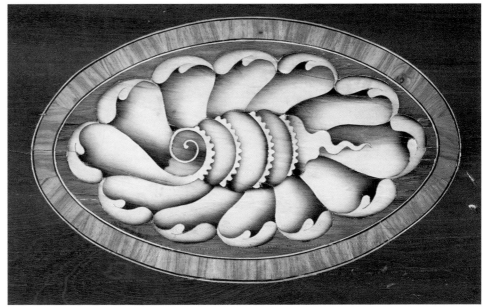

This inlay detail, typical of the work found in the finest period furniture, appears on the inside lid of the Dowling chest, an English toolbox built between 1780 and 1790. Photo courtesy of Birmingham Museum of Science and Industry, Birmingham, England.

world. It is also worth noting that a craftsman's tool chest may have been his most valuable asset, and perhaps the only piece of fine, high-style furniture he would ever own. Perhaps built largely from scraps saved from paying work and embellished over an extended time, this was magnificence that a craftsman of the 18th century could afford.

A Cabinetmaker's Chest

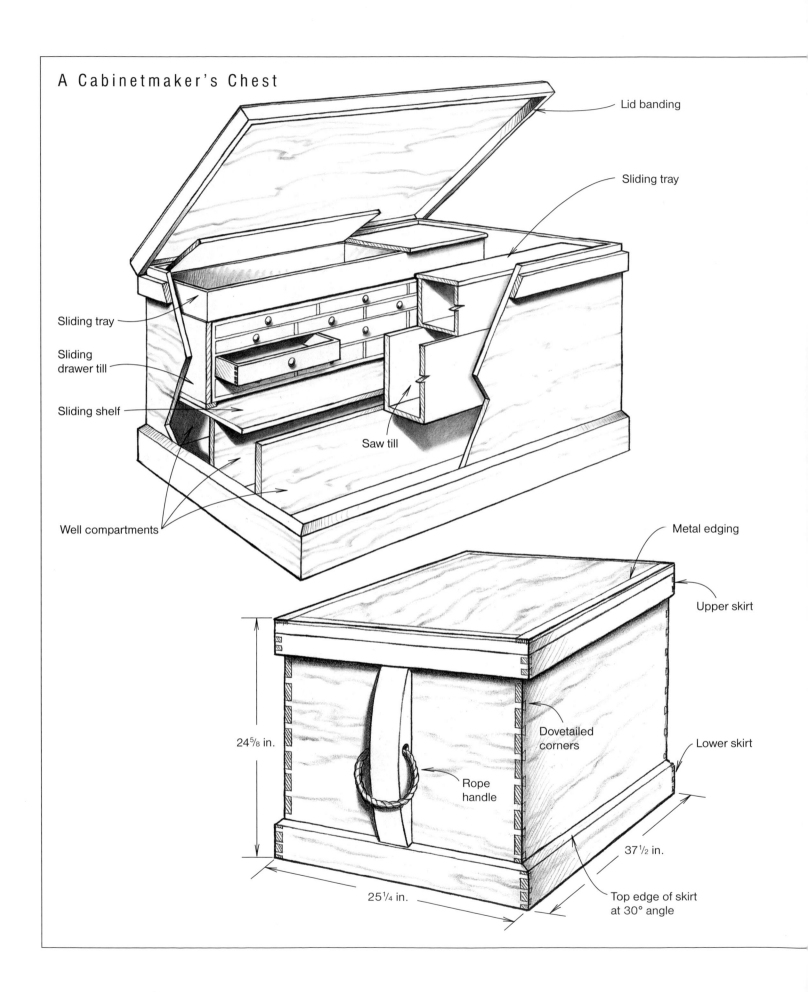

Lid banding

Sliding tray

Sliding tray

Sliding drawer till

Sliding shelf

Saw till

Well compartments

Metal edging

Upper skirt

Dovetailed corners

Lower skirt

Rope handle

24⅝ in.

37½ in.

25¼ in.

Top edge of skirt at 30° angle

CROSS SECTION FROM END

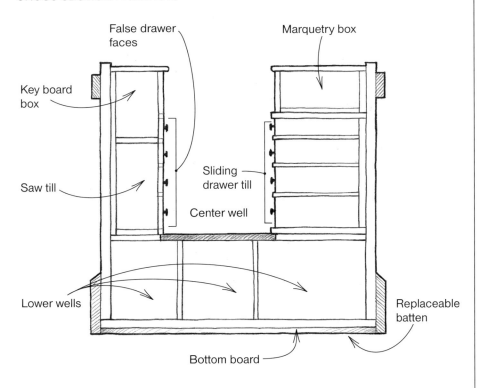

False drawer faces

Marquetry box

Key board box

Saw till

Sliding drawer till

Center well

Lower wells

Replaceable batten

Bottom board

CROSS SECTION OF SLIDING DRAWER TILL

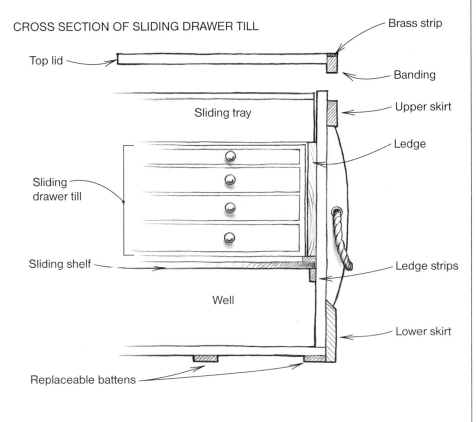

Brass strip

Top lid

Banding

Sliding tray

Upper skirt

Ledge

Sliding drawer till

Sliding shelf

Ledge strips

Well

Lower skirt

Replaceable battens

DESIGN AND CONSTRUCTION OF A CABINETMAKER'S CHEST

Aware of the weight these fully loaded boxes would have to support and of the abuse they would suffer during shipment, the craftsmen who built these tool chests did so with sturdiness foremost in mind. Choosing knot- and defect-free pine boards a full 1 in. thick for the box sides, they joined the planks at the corners with closely spaced (usually less than 1½ in. apart), tight-fitting through dovetails—an exceptionally strong joint for this application. In many boxes, the sides were made from a full-width plank, eliminating the need to join up boards to sufficient width. Single-plank construction also eliminated the potential weak spot created at the juncture of two boards.

It is interesting to note how universal the overall dimensions of these chests appear to be. After measuring perhaps a dozen chests (and noting that the English-made chests were generally a bit larger than the American ones), I found that when averaging the dimensions I came up with a rectangular box measuring approximately 2 ft. wide by 2 ft. high by 3 ft. long. Many of the chests are proportioned according to the rules of the classic golden rectangle, wherein the short side of the rectangle is five-eighths the size of the long.

Like the sides, the tool-chest bottom was also made from 1-in. pine, but instead of using a single-width plank (which could shrink and pull loose from the nails), many cabinetmakers chose to tongue and groove the edges and to run the boards from the front to the back of the box. Though these floor boards were simply nailed to the bottom edge of each

Upper-Skirt Dust Shield

CROSS SECTION AT SIDE

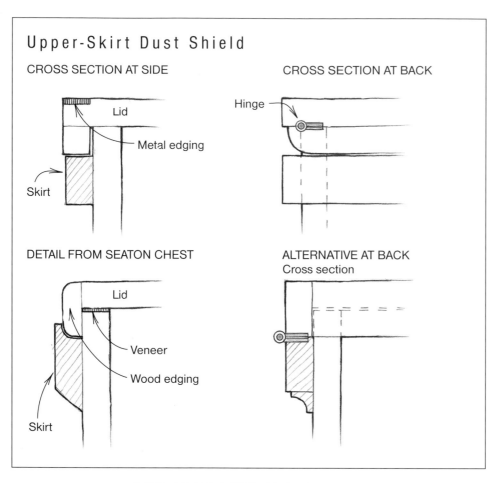

Lid

Metal edging

Skirt

CROSS SECTION AT BACK

Hinge

DETAIL FROM SEATON CHEST

Lid

Veneer

Wood edging

Skirt

ALTERNATIVE AT BACK
Cross section

In this chest, the pins of the skirt board's dovetails oppose the direction of the dovetails on the box sides. A brass rub rail inlaid along the outside edge of the top skirt board protects the edge from damage. Chest courtesy of Leonard Langevin; photo by Vincent Laurence.

case side, they were secured a second time along their edges with nails through the skirting boards.

These skirting boards were made from clear lengths of hardwood (usually oak), and were generally joined at the corners with dovetails. In some instances, as in the photo above, the pins were oriented opposite to those on the case, ensuring that the case joints, should they loosen, would be locked in place by the skirting joints. The bottom skirting not only helped support the floor boards of the box by providing nailing, but also offered abrasion protection as well. Set slightly below the edge of the floor boards, the skirts helped prevent rot by keeping the floor boards off the shop floor. Expendable stretchers (and in some cases a removable covering of thin tongue-and-grooved boards) filled the raised space to support the weight of the tools.

Rule-Joint Hinge Edge

DETAIL FROM DOWLING CHEST

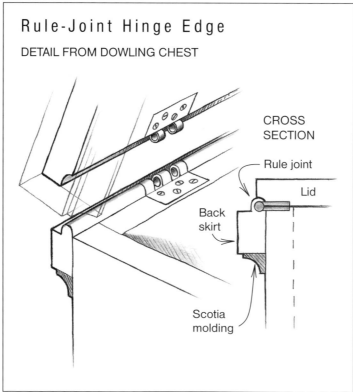

CROSS
SECTION

Rule joint

Lid

Back
skirt

Scotia
molding

The upper skirt board served two functions. First, it helped to lock the open top of the case together and to keep it from racking. And second, the skirt, in conjunction with a strip of wood run around the underside of the lid, formed an effective dust shield. An interesting variation of a top skirting along the hinge side of a box is shown in the bottom drawing on the facing page. Seen occasionally in English chests (including the well-known Dowling chest), the top edge of the skirt has been planed to form a rule joint with the back edge of the lid. This created a highly effective seal, and it also reportedly functioned as a burglar alarm as well. If you purposely did not wax this joint, it would make a piercing squeak each time you lifted the lid—an alarm as effective as hanging bells under the lid (another trick reportedly employed in other English chests).

Most cabinetmakers constructed the lid from a single plank, mortising the ends into a crosspiece to help keep the lid flat and to reduce end splitting. (A lid made from several planks was usually joined with splines and hide glue.) To allow the plank to shrink and expand, some craftsmen cut the tenons toward the outside edges of the lid narrower than their mortises.

Because the edge of the lid protrudes past the rest of the box, it is subject to a certain amount of abuse. The builder of the chest shown in the drawings on pgs. 12 and 13 inlaid a strip of brass bar stock around the outside edges of the lid to absorb the wear and tear that would otherwise destroy the wood. Some other ways builders found to add metal protection are shown in the drawing above right.

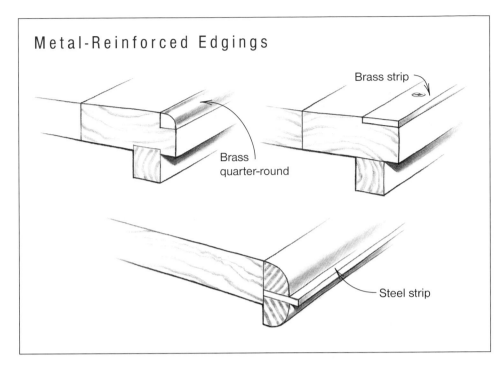

Metal-Reinforced Edgings

Brass strip

Brass quarter-round

Steel strip

The campaign-style lift handles for this chest were hand-forged by the builder, possibly while working on board a whaling ship. The photo clearly shows one drawback of a metal lift handle: The attachment bolts, having passed through the same grain line in the wood, have caused the wood to split in this area. Chest courtesy of Leonard Langevin; photo by Vincent Laurence.

This chest was built by Duncan Phyfe, one of this country's premier cabinetmakers, in the early 1800s. The chest, of pine with interior fittings faced in Santo Domingo mahogany, features a large sliding till containing 16 finely dovetailed drawers. Note the saw till mounted under the lid, an unusual feature for American-built chests.

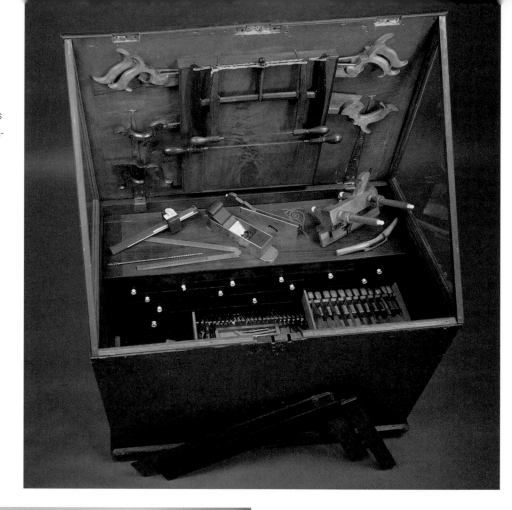

Built by a ship's carpenter in the middle of the 19th century, this chest is unusual in that the saw till acts as a second lid. Though this arrangement adds considerable weight, the saws are safely enclosed behind a drop-down front. Chest courtesy of Leonard Langevin; photo by Vincent Laurence.

To lift the chest, most builders provided some form of handle. Some English chests used a rope passed through a hole in a block attached to each side of the box and spliced into a loop. Several chests have come to light in which the rope was made long enough to reach over the top of the box, perhaps so that two people could lift the box by passing a stout stick through the two loops. Knowing how much 18th-century woodworkers treasured their tools, though, I doubt they would entrust them to a stick, however stout. My guess is that the length of the rope kept the craftsman's knuckles from swinging into the side of the box when tilting it up into a conveyance or carrying it upstairs.

Boxes made in the latter part of the 18th century often were fitted with metal handles. Some were "campaign" style, that is, recessed into their escutcheons (see the photo on p. 15). Though certainly more expensive than a rope handle and perhaps a little less comfortable under load, they were less liable to break.

Trays and tills

Of particular interest in the design and construction of these low tool chests is the use of trays and tills. To make the most use of the space within, cabinetmakers created storage units of stacked trays or a till of drawers that slid back and forth on rails over a divided well at the bottom of the box. This well was usually built deep enough to store molding planes on edge—maximizing the number of planes that could be accommodated and making it easy to see their profiles.

Another till might contain saws and other large tools, such as a layout square. To access this till, you would either lift it out of the box entirely, or open a lid at the top and reach into it from above. The top drawing at right shows an unusual saw till, which was found in a box in the collection of James Delsman, of Ashland, Oregon; here the saws are slid into a rack that pivots out of the lift-out till. Sometimes, as on the Duncan Phyfe chest, shown in the bottom drawing at right, the saw till is not located in the box at all but is instead fixed to the underside of the lid.

In yet another variation, the saw till might form an entire second lid for the chest. The example shown in the bottom photo on the facing page was built by C. A. Pierce, a ship's carpenter sailing out of New Bedford, Massachusetts. According to his grandchildren, Pierce built this chest while on a four-year whaling expedition to the Indian Ocean

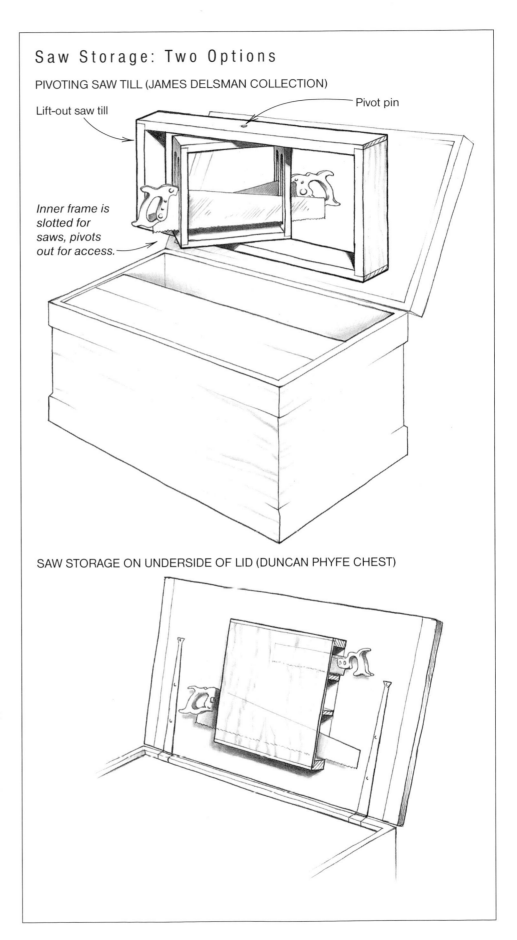

Saw Storage: Two Options

PIVOTING SAW TILL (JAMES DELSMAN COLLECTION)

Lift-out saw till

Pivot pin

Inner frame is slotted for saws, pivots out for access.

SAW STORAGE ON UNDERSIDE OF LID (DUNCAN PHYFE CHEST)

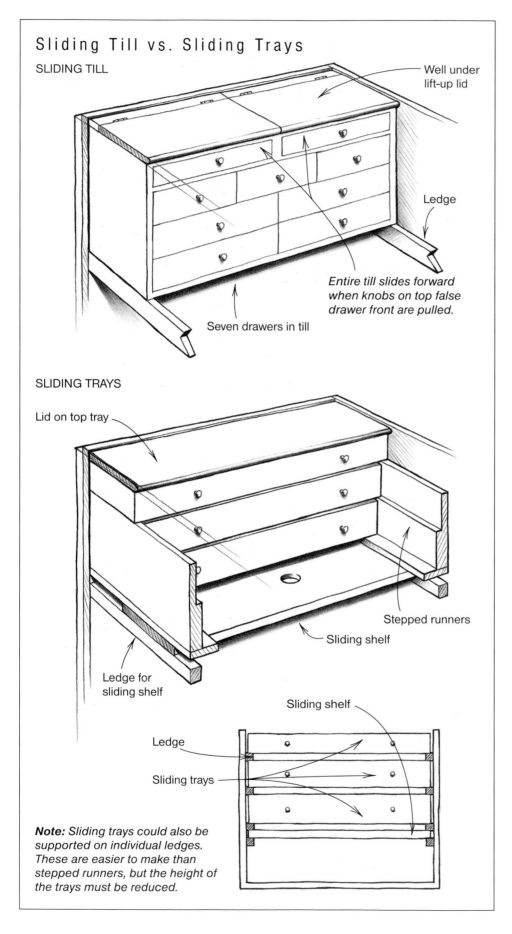

Sliding Till vs. Sliding Trays

SLIDING TILL

Well under lift-up lid

Ledge

Entire till slides forward when knobs on top false drawer front are pulled.

Seven drawers in till

SLIDING TRAYS

Lid on top tray

Stepped runners

Sliding shelf

Ledge for sliding shelf

Sliding shelf

Ledge

Sliding trays

Note: *Sliding trays could also be supported on individual ledges. These are easier to make than stepped runners, but the height of the trays must be reduced.*

on board the *Kensington*, not an impossibility considering the time a carpenter might have on his hands on such an extended journey. The hand-forged handles might have been made in the ship's on-board forge.

With the careful execution of this basic interior layout, it was possible for cabinetmakers to reach many tools within the box without having to remove another tool or storage unit. Often, however, it might take two hand movements—one to slide a drawer out of a till and a second to extract the tool. To get at a tool in the bottommost well, you would slide over the entire till and then reach down into the exposed well. If, however, the box featured a bank of sliding trays (rather than a single till of drawers), you would have to slide over each individual tray to get to the underlying well compartment.

Because ease of movement of the tills is crucial to the efficient use of the chest, the ledges were kept well waxed with a candle stub. On the Duncan Phyfe tool chest, a $1/16$-in. thick steel strip tacked to the top of the ledge prevents wear and adds slickness. A chest that I saw in the private collection of Donald Wing, of Marion, Massachusetts, has strips of whale baleen on the ledges, probably for the same reasons. There have even been reports of chests with miniature casters fitted to the bottoms of the sliding tills. Some obviously slid so well that the builder felt the need to add sliding bolts to prevent them from moving during shipping (see the photo on p. 21). Most cabinetmakers did not resort to this strategy. Instead, they would temporarily fill the open well with loose items like work aprons and tools wrapped in cloth.

It was astonishing how many tools these cabinetmaker's chests could hold. Some had inventories of nearly 400 tools—there are over 61 planes alone in the Duncan Phyfe chest. And most of

Ease of Access: Trays vs. Till

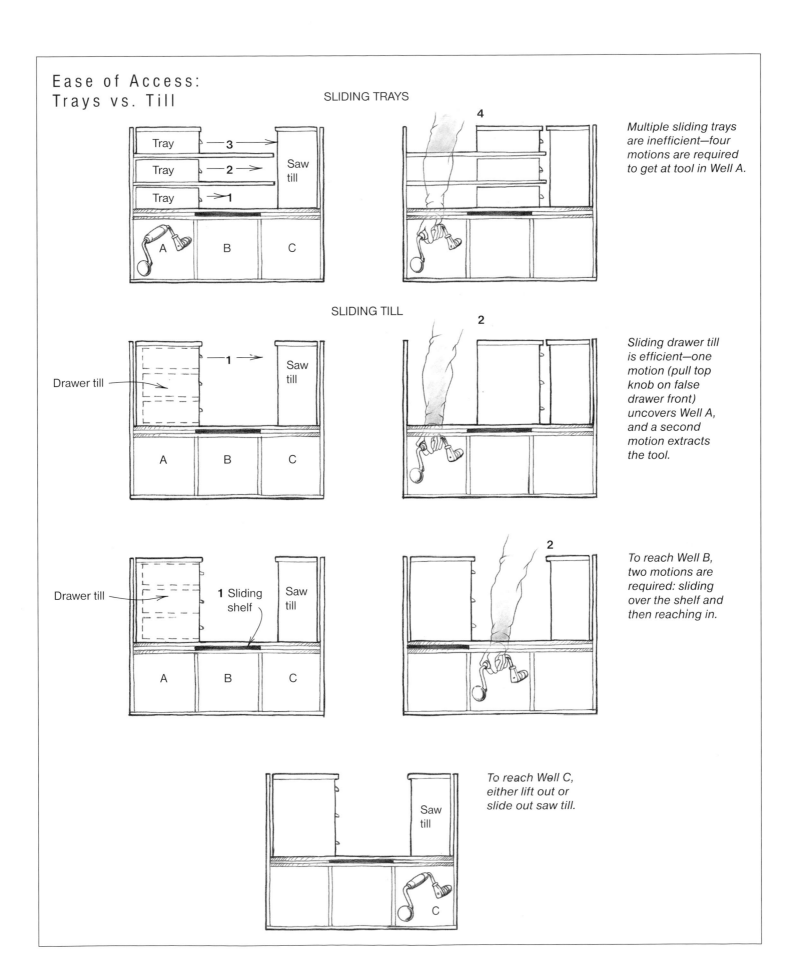

SLIDING TRAYS

Tray — 3 →
Tray → 2 →
Tray → 1
Saw till

A   B   C

4

Multiple sliding trays are inefficient—four motions are required to get at tool in Well A.

SLIDING TILL

Drawer till
— 1 →
Saw till

A   B   C

2

Sliding drawer till is efficient—one motion (pull top knob on false drawer front) uncovers Well A, and a second motion extracts the tool.

Drawer till
1 Sliding shelf
Saw till

A   B   C

2

To reach Well B, two motions are required: sliding over the shelf and then reaching in.

Saw till

C

To reach Well C, either lift out or slide out saw till.

While we know quite a bit about how cabinetmaker's chests were built, we know very little about how they were used on a daily basis. To a modern woodworker (myself included), the chests look clunky. Having to crouch down and grope about in a deep, dark box, sliding the tills and drawers to and fro to get at a single tool, seems awkward and time-consuming.

At first I speculated that at the start of each workday, the cabinetmaker would remove the tools he thought he would need for that day's tasks. To maximize efficiency, he would then either place them on his workbench or set them nearby on an open shelf. But after talking to several researchers and to one woodworker who has spent many years working out of a traditional chest, I came to a different conclusion. While it's possible that many tools may have been left out in a one-man or a small family-type shop (see the photo of the Dominy family's shop on p. 64), it seems more likely that most cabinetmakers worked out of their toolboxes on a tool-by-tool basis. Indeed, judging from the wear seen on the runners of many chests, the tills experienced a great deal of sliding back and forth.

A woodworker at the bench at Colonial Williamsbug. Photo courtesy of Jay Gaynor, Colonial Williamsburg.

To get a better feeling for how these toolboxes were used—which means understanding a toolbox-to-workbench relationship that essentially no longer exists—put yourself for a moment in the hobnailed shoes of an 18th-century cabinetmaker. As you take your first look around, you may be amazed at how small your workspace is, until you realize that it doesn't have to be large because there is no machinery. Because you are not using machines, you discover an entirely new relationship between the tools and the wood: Instead of having to carry lengths of wood around your shop to feed to the machines, you can bring the tools to the wood. And the wood generally sits clamped to your workbench while you size and shape it by hand.

As you work on the wood over the course of the day, you realize you rarely move very far from the bench—or from your toolbox, which is just a step or two away. Your hands, now familiar with your tool chest (not only did you make it, but you also use it constantly), can find any tool almost instantaneously. With this kind of efficiency, then, what need is there to clutter the bench with hand tools or to leave them lying where another cabinetmaker might mistakenly pick them up or accidentally knock them to the floor? Knowing the value and expense of hand tools, the 18th-century cabinetmaker probably kept them secure in his tool chest most of the time.

On this tool chest, sliding bolts keep the trays from opening when the chest is being transported. Toolbox courtesy of Donald Wing; photo by Vincent Laurence.

these tools had their own specific niche within the chest. With a little practice, the working craftsman could find any tool within his toolbox on the first try and usually without even looking.

The interior fittings for storing tools in such a well-organized way were made as light as possible—most of the till components were ⅜ in. or smaller in thickness and often made from pine—to maximize the amount of room left for tool storage and to minimize the weight of the chest itself. For beauty's sake, however, the faces of the drawers, tills and tray lids were faced with thin veneers of exotic furniture woods such as mahogany or walnut and were embellished with inlays and stringing of boxwood, holly, satinwood and ebony. The joinery of the drawers and trays was almost universally fine dovetails, even if it was permanently hidden from sight under a facing. (Showing off joinery is, it seems, a relatively modern phenomenon.)

The End of an Era

In the early 1800s, a group of workers in Leicestershire, England, gathered together under the leadership of a craftsman named Ned Ludd. The Luddites, as they were called, attempted to destroy the machines that threatened to put an end to hand-tool craftsmanship. Their noble, but woefully naive, campaign failed absolutely. Inexorably, machines began to transform the workplace, and the golden age of hand-built furniture drew to a close, not only in the Old World but here in the United States as well. Though fine hand-built furniture persisted late into the 19th century (as did the building of a number of traditional, ornate tool chests), by the Civil War the era of hand-tool craftsmanship was all but over. Cabinetmakers building fine furniture with hand tools alone couldn't compete in production or in price with factories fitted out with the latest in machine woodworking tools.

Probably with great reluctance, cabinetmakers and their offspring left their quiet shops behind to find work in the din of mechanized furniture factories. Because most of these shops supplied the basic tooling to size and shape the wood, many craftsmen probably also left behind their tool chests. Young woodworkers just entering the trade had little reason to build more than a rudimentary box in which to keep their personal tools at work.

By the turn of this century, in factory shops across this nation, the traditional, embellished cabinetmaker's tool chest was rarely seen by a craftsman's side. But the tradition didn't die entirely; patternmakers, coachwrights and piano builders continued to build their own wall-hung tool cabinets (see Chapter 5). Some, like that of patternmaker H. O. Studley, were magnificent.

Today, likely just in the nick of time, a widespread resurgence of interest in fine woodworking has brought the building of toolboxes back to life. The boxes shown in the balance of this book are the work of woodworkers all over the United States and represent a variety of solutions to the craftsman's age-old problem of storing tools. The quality of the workmanship is high, the designs eminently practical—a worthy continuation of the tradition.

2

TRADITIONAL-STYLE
TOOL CHESTS

If you are an ardent collector of hand woodworking tools, you probably already keep them in a traditional tool chest. If not, finding one is likely high up on your wish list. Unfortunately, chests in good condition and of an efficient design are not only hard to come by but expensive, too. But instead of discouraging you, let me offer a few words of encouragement: Building a traditional tool chest, while certainly time-consuming, is not that difficult an undertaking. Unless you intend to do fancy inlay or banding work (which you could always add later when you feel up to it), you need only be familiar with basic woodworking tools and skills.

Building a reproduction of any period piece is an engrossing and enjoyable experience. When I make a reproduction piece, as the object of another era begins to take form beneath my hands I sometimes have the sensation of reaching back into the hearts and

Tim Kimack's tool chest is modeled after traditional master cabinetmaker's chests of the early 19th century. Photo by Vincent Laurence.

minds of the craftsmen who first built the piece. This experience deepens as I slow down to shape the various parts using only hand tools—perhaps because it gives me the time I need to observe how the elements of the piece go together. Watching closely, I can see how the various components of the piece proportion themselves elegantly and harmoniously with one another. I admit, too, that I relish the epiphany that sometimes comes in doing reproduction work. I love that sudden gut understanding of why something was done in a certain way.

While for me these experiences are often reason enough to build a period piece, there is at least one strictly practical reason that might entice you to go to the trouble of building a traditional-style tool chest: Such a box offers you one of the most secure ways to keep and to transport a cherished set of hand tools. In size, shape, and construction, a traditional joiner's chest is ideally suited to this purpose. And even if you intend only to display your tools, a classic cabinetmaker's or machinist's chest offers you the most authentic manner in which to do so.

In the rest of this chapter, you'll see how five different woodworkers went about creating traditional-type toolboxes for themselves. None, however, is an exact copy of a surviving period piece. This means the boxes are reproductions not in the strict sense of the word, but in spirit. Just as the toolboxes of old were designed to suit their owners, these five examples have been designed with special fittings, unique interior layouts and original decorations to suit the needs and fancies of their makers. If you decide to make one of these boxes, you don't have to limit yourself to the exact design shown here. Don't be afraid to make your toolbox your own.

Tim Kimack's tool chest features extensive inlays, crotch walnut veneer and a sliding drawer till. Photo by Ray Fischer.

A Cabinetmaker's Chest Built with Hand Tools

Finish carpenter and furniture maker Tim Kimack, of Simi Valley, California, added to the challenge of building a typical early 19th-century master cabinetmaker's chest by using only hand tools to do so. Though he lost track of his hours after counting to 250, Kimack figured that he probably put at least 400 hours into the project. Why did he do it? Much of his inspiration came from the magnificent Studley tool chest (see the photo on p. 76); after viewing it, Kimack came away convinced that he had to own a similar box. Kimack also liked the idea of using his cherished collection of hand tools to craft elegant and secure storage for those tools. So, like the craftsmen of old, he accepted the challenge of building his own tool chest, and the result is shown in the photo on the facing page.

In designing his chest, Kimack stuck closely to the traditional layout of an early 19th-century cabinetmaker's chest: three wells in the bottom of the box, one each for bench, specialty and molding planes; a sliding till of seven drawers (constructed using half-blind dovetails) running on a ledge from the front to the back of the box; and a till for saws resting against the inside front. For an impressive decorative effect, he designed his own unique pattern of inlaid maple bandings and burl and crotch walnut veneers, and created a total of 18 false fronts on the sliding till faces. He finished this interior woodwork with many coats of hand-rubbed tung oil.

Like most builders of traditional cabinetmaker's chests, Kimack chose to use wide pine planks for the carcase, joining them at the corners with through dovetails around a bottom also made from pine planks. He made the top and bottom skirt boards of solid walnut, mitering them at the corners. However, unlike the skirting joints on most traditional chests, Kimack inserted mock dovetails across the miter—a decorative, yet secure, technique for ensuring a tight miter joint. Though this joint is rarely seen in period work (probably because its security depends so much on the strength of the glue holding the mock dovetail in place), it is easy to produce with hand tools. Modern glues ensure that it won't loosen over time. Kimack cut the mock dovetail with a handsaw and cleaned out the slot with a paring chisel. The sidebar on p. 26 shows how to make a mock-dovetail miter joint using a table-mounted router.

While Kimack painted the outside of the pine case with milk paint, he again deviated somewhat from tradition by varnishing the skirt boards. It seems he just couldn't bring himself to hide that beautiful walnut. He also lavished attention on the side handles, carving graceful chamfers in the blocks and hand-forging shapely handles.

Kimack's magnificent chest now houses his fine hand-tool collection and also offers a sample of his skills to potential clients. For himself, the chest is an unending source of pride and inspiration to do high-quality work.

Forged iron handles are set into sculpted walnut blocks on the sides of the chest. Photo by Ray Fischer.

ROUTING A MOCK-DOVETAIL MITER JOINT

The mock-dovetail miter joint is easily cut on a table-mounted router fitted with a dovetail-cutting bit and a shop-built sliding carriage that holds the assembled skirt boards securely at a 45° angle to the table. Begin by cutting the mitered ends of the skirt boards to their exact length. Assemble the four boards using glue and clamps. The addition of screws or nails is optional. If you choose to use fasteners, keep them out of the area where you will cut the slot. When the assembly is dry, take off the clamps and remove any glue residue.

Now adjust the depth of the router to cut the slot at the size you wish (the more the bit protrudes above the table, the larger the slot will be), and set the table's fence to guide the carriage at the desired inset. Clamp a piece of scrap with a mitered end into the carriage and make a test cut. Be careful to keep the carriage riding tight against the fence as you slide it along. Adjust the bit and fence until the slot is located where you want it. Again note that the deeper the cut, the larger (and more conspicuous) your mock dovetail will be.

When you are satisfied with the settings, set the skirt assembly against the carriage. Carefully align the mitered corner of the skirting to the bottom edge of the fixture and then secure it firmly in place with two hold-down clamps. Run the assembly through the bit, then lift the carriage away from the table. Unclamp, shift the skirting to the next corner and repeat the process.

After the slots are cut, make the four mock dovetails from a single length of stock. Cut the side angles to match the slots you have cut in the skirting. To ensure a tight joint, rip the stock oversize on the table saw and then hand-plane it to fit. Cut the length into four pieces (cut them oversize) and glue them into the slots. When the glue is dry, use a sharp paring chisel to trim the mock dovetails flush to the face of the skirt boards.

Mock-dovetail miter joints at skirt-board corners add a decorative touch when contrasting woods are used. Here, the mahogany dovetail contrasts nicely with the walnut skirting. Photo by Ray Fischer.

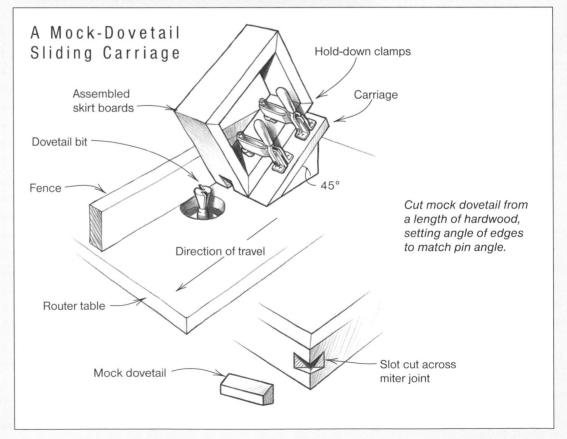

A Mock-Dovetail Sliding Carriage

Hold-down clamps

Assembled skirt boards

Carriage

Dovetail bit

Fence

45°

Direction of travel

Router table

Mock dovetail

Slot cut across miter joint

Cut mock dovetail from a length of hardwood, setting angle of edges to match pin angle.

A Shipwright's Chest Built to Fly

Having been accepted into a four-week boatbuilding class at the WoodenBoat School in Brooklin, Maine, Superior Court Judge Bill Tinney, of Tucson, Arizona, realized he would need to build a toolbox to carry his tools across the continent. After some research, he settled on a design of an 1820s shipwright's box whose plans were published by Roy Underhill of Colonial Williamsburg. Tinney then proceeded to modify the overall dimensions, not only to fit the tools he was required to bring to the boat school, but also to accommodate the baggage size limitations set by commercial airlines.

After some hesitation, Tinney decided to build the case sides and top, as well as the inside trays of the box, from a prize piece of 16-in. wide mahogany he'd been treasuring for years, even though it was a much fancier wood than the white pine used by the original maker. Tinney justified his choice by thinking of all the work he would be putting into the box and of how he would treasure its use over the years. Since it takes the same effort to build with cheap wood as with rare and beautiful wood, he figured, why not use the latter and enjoy it?

After observing how baggage is handled at airports, Tinney made another modification to the design: the addition of three steel reinforcing bolts across the grain of the tongue-and-groove beechwood floor. This reinforcement keeps the floor of the box from breaking through from the weight of the tools, no

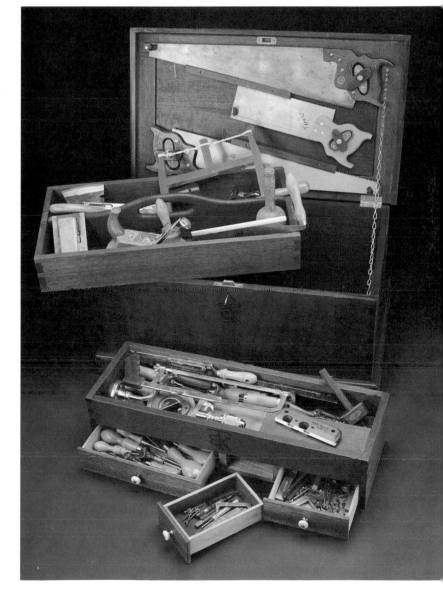

Bill Tinney's shipwright's chest was designed to contain boatbuilding tools. A raised frame-and-panel top prevents splitting (above). Other features include a tray with fold-down handle and a sliding three-drawer till (right). Photos by International Photographic Associates.

Reinforced Floor

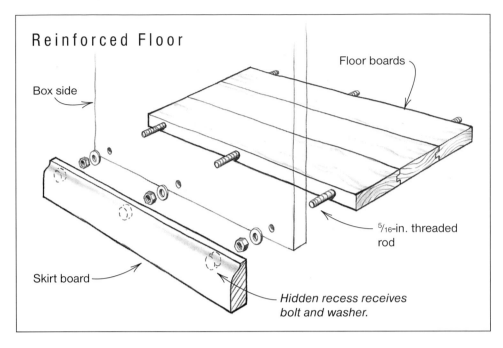

Box side

Floor boards

⁵⁄₁₆-in. threaded rod

Skirt board

Hidden recess receives bolt and washer.

Saw Retainer

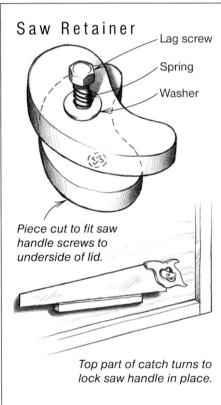

Lag screw

Spring

Washer

Piece cut to fit saw handle screws to underside of lid.

Top part of catch turns to lock saw handle in place.

matter how roughly the box is handled. As you can see in the drawing above, the ends of the bolts are covered by the lower skirt board. Tinney also designed his own spring-loaded saw retainers, shown in the drawing at left, to hold his assortment of handsaws to the underside of the lid.

Tinney designed the interior of the box not only to fit his particular assortment of tools, but also to suit how he would be using them at the boat school. First, he designed the well in the bottom of the box to be just deep enough to clear his planes. Then he covered the well with a tray featuring a fold-down handle that would allow the unit to convert quickly into a hand tote for carrying an assortment of tools. At the school he could haul this tote up into a boat under construction, then return the tray to the box at the end of each workday. A three-drawer sliding till fits between the tray and the top lid (clearing the saws). The till is narrow enough to slide back and forth in the box, allowing access to the hand planes in the well below.

Building a Masterpiece Tool Chest

When you understand that Tony Konovaloff, of Bellingham, Washington, once made a living building Shaker-type furniture entirely by hand, it is not too surprising to learn that he built a most impressive tool chest with hand tools only. The chest, shown in the photos on the facing page, is made primarily of black walnut and contains more than 400 tools—nearly all the tools of his trade. From the outside, Konovaloff's toolbox is similar in shape and size to a late 18th-century cabinetmaker's chest, but inside there are many significant alterations to the traditional design.

The most immediately obvious design deviation is the unusual orientation of the drawer tills—they slide across from side to side within the box rather than from front to back. Why this change? After working with a traditional layout for a few years (and hating it), Konovaloff decided that narrower tills would bind less than wider front-to-back tills, and that they would require only one hand to manipulate. He was tired of constantly having to withdraw tills entirely from the box to make them easier to access, and then balancing them precariously on the corner of the box or on his tool bench. After working with the new box for a few years now, he feels the change in orientation was a good idea. The side-to-side tills are definitely much easier to get into, and they tend to stay in the box where they belong.

In addition, these tills, which are smaller than was traditional, leave ample room for another innovation: lift-out sharpening and drill boxes (see the top photo on p. 30). To get at the tools stored in the bottom well, Konovoloff removes these boxes and reaches down between

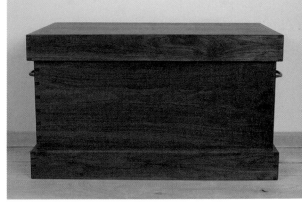

Tony Konovaloff's tool chest holds more than 400 tools and weighs close to 400 lb. when fully loaded. In the photo at left, the tills and boxes have been lifted out. Note the drill box (shown open at right). Photos by Vincent Laurence.

the sliding tills. The lift-out boxes are normally removed at the beginning of a typical workday and set next to the chest. At the end of they day, they're the last items to be returned to the box.

In yet another departure from traditional chests, Konovaloff created storage for many of his most frequently used tools independent of tills or trays. Because he was going to attempt to make his living working out of this tool chest, one of his prime design objectives when creating it was to make the tools as readily accessible as possible—a single hand motion was the goal.

Beneath the lift-out boxes, drawknives and spokeshaves hang on perches at one end wall of the box while several marking knives and a straightedge hang along the back board. (Also exposed on perches when the lift-out boxes are removed are a folding rule, a

framing square and the beam of a panel-marking gauge.) At the other end of the box Konovaloff placed a wide variety of chisels, their handles set upright and immediately accessible. Since the blades aren't visible, he has to rely on memory to grab the one he wants.

In a departure from tradition, the tills and boxes in this chest slide side to side, creating easy access to the bottom of the box. The Latin motto "Art endures, life is short" is a fitting testament to this lengthy, painstaking project. Photo by Vincent Laurence.

Like Tim Kimack, Tony Konovaloff stopped counting his construction hours after about the first 250—art to last the ages obviously takes time. But art won't happen at all until you take the first step, and for Konovaloff that meant laying out all the hand tools he used in furniture building to determine how big a chest he would need to contain them. In essence, Konovaloff designed his box from the inside out.

It is interesting, though not surprising, to note the size of the box Konovaloff wound up with: $21\frac{5}{8}$ in. wide by $39\frac{5}{8}$ in. long by $22\frac{5}{8}$ in. high—dimensions that are well within the range of a number of measured traditional cabinetmaker's chests (see the discussion on p. 13). To determine the footprint of the box (the width and length), he laid out the hand planes and other large tools that would be kept in the bottom well, nesting them closely to minimize the space they would take up. (He represented the dividers with masking tape.) The inside height of the front case had to be at least 16 in.— enough for the standard framing square that would hang against it.

Konovaloff had to take two things into consideration when he developed the size of the two sliding tills. The first was the size of the tools they would contain. The second was the amount of room he needed to leave between the opposing tills to allow him to lift his largest tool, a #7 jointer plane, out of the bottom well of the chest. Once he knew how much space he had to leave between the two tills, he designed the lift-out sharpening and drill boxes to fit. He was careful to leave room for the rack of chisels and the perches for the drawknife and spokeshaves. Finally, Konovaloff designed the size of individual drawers within the tills to contain certain groupings of tools.

Lift-out boxes (above) hold a variety of small hand tools; note the French-fitted tray at left. The hollow lid (right) stores 15 saws. Photos by Vincent Laurence.

Finally, take a look at the inside of the chest's hollow lid (see the photo above). While you occasionally see hollow, or even double, lids in traditional chests (see the bottom photo on p. 16), it is rare to see one that contains this number and variety of saws—there are 15 mounted here! To support the weight of this saw-studded lid, Konovaloff added a pair of sturdy hinged supports to the back of the box. While lid supports are undoubtedly a useful feature in any lidded box to prevent the hinges from pulling out or racking, it's surprising how rarely one sees them in traditional boxes. When you do they are often only in the form of a narrow ledge, which, because it acts as a fulcrum for the stress against the hinge, often does more harm than good.

Tony Konovaloff's Tool Chest

All chest parts are 3/4 in. thick except where noted. Drawer sides are 1/2 in. thick, and drawer bottoms are 3/8 in. thick. Size drawers to suit your needs.

Inside of chest, 18 1/2 in. by 18 1/8 in. by 36 1/2 in.

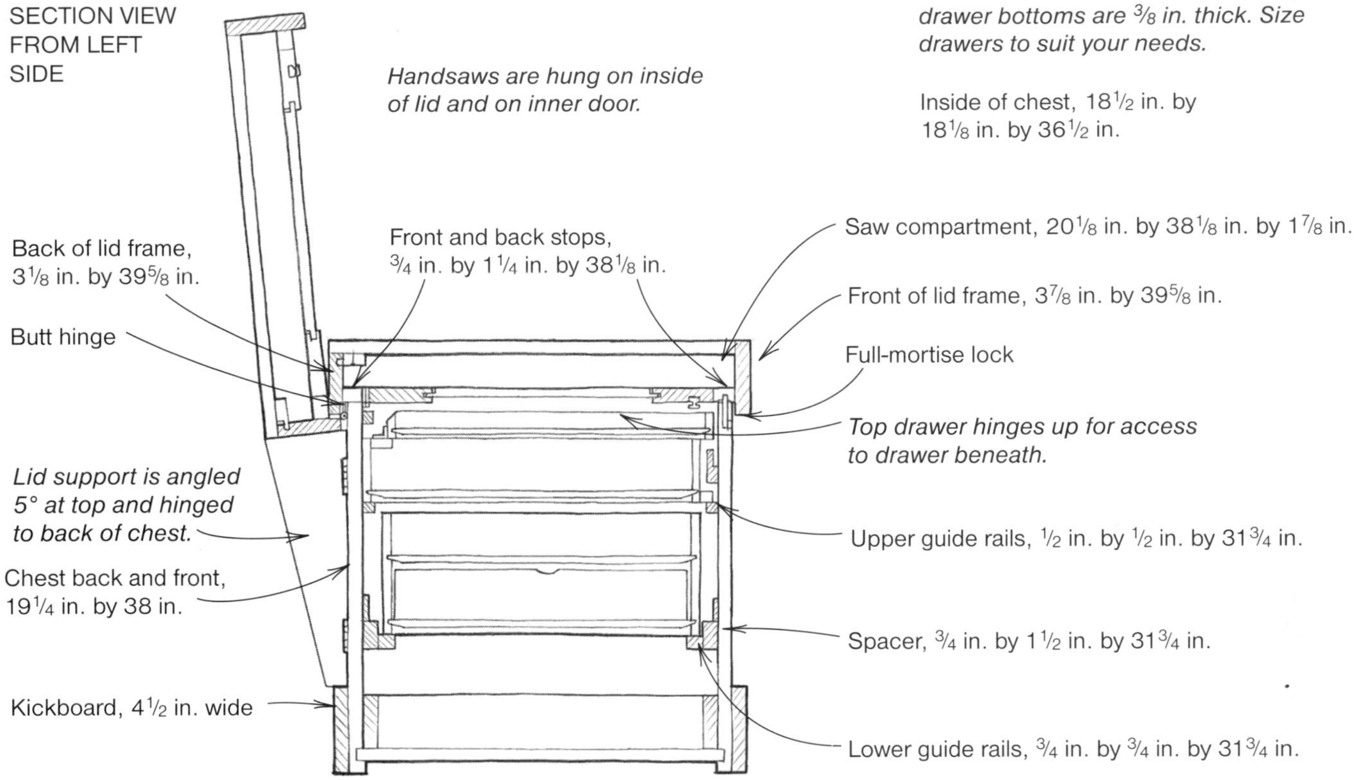
SECTION VIEW FROM LEFT SIDE
Handsaws are hung on inside of lid and on inner door.
Back of lid frame, 3 1/8 in. by 39 5/8 in.
Front and back stops, 3/4 in. by 1 1/4 in. by 38 1/8 in.
Saw compartment, 20 1/8 in. by 38 1/8 in. by 1 7/8 in.
Front of lid frame, 3 7/8 in. by 39 5/8 in.
Butt hinge
Full-mortise lock
Top drawer hinges up for access to drawer beneath.
Lid support is angled 5° at top and hinged to back of chest.
Upper guide rails, 1/2 in. by 1/2 in. by 31 3/4 in.
Chest back and front, 19 1/4 in. by 38 in.
Spacer, 3/4 in. by 1 1/2 in. by 31 3/4 in.
Kickboard, 4 1/2 in. wide
Lower guide rails, 3/4 in. by 3/4 in. by 31 3/4 in.

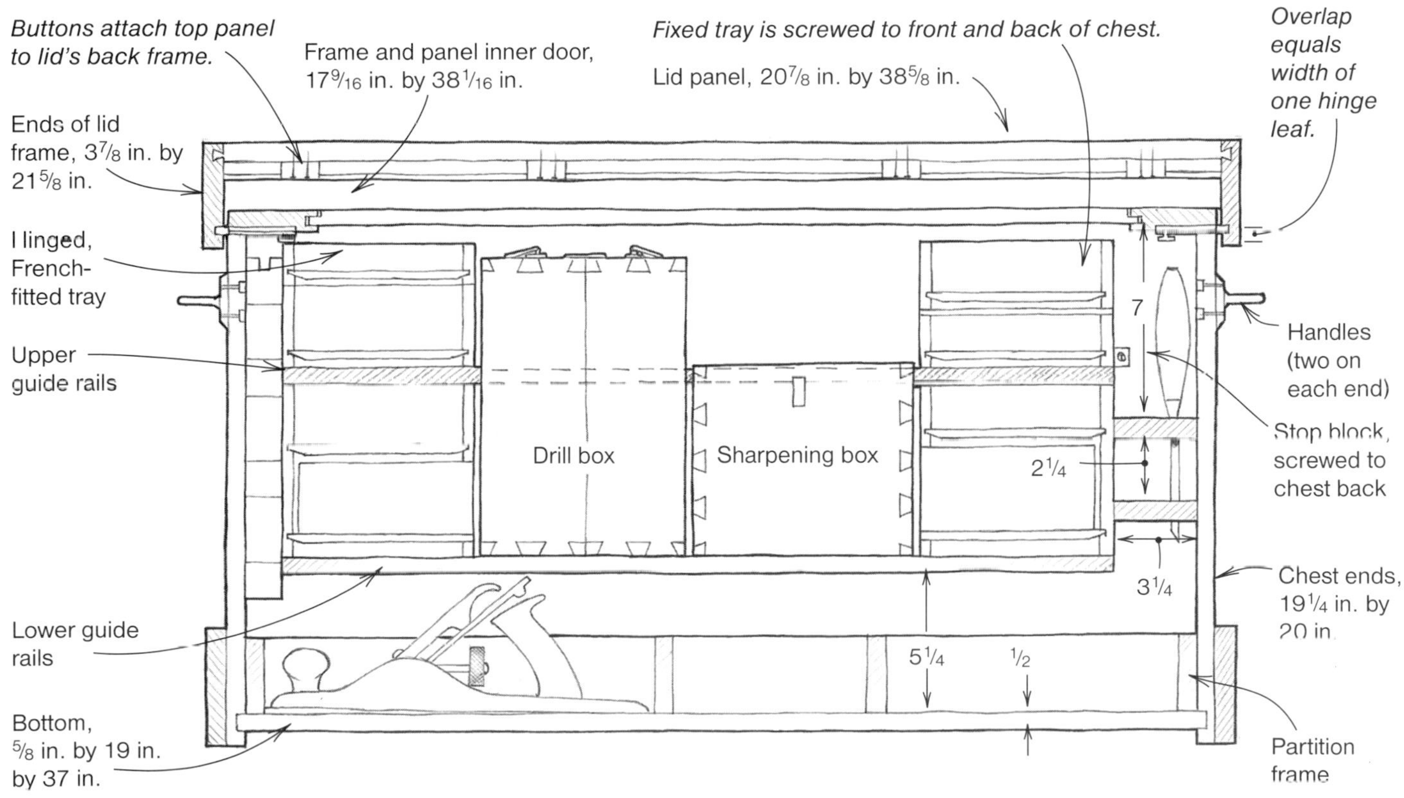
SECTION VIEW FROM FRONT
Buttons attach top panel to lid's back frame.
Frame and panel inner door, 17 9/16 in. by 38 1/16 in.
Fixed tray is screwed to front and back of chest.
Lid panel, 20 7/8 in. by 38 5/8 in.
Overlap equals width of one hinge leaf.
Ends of lid frame, 3 7/8 in. by 21 5/8 in.
Hinged, French-fitted tray
Upper guide rails
7
Handles (two on each end)
Drill box
Sharpening box
2 1/4
Stop block, screwed to chest back
3 1/4
Chest ends, 19 1/4 in. by 20 in.
Lower guide rails
5 1/4
1/2
Bottom, 5/8 in. by 19 in. by 37 in.
Partition frame

CONSTRUCTION PROCEDURES

Tony Konovaloff built his box exclusively with hand tools, following the old-fashioned procedure of cutting and fitting one piece at a time. When working with modern power tools, it's generally more efficient to cut out all the pieces at once, but with hand tools, there is no particular advantage to using production-style techniques to prepare or mill the wood. The instructions that follow assume that you will, like Konovaloff, build this box exclusively with hand tools. You may, of course, use power tools wherever you like.

Making up the case

After determining the overall size of the box and its interior fittings, sketch out various aspects of the box. When you are happy with the design, you can begin construction. Choose boards for the sides of the box and edge-glue them to width. Hand-plane them flat with a scrub plane and then finish the board's surfaces with a smoothing plane. Next, plow grooves (with a combination plane) near the base of the side and end boards to accept the bottom panel. To bring both visual and physical lightness to the box, you can make this panel up of several edge-joined boards of light-colored alder.

The next step is cutting the through-dovetail corner joints. Cut the tails first, and trace them to mark out the pins. Trim the pins to fit between the tails with rasps followed by files, then dry-fit the sides together around the bottom panel. When you are happy with the fit, reassemble the box, this time using glue in the corner joints and in the middle area of the bottom panel (so it can shrink and expand in its slot from either end). Insert notched cauls under the clamp pads to hold the dovetail joints tight—see the drawing above. Check diagonal measurements to ensure that the chest is absolutely square before setting it aside to dry.

Remove the case clamps once the glue has set and then cut the bottom skirt boards to width and thickness. Cut the end pieces to length and make the pins. Attach these pieces to the box by driving in screws from the interior of the box. Working in this order will help you accurately lay out the tails on the front and back skirt boards and will ensure that these pieces will fit tightly to the case after you cut these joints. Now cut the tails and install the skirts to the case, also screwing them in place from the inside of the box.

Making and installing the drawer tills and other storage fittings

Begin work on the chest interior with the bottom well—a 3-in. high framework of dadoed partitions sized to fit precisely within the box. Then make up and install the array of hangers designed to hold various tools. Finally, build the four drawer tills, the two open trays and the two removable boxes. Construct these all in similar fashion: hand-dovetailed sides joined around a beveled board inserted into a plowed groove. To support the tills in the case, screw guide rails into the front and back of the case. Note that the top tray on the right is fixed permanently into the box and the top tray on the left is hinged to the

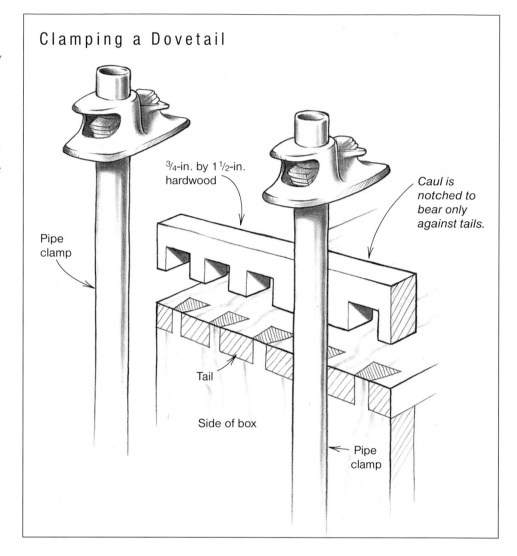

Clamping a Dovetail

¾-in. by 1½-in. hardwood

Caul is notched to bear only against tails.

Pipe clamp

Tail

Side of box

Pipe clamp

Cradling your tools in a French-fitted drawer or tray is an excellent way to show your love for them. The close-fitting compartments keep the tools from rolling about and damaging themselves and their neighbors. Even if the drawer is knocked about or tilted almost on end, the tools will stay safely in place. Best of all, French-fitting is not all that mysterious or hard to do.

Begin by cutting the tool board to size from a piece of clear 3/4-in. thick wood or hardwood plywood. In most cases, the width and length dimensions will be the inside diameter of the drawer box or tray banding. Lay out the tools you wish to carry in the board, drawing their outline with a pencil. Add a bit to allow for the lining material (1/16 in. for leather, a little less for felt). Draw in a notch for a finger pull near the balance point of the tool.

Drill starting holes for your jigsaw, coping saw or fretsaw, and cut to the inside of the outlines. If you can't get into tight corners with the sawblade, file or chisel to the line. If you intend to apply finish to the top surface of the tool board, do it now.

Now cut strips of lining material to the thickness of the tool board, adding about 1/8 in. for trimming. Apply contact cement to the inside perimeter of the tool outlines

French-Fitted Compartment

STEP 1: OUTLINE THE TOOL BOARD

Outline of tool plus a fraction for material lining

Notch for finger

3/4-in. wood or plywood tool board

STEP 2: CUT TO INSIDE OF OUTLINE

STEP 3: ADD THE LINING

Leather lining

Press lining tight into corners.

STEP 4: ADD THE SUBSTRATE

Screw on 1/4-in. plywood substrate.

Tool board

STEP 5: CREATE A DRAWER OR TRAY

Substrate

Dado substrate into side.

and to the material, and then glue it in place. Press the material into the tight corners (use the side of a file or nail set to apply pressure) as you work your way around the edge. Using a sharp razor blade, trim the material flush to the top and bottom surfaces of the board. If you are working with leather, bevel the top edge so it won't catch on the tool as you lift it in and out.

To cut the material to line the bottom of the tool compartment, trace its shape through the cutouts. You can also skip this step and apply the material to the entire face of the substrate.

Next, cut out the 1/4-in. plywood substrate. To use the substrate as a tongue into the surrounding banding or drawer box, let it protrude 3/16 in. to 1/4 in. all around.

Attach it to the tool board from below with screws (and glue if you chose not to surface it first with material). If you cut the bottom linings for each tool compartment to shape, glue these in place now.

Finally, cut the drawer box sides or the tray banding to size. Install them around the completed tool board. Now you can put your tools in their softly lined nests.

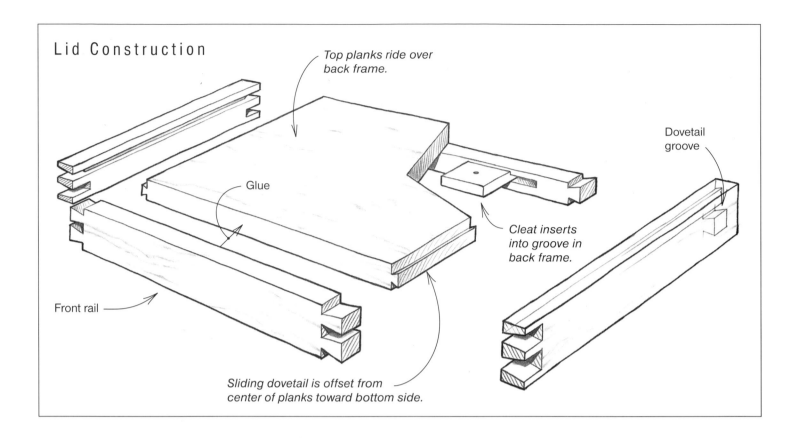

Lid Construction

Top planks ride over back frame.

Glue

Dovetail groove

Cleat inserts into groove in back frame.

Front rail

Sliding dovetail is offset from center of planks toward bottom side.

underlying sliding drawer till. The tools in the hinged tray don't fall out when the tray is tilted because they're held tightly in place in French-fitted recesses. This type of tray provides a felt- or leather-lined, close-fitting compartment for each tool. (For details on French-fitting, see the sidebar on p. 33.)

Making up the top lid

Build the top lid much like a drawer by dovetailing the box-like sides around the floating panel forming the lid. To allow the panel to shrink and expand without splitting or distorting the structure, join it to the side rails with full-length sliding dovetails. Glue the panel to the front rail and screw it to the back rail through a tongued cleat. This cleat holds the panel down to the rail but allows the former to move back and forth.

Begin work on the lid by edge-gluing the panel stock to the necessary width and then cutting it to exact length. Next,

using a dovetail plane designed specifically for this purpose, plane the full-length tail along either end (see the bottom photo on the facing page). (Unfortunately, these specialized planes are becoming hard to find, though they are still manufactured in Germany. Antique dealers may have old ones while some mail-order sources of new tools may still carry them in stock.)

To cut the matching groove in the side rails, plow a dado (see the top photo on the facing page), then undercut the sides with a side rabbet plane, eyeballing the dovetail angle. Note in the drawing above that the tail is offset toward the bottom of the panel, which ensures that the top of the rail above the groove will not be too weak. After cutting the pins in the ends of the side rails, wax the groove, slide the rails in place, and then mark for the tails on the front rail. With these cut and tested for fit, glue them to the side rails and to the front edge of the panel.

With the lid assembled, measure for and build the frame-and-panel inner lid/door and the spacers for attaching it to the lid. Join the frame with haunched mortises, and float the panel in a groove plowed in the frame.

Hanging the lid

With the lid fully assembled, chisel the hinge mortises into the inside edge of the back frame and install the hinges. Then hold the lid to the chest to mark the hinge locations on the back wall. After chiseling for the hinges on the chest, remove the hinges from the lid (if they are not the loose-pin type) and install them on the chest. Then, propping the chest on your workbench, bring over the lid and screw the hinge leaves to it. Finally, check the operation of the lid to be sure it closes over the chest without rubbing, and that, in the open position, it rests equally on the two back lid supports. Note that these supports hold

A Stanley side rabbet plane (No. 79) works a dado into a sliding dovetail groove. Konovaloff eyeballs the angle—a less experienced woodworker could make the cut with the tool held to a guide board. Photo by Craig Wester.

the lid at an angle 2° past 90°. This prevents the lid from self-closing, and it holds the inner lid in place even if the catches are undone.

To stabilize and add beauty to the wood both inside and out of the box, mix up a batch of beeswax and boiled linseed oil (2 oz. of beeswax per gal. of oil). Once a day for at least a week brush the mixture generously onto the wood, rubbing it in briskly with a rag (the more heat generated from rubbing, the greater the sheen). Wipe off the excess with a rag. Finally, install the mortise lock and its striker plate and bolt on two pair of marine-type bronze handles. (Do not use screws—they won't be strong enough.)

An Ulmia dovetail plane cuts the sliding dovetail on the end of the lid board. Sliding dovetails allow the plank of the lid to shrink and expand without splitting. Photo by Gary Weisenburger.

Patternmaker's and Machinist's Chests

Sometime around the turn of this century, Henry A. Leigh, while working as a patternmaker at New York's Brooklyn Navy Yard, built the chest shown in the photo at right to house the tools of his specialized trade. Though similar in shape to a traditional cabinetmaker's chest (and a bit smaller), there are, as you can see, a number of distinct differences. The most obvious is the drawers, which all open to the outside of the chest. The materials and construction are also different. Leigh selected oak and ash over the traditional pine planks, and used frame-and-panel construction instead of dovetailed planks to form the case.

If Leigh's toolbox were an isolated example, you could write off these design variations as idiosyncratic. But many other similar examples built by patternmakers and machinists (trades that were an integral part of the Industrial Age) have survived. Most of these chests feature drawers that open to the outside, use frame-and-panel construction, and are considerably smaller than the classic cabinetmaker's chest.

Why are patternmaker's chests different? The answer may be found by looking at how and where these tradesman worked. By the mid-1800s, the encroachment of machines into the workplace was bringing the era of hand-built furniture to a close. Some cabinetmakers accepted the inevitable, brought machinery into their shops, and shifted toward production furniture making. Others went a step further and found work making the machines themselves, carving the casting patterns for the machine components from wood.

When these craftsmen went to work in the new factories, they usually found that many of the hand tools they were expected to possess as journeyman woodworkers were no longer required. Gone, for example, was the need for bowsaws or panel saws, hand braces, and jointer planes—the work these tools performed was now done by machine. These particular hand tools happened to be among the largest tools a worker might need to contain in his chest; their absence allowed the use of a chest so small it could sit on its owner's

workbench. Since the tool chests had to hold a collection of mostly smaller hand tools, had no need for a saw till and could sit at elbow height, slide-out drawers under a single layer of trays or an open well made good sense.

It is also possible that the configuration of the "gentleman's chests" of the 18th century, such as those shown in the top photo on the facing page, may have served as an inspiration for patternmakers and machinists when they set about to design their tool chests. These chests were offered in late 1700s tool catalogs. Since they are considerably too small for professional tradesman, it is assumed they were intended for

This all-drawer chest, made by master patternmaker Henry A. Leigh around 1900, housed most of the hand tools he needed to practice his specialized trade. Though larger in scale, the chest's design is reminiscent of the gentleman's chests of a century earlier. A locking front lid, which has been removed for this photo, covers the drawer faces. Photo courtesy of The Mariners Museum, Newport News, Va.

Gentleman's chests from Williamsburg. Judging from the similarity of their layout and style, they may have been the precursor of the machinist's-type chests that appeared in the next century. Photo courtesy of Colonial Williamsburg.

gentleman woodworkers (woodworking was an accepted pastime amongst the well-to-do in England).

By the turn of this century, the trades of the patternmaker and machinist had mushroomed in growth—and so did the need for toolboxes to contain their tools. Working for industry, many craftsmen had little time to build their own toolboxes, and so had to purchase them from one of the more than 20 companies that produced them. Of these companies, only one exists today: H. Gerstner & Sons, of Dayton, Ohio. Working out of the same shop and even with some of the original machinery, Gerstner and Sons makes a wide variety of tool chests. Notice how similar the Gerstner box in the photo at right is to the chest that Henry Leigh built for himself at the Navy Yard.

And what about that diamond-shaped mirror set into the lid? Cabinetmakers used to say that it was put there to serve the vanity of the patternmakers, who fancied themselves

A commercially made machinist's tool chest. Note the felt lining and diamond-shaped mirror. Photo courtesy of H. Gerstner & Sons.

David Winter's 10-drawer tool chest, made entirely of pecan, features a drop-front panel and a locking lid. Note the decorative inlay banding and oak leaf carving. Photo by Sandor Nagyszalanczy.

at the top of the woodworking trade. Patternmakers said it was there for the machinists (who also work out of this type of box) to tidy themselves up at the end of their greasy workdays. (Also, machinists often got metal filings in their eyes, and a mirror would have been helpful in removing them.) An old legend says that the purpose of the mirror was to conceal a shallow cavity in which the tradesman could hide his "burying" money. Indeed, money has been found tucked behind a few mirrors, but usually only enough to buy a fifth of gin, not a casket in which the craftsman could lay himself out permanently.

Building a Machinist's-Type Chest

The mess of tools and junk lying about his shop inspired woodworker David Winter, of Allen, Texas, to organize his smaller and more delicate tools. Having settled on building some kind of locking box with an ample number of drawers, he began by mocking up a number of scaled-down versions in an attempt to come up with a prototype. It didn't take long for Winter to realize that the best way to house his small, fragile and easy-to-lose tools was in a traditional-style machinist's chest. Three boxes later (the first two became Christmas presents for his father and brother), Winter had his box: a 10-drawer chest built from over 40 bd. ft. of solid pecan. The box, shown in the photo at left, features solid brass hardware, a drop-front panel that slips under the bottom drawer when not in use, and a locking lid over a tool well deep enough to contain not only planes but a collection of finger-jointed boxes containing drill bits and other small items as well.

DESIGN NOTES

Though a typical machinist's toolbox looks complicated to build because of the formidable number of diminutive drawers and the tricky-looking disappearing drop-down panel, Winter found that with some careful planning all the construction steps could be broken down into a series of straightforward procedures. To add both precision and efficiency to the process, he made templates and jig setups for cutting identical components and forming joints.

His first, and perhaps most important, task was to make a full-scale drawing of the front and side of the box (see pp. 72-75 for details on creating full-scale renderings). Drawing to full scale, Winter was able to double-check the design to make sure, for example, that the top rails that defined the well were high enough to enclose his hand planes and to provide room for the lid stay hardware. The drawing (see pp. 40-41) also provided him with a fail-safe method of establishing the cutting dimensions of all the parts.

CONSTRUCTION PROCEDURES

Once you have a full-scale rendering of the chest you intend to make, you can then develop your cut list and get right down to work. Start by cutting the carcase, getting out the following parts to their specified thickness, width, and length: the bottom board, the two end panels, the interior partition panels, and the front and rear rails.

Milling the components

Starting with the bottom board, dado one groove to receive the tongue of the drop panel and another to receive the back panel. Then cut holes for the assembly dowels using a doweling jig. You can also choose to use biscuit joinery

Cut the stopped sliding-dovetail groove on a table-mounted router equipped with a dovetail bit. The same router-table setup, with a straight bit, is used for making grooves for drawer guides and dadoes for partitions. Photo by Craig Wester.

Rout sliding dovetails on the ends of the rails, using a vertical carriage to move the workpiece past the router bit. Photo by Craig Wester.

to assemble the case components (see pp. 84-86).

Moving on to the side panels, cut grooves to receive the sliding dovetails on the end of front and rear rails. The photo at top right shows what this setup looks like on a table-mounted router. Next drill holes for the assembly dowels after marking their locations from the centerlines of the dowel holes on the bottom board. Returning to the table-mounted router—this time fitted with a straight bit—cut the blind grooves to receive the drawer guides and the horizontal partitions. To ensure precise alignment, cut the grooves for each drawer level before moving the fence setup and setting stops to limit the length of the grooves. You can also use this setup for cutting the guide grooves in the vertical dividers of the interior partition assembly.

David Winter's Tool Chest

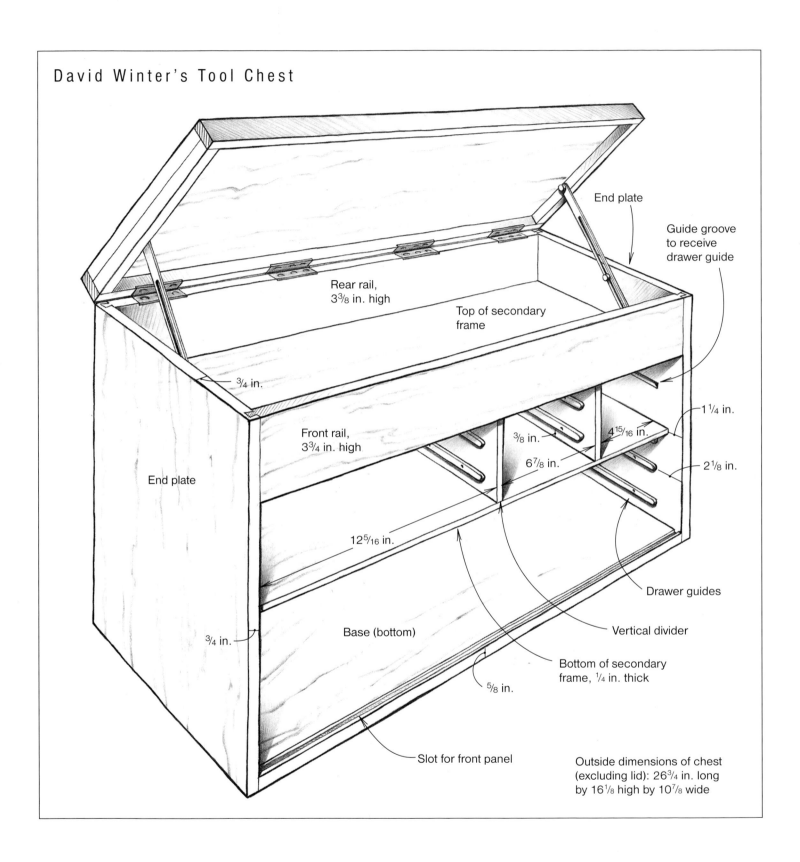

End plate

Guide groove to receive drawer guide

Rear rail, 3⅜ in. high

Top of secondary frame

¾ in.

Front rail, 3¾ in. high

1¼ in.

³⁄₈ in.

4¹⁵⁄₁₆ in.

6⅞ in.

2⅛ in.

End plate

12⁵⁄₁₆ in.

Drawer guides

Vertical divider

Base (bottom)

¾ in.

Bottom of secondary frame, ¼ in. thick

⅝ in.

Slot for front panel

Outside dimensions of chest (excluding lid): 26¾ in. long by 16⅛ high by 10⅞ wide

Chest without Front Cover

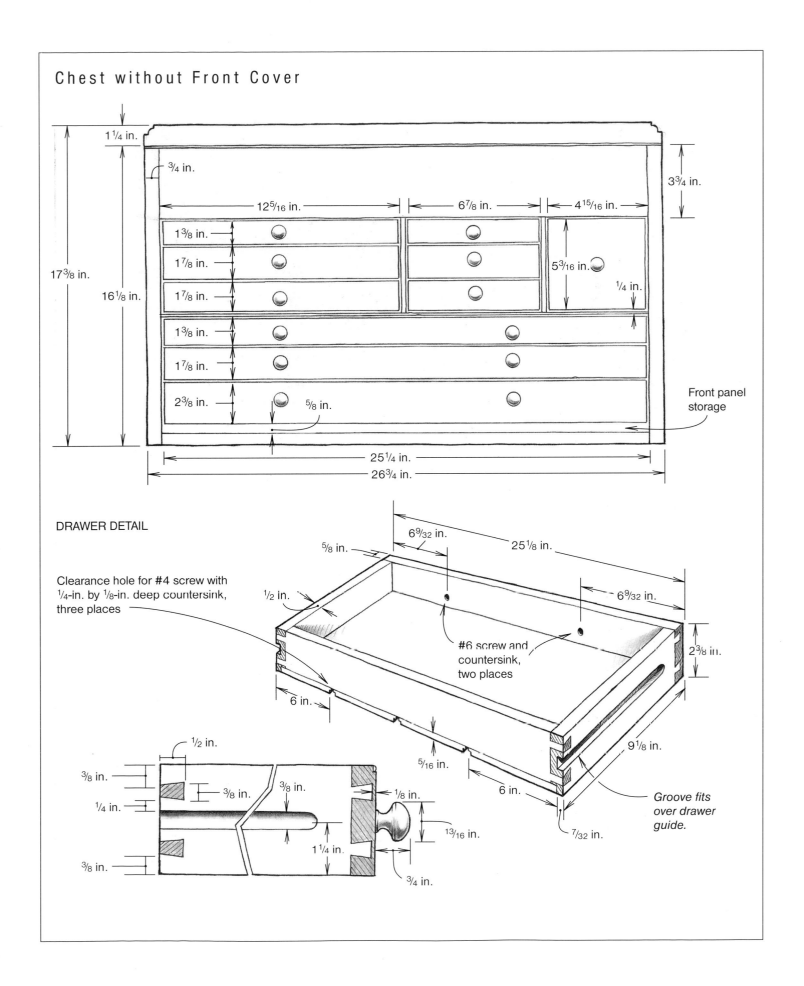

1 1/4 in.

3/4 in.

3 3/4 in.

12 5/16 in.

6 7/8 in.

4 15/16 in.

1 3/8 in.

1 7/8 in.

1 7/8 in.

5 3/16 in.

1/4 in.

17 3/8 in.

16 1/8 in.

1 3/8 in.

1 7/8 in.

2 3/8 in.

5/8 in.

Front panel storage

25 1/4 in.

26 3/4 in.

DRAWER DETAIL

Clearance hole for #4 screw with 1/4-in. by 1/8-in. deep countersink, three places

6 9/32 in.

25 1/8 in.

5/8 in.

6 9/32 in.

1/2 in.

#6 screw and countersink, two places

2 3/8 in.

6 in.

5/16 in.

9 1/8 in.

6 in.

Groove fits over drawer guide.

7/32 in.

1/2 in.

3/8 in.

3/8 in.

3/8 in.

1/4 in.

3/8 in.

1/8 in.

13/16 in.

1 1/4 in.

3/4 in.

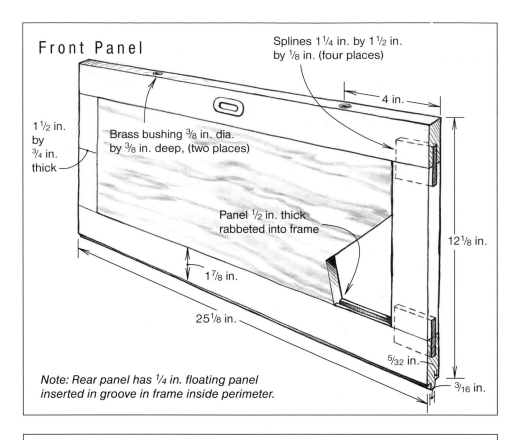

Front Panel

Splines 1 1/4 in. by 1 1/2 in. by 1/8 in. (four places)

4 in.

1 1/2 in. by 3/4 in. thick

Brass bushing 3/8 in. dia. by 3/8 in. deep, (two places)

Panel 1/2 in. thick rabbeted into frame

12 1/8 in.

1 7/8 in.

25 1/8 in.

5/32 in.

3/16 in.

Note: Rear panel has 1/4 in. floating panel inserted in groove in frame inside perimeter.

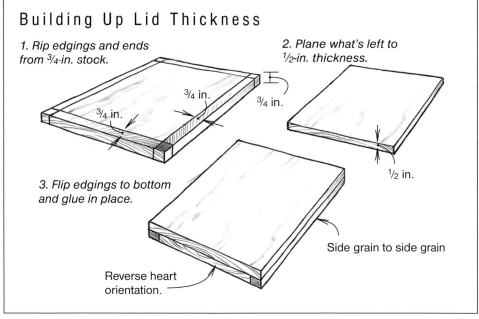

Building Up Lid Thickness

1. Rip edgings and ends from 3/4-in. stock.

2. Plane what's left to 1/2-in. thickness.

3/4 in.

3/4 in.

3/4 in.

3/4 in.

1/2 in.

3. Flip edgings to bottom and glue in place.

Side grain to side grain

Reverse heart orientation.

After cutting the slots in the two vertical dividers to receive the drawer guides, rabbet the edges of the two horizontal partitions to fit the grooves in the carcase pieces. Then cut shallow dadoes to accept the vertical dividers. Now go on to attach the drawer guides to these vertical dividers with screws—countersunk so they don't interfere with drawer sides and slotted to allow the divider to move if it swells or shrinks.

Now you can join the partitions to one another, clamping them up square before drilling the pilot holes for the assembly screws. Brace the assembly square with a stick tacked diagonally across the case, test-fitting the three small drawers between the vertical dividers. (Note that it is easier to make adjustments to the guides before the partition assembly is permanently installed into the case.)

After double-checking that the front and rear rails are cut to the same length (and to the size shown on your rendering), cut the sliding dovetails on the router table (see the top photo on p. 41). Use the same bit that cut the receiving grooves in the side panels. Note that the sliding dovetails are offset from the centerline of the rail toward the inside of the case—a configuration that strengthens the outside corner of the side panel. Next cut a slot in the front rail and a rabbet in the back rail to receive the top horizontal partition board. While the rails are free—and thus easy to hold in a vise—make the mortise for the lid lock mechanism in the front rail, the clearance hole for the lock key, and the relief mortise for the lock escutcheon. Now take the front rail to the drill press to drill the holes for the pair of front-panel lock assemblies. Finally, make the relief mortises for the butt hinge leaves on the back rail.

Making the front and rear panels

Make up the drop-down front panel (see the drawing above left) and the fixed rear panels of the case, cutting the frame-and-panel members slightly overlong so you can later trim them to fit the dry-assembled case perfectly. Use splines both to join the butts of the rails and stiles and to attach the flush-front panel to its frame. Dado the inner edge of the frame of the rear panel to receive its thin recessed panel. Having glued up the frames—being careful to get them square and to keep glue off the panels so they will float freely in their frames—set them aside to dry. Later, sand the joints of the frames flush.

In the next step, dry-assemble the case (being careful to clamp it square) so you can cut and trim the front and rear panel assemblies to size. Then remove the back panel and cut the slots for the splines that will attach this panel to the case. Cut the tongue in the bottom rail of the front panel to fit in the groove you made earlier in the bottom board. Finally, lay out and drill for the brass inserts that will receive the locking pins.

Making up the top lid

To gain a thick lid without the weight, build up the thickness with edgings (see the bottom drawing on the facing page). To hide the change in grain at the lamination joint, cut the edgings and ends from the top board stock (which is ¾ in. thick), being careful to mark the offcuts to show their original position in the board. Now plane the board with the end and edgings removed down to ½ in. (leaving the cutoffs at their original ¾ in.), and cut it to its approximate finished width and length. (To ensure that the lid will fit the case, make the lid slightly oversize at this stage—you will trim it to its finished width and length— 10⅞ in. by 26¾ in.— later.) Next, cut the side strips to length and glue them to the underside of the lid, filling in between with the end-grain cutoffs. To make a pleasing grain pattern, you can flip over the end cuts so the growth rings form an elliptical pattern.

Making up the drawers

The 10 drawers call for a lot of joints, so create them efficiently, either by routing dovetails using a dovetail jig with a hand-held router or cutting finger joints with a shop-made jig on the table saw (see the sidebar on p. 88). Winter cut the through dovetails at the back of the drawer box with a shop-made router jig

Using a shop-made jig, Winter routs dovetails on the drawer backs. Photos by Sandor Nagyszalanczy.

as seen in the photos above right, and cut the blind dovetails that join the sides to the front face with an Inca jig fitted to a table-mounted router. Alternatively, if you have the time, you can cut both with a fine handsaw and a chisel.

The first step in drawer construction is to get out the stock for the drawers. Cut all the drawer fronts from one board to ensure a pleasing grain match across the entire face of the box. After cutting the parts to the dimensions established

on your full-scale rendering, mark them with a symbol indicating the drawer they belonged to and their orientation to one another (see the drawing on p. 44). Now make the pins and tails of the dovetail or the finger joints.

The next step is to rout a slot in the inside face of the front and sides of the drawer box to accept the bottom panel, which in turn receives a rabbet along three sides to fit into this slot. Cut the back board of the drawer box to sit atop

Marking Drawer Parts

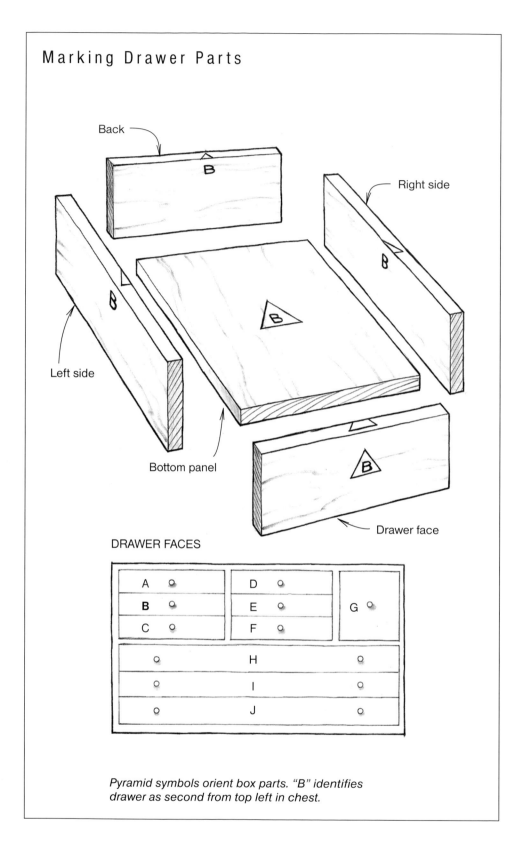

Back

Right side

Left side

Bottom panel

Drawer face

DRAWER FACES

A ○	D ○	
B ○	E ○	G ○
C ○	F ○	
○ H ○		
○ I ○		
○ J ○		

*Pyramid symbols orient box parts. "B" identifies
drawer as second from top left in chest.*

the bottom panel—the panel is screwed to the bottom edge of this board during assembly. This construction method makes it easier to assemble and to square up the drawer boxes, and also allows the drawer bottom to be easily repaired or replaced if necessary.

With all the parts cut and milled, dry-assemble each drawer to ensure that the joints are tight with all the parts of the box sitting square and flat. Now glue and clamp the box together, sliding in the bottom panel and screwing it in place. When the box is dry, remove it from the clamps and sand the joints flush. Then, with a straight-fluted bit set up on the router table, cut the slots for the drawer guides in either side of the drawer. To ensure that the drawers will hang level in the case you must locate the slots precisely. To this end always index the bottom of each drawer to the router table's fence. Finally, rout a bead for decoration along the top edge of each drawer face.

Assembling the box

Now comes the challenge—putting all the parts together before the glue dries. Before you attempt this, do a dry run. In addition to checking the fit of joints, a dry run lets you practice the assembly sequence. On this box, join the bottom board to the two end panels around the back panel and slide in the front rail from the top. Then slide the partition assembly in from the back until it engages in the groove in the back of the front rail. Finish by sliding the rear rail down from the top until it sits over the back of the top partition and fits tightly to the top of the back panel.

Next, temporarily install the still oversized lid by marking for and cutting the hinge mortises and installing the hinges. Then, with the lid closed, trace the shape of the top of the case to the underside of the three overhanging edges. After trimming the lid to size, use a dowel-center marker to mark the two holes for the locking mechanism actuators. Finally, remove the lid and rout in the decorative edge profile.

With the box now permanently assembled, the time has come to final-fit the removable front panel and to install and adjust the drawers. Plane the edges of the panel to form an even gap line between the panel and the case. Then, installing the locking mechanism into the front rail, press down on the pin to mark the center of the holes to be drilled in the top edge of the panel (in which the bushing for the lock pin will be installed). You can make your own mechanism as Winter did (see the drawing at right), or you can obtain one through mail-order sources.

Center the drawers in their openings by adding paper shims beneath the tongues of the guides to bring them out slightly. If the drawers stick, carefully plane down the face of the guides. As a final touch, use spray adhesive to attach acrylic felt to the inside bottom of the drawers (and to the bottom of the upper tool well).

Applying carving and banding

Adding decorative features to your toolbox not only enhances the look of the piece, but also makes the box your own. Inspired by the magnificent oak trees of his home state, Winter decided to carve a pair of oak leaves around the lock escutcheon. To add more visual interest to the front of the chest, he inlaid a decorative banding across the drawer faces.

Winter prepared for the relief carving process with the help of the real thing, photocopying two oak leaves and then reducing the size of the image to suit the scale of the box. After gluing the photocopies in place around the lock escutcheon with white glue, he then set

Panel Lock Mechanism

3/8 in. dia.

5/32 in. dia

Actuator (lid)

3/8 in.

1/4 in.

1 3/8 in.

Top guide (front rail)

3/8 in.

1/8 in.

#6 countersunk hole

3/16-in. dia. hole

3/16 in. dia.

3 3/4 in.

Lock pin (front rail)

.350-dia. by 1/8-in. thick pressed-on disc

5/16-in. dia. x 1-in. spring

#8 washer with drilled-out center hole

3/16-in. dia. hole

3/8 in.

Bottom guide (front rail)

3/16-in. dia. hole

3/8 in.

Receiver (front panel)

Bottom guide and receiver, 3/8-in. dia

to work to carve the relief. He began by using a knife to cut in the outline of the leaves to the desired depth. Then he cleaned out the waste between the lines with a variety of small carving chisels.

Not satisfied with commercial bandings, Winter decided to make his own from leftover pieces of pecan. To create a color contrast, he blended light-colored sapwood with the much darker heartwood. After routing grooves in the face of the drawer fronts and the front rail, he applied glue and pressed the banding into the grooves, being careful to start and end the banding so the patterns would be symmetrical from drawer to drawer.

A Chest with Full-Extension Drawers

Like David Winter, Karen Robertson had to build three boxes before she got to keep one for herself—the first two went as presents to family members. Designed primarily to hold her collection of drafting instruments and precision layout tools, Robertson's yellow cedar machinist's-type box has some unusual features: a drop-down lid with a leather-covered writing surface, a shop-made ebony latch system, and full-extension drawer slides made entirely from wood. To personalize and decorate the chest, Robertson, of Saanichton, British Columbia, Canada, inlaid a floral pattern into the top of the lid.

Not finding latch hardware that was either small enough or of high enough quality to use on her chest, Robertson decided to design a system of her own. After all, she had inherited from her grandfather a 20-lb. block of ebony, a perfect material for making durable and beautiful hardware. After making a few full-scale mockups of the latch and catch, she came up with the system shown in the drawing on the facing page.

Robertson turned the knobs on a small lathe and then shaped the latch with chisels and small files (the tapered profile allows the latch to clear the mortise in the front rail as the lid is lifted up). Measuring carefully from a full-scale rendering, Robertson marked and predrilled the holes for the knob and the pivot pin. Next, she cut the tapered mortise in the lid and the straight mortise in the front rail by drilling out most of the waste and then cleaning up with a chisel. She cut the elongated opening for the knob in the face of the top rail using a router template. Finally, Robertson drilled pilot holes for both the pivot pin and the lock pin from the

Karen Robertson's mechanic's-style box in yellow cedar features full-extension drawers, frame-and-panel sides, a leather writing surface and ebony feet and pulls. Photo by Charley Robinson.

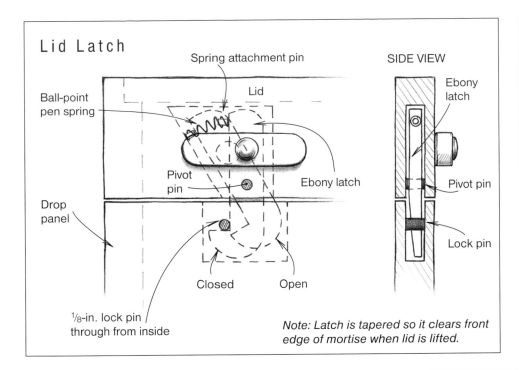

Lid Latch

Ball-point
pen spring

Spring attachment pin

Lid

Pivot
pin

Ebony latch

Drop
panel

Closed   Open

1/8-in. lock pin
through from inside

SIDE VIEW

Ebony
latch

Pivot pin

Lock pin

Note: Latch is tapered so it clears front
edge of mortise when lid is lifted.

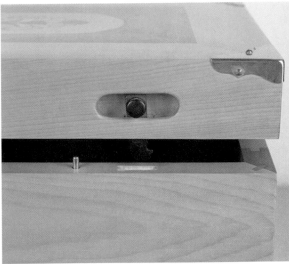

An ebony latch holds the chest closed. Photo
by Charley Robinson.

The top of the box is
inlaid with a floral
pattern. Brass cor-
ner protectors are
both decorative and
practical. Photo by
Charley Robinson.

Start by making a full-size drawing of the side of the toolbox and the drawers. Also draw front views to determine the layout of the sliding dovetails and the grooves. Draw in the parts of the extension system, including the runner (which is fixed to the case side), the slider (which runs between the runner and the drawer box) and the side of the drawer box. If you need more clarification, also draw the box fully extended out of the case.

Measure the size of the parts on the rendering and then cut them out of clear, stable hardwood stock. (Teak would be a good choice because of its self-lubricating qualities and its inherent stability.) To keep things simple, make the slider the same thickness as the drawer side. Note that the drawer face will overlap the end of the runner, hiding it from view. Also note in the cross section that the slider is slightly narrower than the drawer side. This difference in height prevents the slider from binding against a cross rail or a tightly fitted neighboring drawer as it moves out of the case.

Set up a dovetail bit on a table-mounted router to cut the dovetailed edges of the runners and sliders. Use the same bit—set to the same

All-wood slides allow the drawers to extend fully for full access. Photo by Charley Robinson.

height—to produce the angled sides of the grooves. When cutting these grooves in the sliders and drawer-box sides, make successive cuts toward either side, starting at the piece's centerline. This way

the grooves will be exactly centered. Now size the sliding dovetail to fit. Though you want the fit to be tight to reduce wiggling, you need it loose enough for a smooth sliding action. Make trial cuts

in scrap stock first to test the action.

Cut the slots for the stop pins in the sliders. A cutting jig to guide a plunge router fitted with a straight bit will help make this task go quickly and with the necessary precision. Note in the slot/pin layout drawing below that the slots run from 1 in. in from the end of the slider to 1 in. on the far side of the centerline. These distances must be equal for the slider to extend exactly half its length out of the case. (The drawer will also pull out half its

All-Wood Extension-Slide System

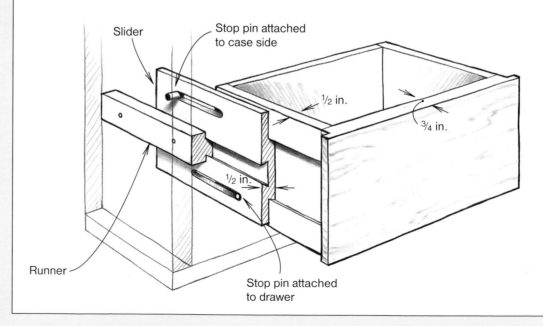

Slider

Stop pin attached to case side

1/2 in.

3/4 in.

1/2 in.

Runner

Stop pin attached to drawer

length along the slider (and thus fully out of the case).

After assembling the drawers and installing the runners in the case, the next step is setting the stop pins. Karen Robertson made her pins by modifying a brass wood screw: After running in the screw to establish the threads, she backed it out and filed the head flush to the shank. To find the location of the pin on the case side, install the slider on the runner. Push it all the way in and then make a mark at the front end of the upper slot. In a similar fashion, mark the pin location on the drawer side with the slider installed tight against the face of the drawer. This time make the mark at the rear end of the lower slot.

Predrill for the screws at the marks.

Install the drawers by sliding in the sliders on their runners. Screw the stop pin in through the slots into the case sides. Now fully extend the sliders from the case and slide in the drawer box, and screw the stop pin into the side of the drawer box. Rub wax from a candle stub liberally on the sliding surfaces. Test the action. If they bind, the runners may not have been installed parallel. You can remedy the problem by using a scraper blade along the edges of the sliding dovetails where binding is evident (you can usually see a burnished surface where rubbing occurs).

inside of the box (stopping before penetrating the outside).

To install the latch, Robertson epoxied a ball-point pen spring to an attachment pin on the latch, put a gob of epoxy on the free end of the spring, and then slid the latch and spring into the wedge-shaped mortise. Aligning the hole on the latch with the pivot pin hole, she slipped in the dowel to hold the piece in place. After the epoxy dried she installed the lock pin and worked the catch, carefully reshaping the end until it engaged the pin smoothly and positively.

Because the drawers of a traditional mechanic's chest are so shallow, you often find that you have to remove them entirely from the chest to get at some of their contents. Robertson felt that the repeated removal of the drawers would lead to excessive wear on the box over time and, worse, could cause their valuable contents to spill. As a solution to this problem, she came up with an all-wood, full-extension drawer slide (see the sidebar at left). As long as the box is kept in an environment where the humidity and temperature are relatively stable (to minimize swelling of the wood slide components), these slides work extraordinarily well. The drawers slide smoothly in and out of the chest and give you access to the full depth of the drawer box.

In essence, the system is made up of two sliding dovetailed guides—one between the guide rail attached to the case and the intermediate slider, and one between this slider and the side of the drawer box. In the intermediate slider, the slots stop against pins set into the drawer and the case side. To make sure that the system would work well for a long time, Robertson used a stable hardwood (cherry) for all components, including the drawer sides. Feeling that any finish might cause stickiness, she applied wax only to the moving parts.

LAYOUT OF SLOTS AND PINS

CROSS SECTION

Slider (pulls out of case to its centerline)

Stop pin in case side

Distance A (1 in.)

Distance B (1 in.)

Drawer (pulls fully out of case)

$1/16$ in.

$1/16$ in.

Runner

1 in.

1 in.

Stop pin in drawer side

Case of box

Centerline

Note: A is distance between end of slot and end of slider. B is distance between opposite end of slot and centerline of slider. A must equal B for slider to extend out of box to midpoint, and for drawer to extend fully out of case.

3

A STUDENT
TOOL-CHEST PROJECT

When the students of the cabinet and furniture-making program at the North Bennet Street School in Boston, Massachusetts, have completed their six-week introduction to the fundamentals of drafting and benchwork, they are given the opportunity to embark upon their first start-to-finish project—the building of a tool chest.

At the outset of the project, the students are given five parameters to guide the building of their chests. The outside dimensions of the case must be 17 in. high by 33 in. long by 20 in. wide (a size that will fit under the school's workbenches). The carcase must be dovetailed. Drawers should be relatively few in number—six is recommended, although this requirement is not always strictly insisted upon. The wood chosen must be appropriate, with good working characteristics. Finally, hardware may be individually selected, but there must be a simple means of locking the chest. Complex construction systems

Tool chest by William Clayton, built while he was a student at North Bennet Street School in Boston, features fine, handcut dovetails on the drawer boxes. For other views of this chest, see p. 53.

and embellishments are discouraged to keep the student's involvement in the project within a two- to three- month time frame.

On a practical level, the students will need this chest to store their personal collections of hand tools when working in the school shop. But the project provides much more: Through the building of a relatively straightforward tool chest, the students learn fundamental woodworking skills, as set forth in the official school prospectus. These include:

♦ blending machine and hand woodworking techniques—with the emphasis on handwork as a way to create a broade range of design and construction solutions on a project.

♦ practicing safe, efficient benchwork and machine-room techniques in the areas of layout, sizing and milling of stock, and applying finishes.

♦ basic joinery, including the dovetail and the mortise and tenon.

♦ other basic woodworking procedures, including dadoing, rabbeting, edge joining, making and fitting divider frames and partitions and door construction (both frame and panel and cleated).

♦ learning about grain and growth-ring considerations, and designing to allow movement.

♦ accounting for time and cost in the planning of a project.

The photos that follow, which were taken by Lance Patterson of North Bennet Street School, represent 17 student projects. As you can see, the restrictions do not resulted in bland, homogenous toolboxes. Instead, students create chests that strongly reflect their own sense of design—and sometimes their sense of humor as well. (Notice that Stephen Alexander's box , shown in the top photo on p. 54, protrays the face of the North Bennet Street School building.) Though humble in dimension and function, the tool-chest project has carried scores of students from theory, through woodworking practices, to the creation of an attractive, functional object.

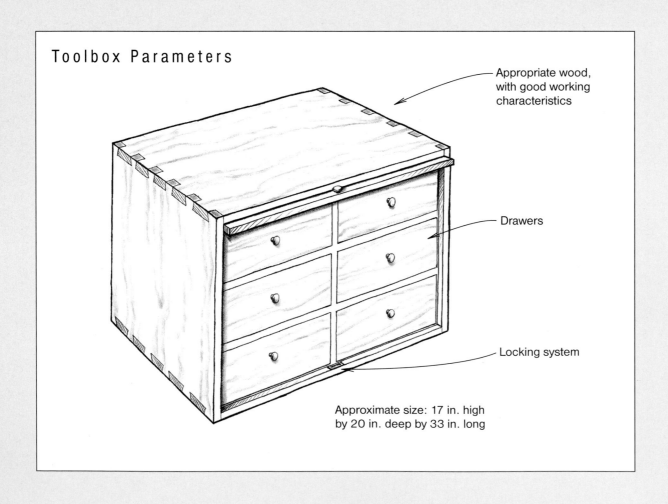

Toolbox Parameters

Appropriate wood, with good working characteristics

Drawers

Locking system

Approximate size: 17 in. high by 20 in. deep by 33 in. long

William Clayton's tool chest has an unusually well-proportioned case. Its design is securely founded in the Arts and Crafts era, with primary woods of quartersawn white oak and birds-eye maple. Altogether the box features 160 hand-cut dovetails. Note the handmade solid-copper pulls and the inlay work of copper, pewter and dyed beech on the doors.

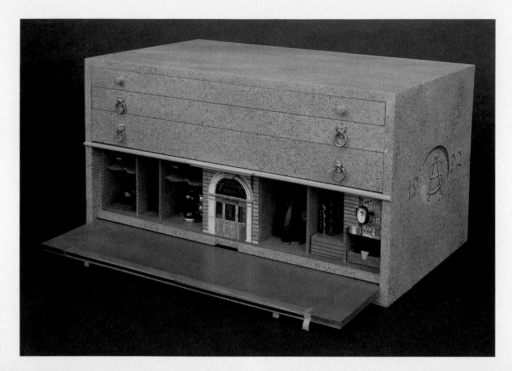

Stephen Alexander employed a painted trompe l'oeil finish to mimic the stone exterior of the North Bennet Street School building on the outside of his toolbox. The "carving" on the end board of the box is also false—the date and symbol are painted, not carved. Faux brickwork and a painted front view of the school's entryway complete the illusion.

Drawing on the techniques used in period furniture designs to create hidden compartments, J. Fischer disguised the side trays containing his chisels as pilaster moldings. A drop lid slides open to reveal the drawers.

Eric Englander drew heavily on the Arts and Crafts style for inspiration when he built his tool chest. The basic form of the box comes from a Gustav Stickley furniture piece, and the inlay is inspired by the work of Harvey Ellis, a colleague of Stickley. The side-opening doors and long, narrow central drawers give the chest a pleasing, stable appearance.

Enchanted by the furniture of the Ming Dynasty, Peter Cabot incorporated many Chinese elements in the design of his chest, above. A campaign chest influenced the shape of the box, a tea table inspired the top, and an emperor's bed suggested the form of the stand. The box is finished with a traditional tung-seed oil.

The chest at right, by Tom Sulvalskas, is influenced by the Baroque furniture of Louis XV. More a miniature piece of furniture than a toolbox, the chest is reminiscent of a classic bombé commode.

Joe Barbeau used a drop lid to add a touch of beauty and craft to his project, shown above and at right. The triptych of Americana was painted using artist's acrylics for the panels and a modern oil stain to color the rest of the chest.

On Jane Swanson's tool chest (above), the drop lid is embellished with an inlaid floral design.

The tool chest of Adam Manes features an open compartment topped by three drawers that run the length of the box. The box closes with lockable, side-opening doors.

Todd Hobday was one of the few students who decided to use the top of the chest as a lid—a design solution that maximizes the amount of usable space within the limited parameters of the project. On his tool chest, an inlaid, lockable drop lid covers the drawer faces for security.

The tool chest of Judith Hanson is pleasing in its thoughtful simplicity of form. A bank of drawers is concealed behind a pair of side-opening doors.

Several students arrived at unique and pleasing solutions for putting handles on the drawer boxes. The chests shown on this page are by Beth Ann Harrington (left), Peter Bartell (below left) and Sean O'Rourke (below). On the facing page are chests by Frances Diemoz (top left), Sam Robinson (top right) and Mario Rubio Ospina (bottom).

Cubbyhole shelving, brimming with power tools, sweeps across an entire wall of Timbercraft Homes' timber-framing shop in Port Townsend, Wash. Photo by Craig Wester.

4
DESIGNING IN-SHOP
TOOL STORAGE

Walking through the cabinetmaker's, wheelwright's and cooper's shops of Colonial Williamsburg in Virgina, I was struck by one thing that each of these pre-industrial woodworking shops hold in common: the ubiquitous presence of countless hand tools hung or shelved along nearly every square inch of wall surface. When I asked the craftsmen about this, they replied that working exclusively with hand tools demanded that the tools be immediately accessible— anything less markedly affected the efficiency of their work. While larger tools such as planes or fragile layout instruments might be stored in their personal chests at the end of the workday, they found it best to leave such tools as screwdrivers, hammers, chisels, saws, and bits and braces permanently set out close at hand on the walls of the shop. And because they worked either alone or among family or close associates (not among strangers in a factory), they felt safe leaving their tools out in the open.

While this ready accessibility made sense to me, I couldn't help comparing these shops to my own, where fine wood dust quickly forms a film over any tools left out for more than a day. Then it dawned on me that my shop contains something completely foreign to these historical shops: machines. It is, of course, power tools that produce most of the fine wood dust in a woodworking shop. Because pre-industrial woodworkers created mostly shavings working with hand tools, they did not have to worry about the handles of their stored tools (or their lungs for that matter) becoming coated with an annoying—and potentially dangerous— slick film of dust.

Nowadays, however, powered hand tools are a necessary part of the work, and they too need a home within the shop. One excellent solution is to create open-faced bins—or cubbyholes—for each tool, its accessories and its snag-prone power cord. The timber-framing shop at Timbercraft Homes in Port Townsend, Washington, features cubbyhole tool storage (see the photo on p. 62). These bins don't block out all the dust and debris of a busy shop, but they do organize the tools and also provide easy access to them. The heavier power tools can be located in the lower bins to make them easier and safer to remove and replace. Be careful, however, to place the

heaviest tools (at Timbercraft, these are the chain mortisers) at about elbow height to protect your back. Small hand and power tools and their accessories can go in the upper bins.

Types of In-Shop Tool Storage

To protect and organize hand tools while keeping them handy, you may choose to build one or more of these varieties of toolboxes: wall cabinets, standing cabinets and rolling carts. To make a good decision about which of these boxes might best suit your needs, you should first make a list of all the tools that need to be easily accessible, yet protected. Then think about where in the shop—and how often—you most often use these tools. After reading the descriptions below, you should have a pretty good idea of which box (or combination of boxes) is right for you.

WALL CABINETS

If you have a shop in a two-car garage or smaller area, you've likely learned that open floor space is at a premium, and you'll probably want a storage system that doesn't take up too much space. In my own shop of less than 500 sq. ft., I'm careful to preserve areas where clamped assemblies can be set against a wall to dry and where milled parts can be stored prior to assembly (and where my kids will invariably lean their bicycles for me to fix). In shops of limited size, the best place for storing tools is generally in an area where floor space is already committed. Rather than sitting a toolbox on the floor, then, you can instead choose to hang a tool-storage cabinet on the wall. One exceptionally efficient location for a tool cabinet is over a workbench. Depending on the size box you choose to make, you could keep a wide variety of bench tools there—from a small box containing only a set of carving or mortising chisels to a larger box for storing a full selection of planes, hand saws, chisels and layout tools.

However, hanging a cabinet over a bench can impose some limitations. If you have to lean over the bench to reach the cabinet, for example, the height to which you can reach is less than if the bench were not in your way, so you'll have to adjust the cabinet's height accordingly. In addition, when you lean over a bench you must extend your arms, which throws you off balance and reduces your lifting ability. Because of these limitations, you may not want to keep heavy power tools (such as a circular saw or a plunge router) in this

Since the turn of this century, resident patternmakers of Wing and Sons machine shop in Greenfield, Mass., have come to this wall-hung toolbox for chisels, measuring instruments and various other tools of their trade. The box is located close to a pattern-maker's vise fixed at the end of a massive workbench. Photo by Vincent Laurence.

Furniture maker Sanford Buchalter, of Freeland, Mich., built this standing chest for his father in trade for a small travel tool chest his father built for him. Nearly every tool in the chest is readily visible and instantly accessible. The box hanging below in the support frame contains a small drawer and woodworking reference books. Photo by Jonathan Binzen.

cabinet. However, there is no limitation on the volume of the cabinet. You can design it as wide as you like (even as wide as your workbench), and you can also outfit the doors to hold a surprising number and variety of tools. Wall cabinets are discussed more fully in Chapter 5.

STANDING TOOL CABINETS

In some specialty woodworking trades the classic cabinetmaker's tool chest evolved from a trunk-like box to a considerably larger, though shallower, standing cabinet. In everyday use, a tall and shallow shape has obvious advantages. Orienting the tools along a tall, vertical surface allows many, if not all, of the tools to be instantly accessible. Unlike the trunk-type box, you don't have to lift or slide trays or a till of drawers to get at tools buried in a well below. And, as a blessing to your back, you don't have to scrunch over to get into the box—instead you can set the tools at a comfortable height above the floor. To make the most of a standing cabinet's ease of access, you should locate it close to where you normally stand at your workbench.

Unlike traditional cabinetmaker's chests, however, standing tool cabinets take up a lot of wall space. In a small shop (say a one-car garage-size space), you may have trouble finding room for one. And if you do, you must be careful to place it so that it doesn't block precious natural light coming in from a window. The standing tool cabinet, when open, also exposes all your tools to dust— and to view. I would have second thoughts about keeping my tools in this type of box if I worked in a busy shop filled with lots of workers and production machinery.

Standing cabinets are difficult to move. Unless you build the box rather small (which severely limits the number of tools it can contain), these bulky chests are definitely awkward to handle. Also, the same clips and cleats that make the tools easy to extract are often too loose-fitting to secure the tools properly during shipping. If you need to move your tools frequently, or even periodically, this probably isn't the best type of tool storage for you. Standing tool cabinets are discussed more fully in Chapter 6.

ROLLING TOOL CARTS

A rolling cart is another good way to provide easy bench-side access to your tools. You can design a cart to contain a great number and variety of tools, but you don't have to worry about overloading it with the heavy ones. Best of all, a rolling cart can follow you anywhere you go in the shop, offering up the necessary tools when and where you want them.

It is tempting and fun to design the cart to carry every tool you think you might need for any purpose throughout the shop. But if you are an obsessive tool collector like most woodworkers I know, your cart would have to be huge. Unfortunately, in a small woodworking shop, an all-inclusive monster cart would be unwieldy and constantly in the way. In general, then, I suggest designing the cart to serve only certain shop operations. (As you'll see in Chapter 7, I designed my cart to contain the tools I would use primarily for assembling cabinets and furniture.) That way you can plan the design around a limited number of tools, making access to them as efficient as possible and limiting the cart's overall weight and dimensions. With this approach, you are using the rolling cart to augment the primary tool-storage systems in your shop.

Craftsman George Snyder, of West Creek, N. J., built this rolling cart to carry his tools to work areas throughout his shop. Constructed largely of quartersawn red oak, it has solved the problem of scattered and misplaced tools. Photo by New Image Photography.

STATION BOXES

A good way to supplement tool storage in any size shop is with a variety of station boxes. Located at the major stationary power tools and workstations throughout the shop (see the drawing below), these boxes hold a collection of tools essential to the work generally performed in that area. Station boxes can be sized to suit the needs at hand. Charles Platt, of Glenmoore, Pennsylvania, built his table-saw tool station entirely around his 10-in. saw (see the photo at left), creating five separate compartments to store a wide selection of sawblades and all the tools and accessories he needed to deal with the general operation of that machine. (These include a set of blade-changing

Cabinetmaker Charles Platt built this storage station around his 10-in. table saw, entirely replacing its metal stand. Making the most out of floor space that is typically wasted, he was able to create separate areas to store table-saw related tools, sawblades, power hand tools and a removable dust bin. Photo by Dick Fellows Photography.

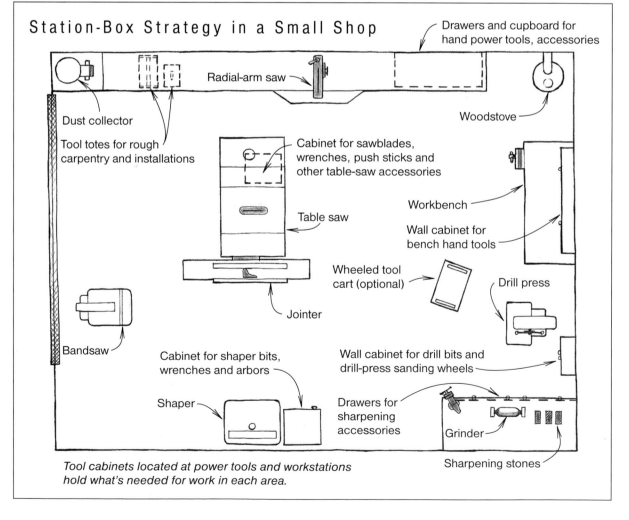

Station-Box Strategy in a Small Shop

Drawers and cupboard for hand power tools, accessories

Radial-arm saw

Dust collector

Tool totes for rough carpentry and installations

Cabinet for sawblades, wrenches, push sticks and other table-saw accessories

Table saw

Woodstove

Workbench

Wall cabinet for bench hand tools

Wheeled tool cart (optional)

Drill press

Jointer

Bandsaw

Cabinet for shaper bits, wrenches and arbors

Shaper

Wall cabinet for drill bits and drill-press sanding wheels

Drawers for sharpening accessories

Grinder

Sharpening stones

Tool cabinets located at power tools and workstations hold what's needed for work in each area.

wrenches, Allen wrenches for fine-tuning the rip fence, a push stick, clamps for the featherboard, and extra saw-kerf inserts.) Plenty of space is left over for a removable sawdust bin, as well as cabinet space for storing other tools that find use in that general area of the shop.

It's impossible to appreciate how much time and effort these station boxes will save you until you've worked with them. Certainly your feet will thank you for the miles of walking you no longer have to do. Your other tool-storage units become more useful as well, since they no longer have to house station-specific tools.

Design Considerations

Perhaps the most fundamental concept to keep in mind when designing tool storage for your shop is this: Provide a specific place for each item to be stored, and consistently return each item to its place. Using a toolbox built according to this principle quickly becomes second nature. Your hands, independent of your eyes, soon know where to find a tool—in its place. And your eyes know at a glance if any tool is missing—it's out of its place.

Another fundamental principle is simplicity. Inevitably, the more complex the storage system, the more difficult it will be to get at an individual tool. Back in my finish-carpentry days, I remember hanging off the end of a scaffolding board trying to fit a piece of molding along a ceiling line. Needing a certain chisel to make the final trim cut, I yelled down to my partner to get it for me out of my toolbox. By the time he waded through the overlying trays of tools and miscellaneous odds and ends to get at it, I had given up waiting and whacked the poor molding into place with a hammer.

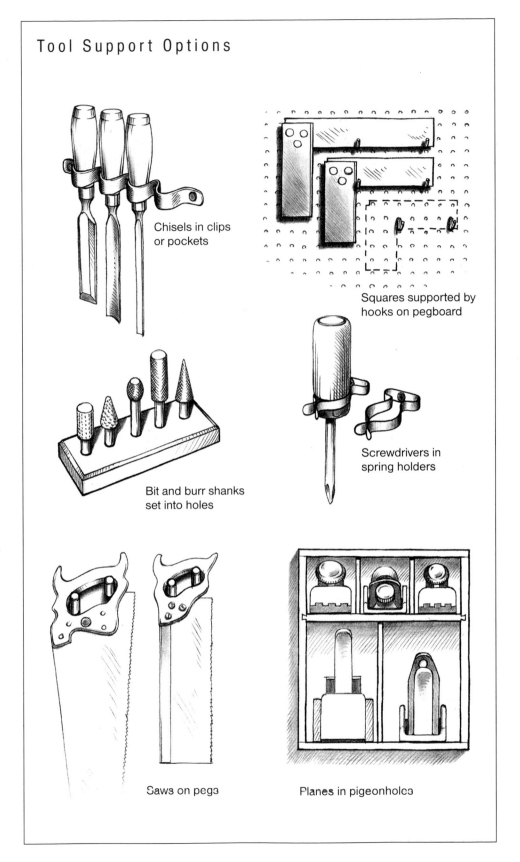

Tool Support Options

Chisels in clips or pockets

Squares supported by hooks on pegboard

Bit and burr shanks set into holes

Screwdrivers in spring holders

Saws on pegs

Planes in pigeonholes

No, it was not a very good fit. And yes, I redesigned my toolbox.

The goal, then, is to find a way to contain all the tools you need without creating toolbox gridlock. Unless you are building a traditional cabinetmaker's chest, avoid creating compartments that require removing other components for access. I also avoid complex holding mechanisms for the tool handles. If a mechanism is necessary at all, be it a turnbutton or some type of catch, it should be operable blindfolded with one arm tied behind your back. A strip of magnetic tape may be all you need to hold light tools like small screwdrivers securely in place. Some typical tool-support strategies are shown in the drawing on p. 69.

THE DESIGN PROCESS

After you've decided on the type of toolbox that would best suit your specific needs and shop situation, begin the design process by thinking about the work you will be doing in proximity to the proposed storage unit. This will tell you what tools you probably should store there. Now make a list of the tools that seem most appropriate to store in the unit. Consider that some tools may not store well (bulky and heavy power tools like plunge routers or circular saws in a wall-hung cabinet for instance), and that some of the tools (such as screwdrivers and hammers) may be equally necessary in other parts of the shop. These might best be placed on a rolling cart or in a station box. Since I do a fair bit of hand-tool woodworking, I place most of my layout tools and hand planes in a wall box located by the vise end of my workbench.

This divided drawer in Jim Tolpin's rolling tool cart has a sliding tray. Photo by Craig Wester.

Once you have your tool list, think about the placement of each tool within the box. To prevent back strain when lifting them out, I locate heavy tools toward the bottom of the unit, with the heaviest placed at just below elbow height. I place a wide assortment of lightweight tools on the doors of the unit—they're easy to see and get at here, and they don't stress the door. Tools with pierced handles (such as spokeshaves, saws, files, and wrenches) go on pegs; other small hand tools (such as screwdrivers) fit easily into clips, brackets or pockets. You can slide planes into small pigeonholes in the interior of the box, but remember that you can't see their lengths this way, so you'll have to memorize where each plane goes. Another option is to set the planes on pegs or narrow shelves, or to pierce their

bases with a hole (collectors will shudder) and hang them. Small tools, especially cutting tools like router and drill bits, are best placed in drawers or pull-out bins.

In a rolling cart, I like to use drawers for most, if not all, of the storage area. As the cart is trundled over the uneven floor of my shop, I want the drawers to provide good protection for my tools—more than they might have if they are hung on pegs or set on shelves. Closely confined between the dividers set within the trays, the tools can't roll about and damage themselves or one another. Notice in the photo above that I have added a divided tray to the drawer. Sliding back and forth on ledges over the divided compartments below, the tray maximizes the use of the space within the drawer, yet barely interferes with

David Powell's tool cabinet features a French-fitted tray. Photo by Vincent Laurence.

Gather the tools you want to store in your toolbox and spread them out on a clean sheet of plywood. Start playing with the arrangement, grouping the tools together according to their function and to the suggestions outlined above. If necessary, hold your experiments in place with wood scraps or nails. Remember to account for the thickness of compartment dividers and tool supports—indicate them on the plywood with strips of wood. Your goal is to discover the layout that maximizes access to the tools in the smallest volume of space.

It won't take long until you begin to see how large—and in what overall configuration—your storage unit must be. (If you don't like what you see, it's still not too late to rethink your tool requirements.) Now make a rough sketch of the unit, drawing in the location of any major partitions, drawers or bins. If you have an "instant" camera, consider taking a picture of the layout as well. Commit yourself to the overall dimensions of the box and the size and location of the major interior components, and indicate them on your rough sketch.

The next step is to create a set of working drawings for the box. I strongly suggest drawing the plans to full scale for several reasons. First, you can see clearly what the overall size and proportions of the box are going to be (you can even take the completed drawing into your shop to see how well the unit will fit into its proposed location). Second, you can measure the components directly off the drawing to produce a bill of materials and cut lists. And third, you can lay out details from the drawing such as joint lines directly on the stock (or on a story stick). This is as close to a fail-safe layout system as you can get.

accessibility. You could also add French-fitted compartments to some of the drawer bottoms to help keep tools from rolling about (see the photo above).

Try to avoid creating non-dedicated spaces for tool storage, such as an open well or a length of undivided shelving. This design option theoretically offers you options, but in reality it just gives you a spot to pile junk. Likewise, while adjustable shelving might seem like a good idea, it rarely is. Once you commit tools to their spaces there's no need to tinker with the shelves, and the adjustable feature becomes a liability, increasing the likelihood that a shelf will tilt and dump its contents on your feet.

Even worse than a whacked foot for a woodworker (who is used to such abuse) is losing a favorite tool. To avoid this disheartening experience, I try not to squeeze too many tools into my toolboxes. If I do, I sooner or later end up hiding a smaller tool behind a larger one. If it is a tool I don't use very often (but it is, of course, the only tool worth using for a certain job), I invariably forget where I stored it. Eventually, it is forgotten entirely.

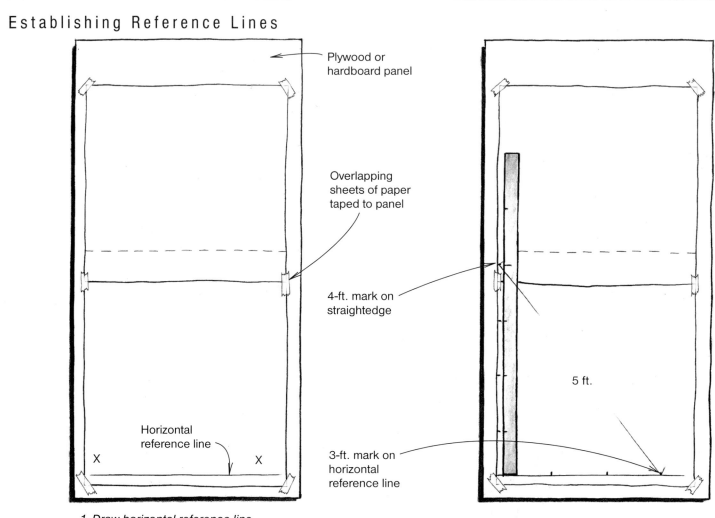

Establishing Reference Lines

Plywood or hardboard panel

Overlapping sheets of paper taped to panel

4-ft. mark on straightedge

Horizontal reference line

X   X

3-ft. mark on horizontal reference line

5 ft.

1. Draw horizontal reference line parallel to bottom edge of panel.

2. Lay out the vertical reference line. Begin by measuring and marking 3 ft. on horizontal line, then hold straightedge at starting point, as shown. Adjust straightedge until distance between 4-ft. mark on straightedge and 3-ft. mark on horizontal line measures 5 ft. Then draw line along edge of straightedge; it will be perfectly perpendicular to horizontal reference line.

Creating a full-scale rendering

To create a full-scale rendering of your toolbox, you will need the following materials and tools: a flat, smooth, and square panel to hold the drawing (¼-in. hardwood plywood or hardboard works well); a roll of butcher paper or a roll of vellum drafting paper (you may have to tape several pieces together to get the width you need); a 2-ft. square; a ruled straightedge that is as long as the longest dimension of the project; and pencils (and an eraser).

Tape a sheet of paper to the plywood panel, building up the width or length if necessary with a second sheet. Remember to allow sufficient paper to draw a side and top view in addition to the face view. If you are designing a standing chest, locate the paper even with the lower edge of the panel so you can use this edge as the base line for the drawing. That will allow you to set the drawing at floor level so you can stand back and get a good idea of the overall size and proportions of your chest when set in normal working position.

Begin the full-scale rendering by establishing reference lines, as shown in the drawing above. Draw the base line—a horizontal reference line close to the bottom of the paper and parallel to the

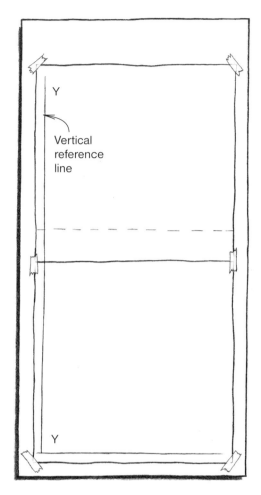

3. The paper is ready for the full-scale rendering.

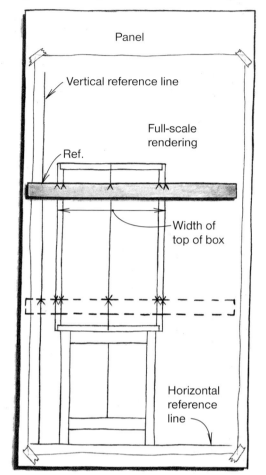

Panel

Vertical reference line

Full-scale rendering

Ref.

Width of top of box

Horizontal reference line

1. Lay out main dimensions of box on stick.

2. Reference story stick to vertical reference line to mark locations of major vertical lines of toolbox.

3. Reference story stick to horizontal reference line to mark locations of major horizontal lines of toolbox.

panel's bottom edge. Then, close to one side of the panel, draw a vertical reference line perpendicular to the base line. If the panel's side edge is perfectly square to its bottom edge, you need only measure over an even amount at the top and bottom of the panel to make this line. Otherwise, use a framing square or the classic 3, 4, 5 measurement trick shown in the drawing. Now, referring to your rough sketch, draw in the outline of the box by measuring over in equal amounts from the reference lines. Draw in the bottom, side and top panels. You can use a straight-edged story stick to ensure accuracy and to speed up the process, as shown in the drawing above right. Continue by drawing in partitions, drawer bins, and any other fixed interior components.

Extend lines up from the face to create the top view, and then to the side to create the side view (see the drawing at left on p. 74). Fill in the details of the drawing on each of the views, drawing in the cut lines of any joints, the outline of any floating panels, and views of drawer boxes, tool attachment cleats, or buttons.

Creating Top and Side Views

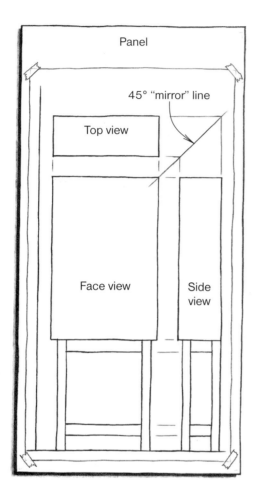

Panel

45° "mirror" line

Top view

Face view

Side view

1. Extend lines up from outside outline of face view to establish width of top view. (Establish depth by measurement.)

2. Extend lines over from top view until they intersect 45° line, then drop vertical lines from intersection points to establish depth of side view.

3. Extend lines over from face view to establish vertical locations and dimensions of side view.

Drawing Up a Cut List from a Rendering

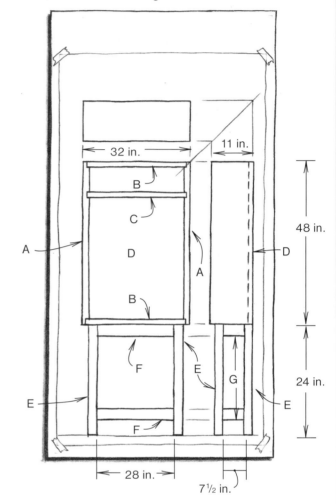

32 in.

11 in.

B

C

A

D

A

B

D

48 in.

F

E

G

E

24 in.

E

F

28 in.

7½ in.

1. Label components on rendering.

2. Make up cut list.

3. Check off labels on renderings as parts are listed on cut list.

CUT LIST FOR STANDING TOOL CABINET						
			Dimensions		**Stock**	
Symbol	**Part**	**Qty.**	**Width**	**Length**	**Solid**	**Ply.**
A	Side	2	11	48	³⁄₄	
B	Top & Bot.	2	11	31	³⁄₄	
C	Shelf	1	10³⁄₄	31	³⁄₄	
D	Back	1	31	47		¹⁄₄
E	Legs	4	1³⁄₄	24	1³⁄₄	
F	Rails	4	2¹⁄₂	30	1¹⁄₄	
G	Rails	4	2¹⁄₂	8¹⁄₂	1¹⁄₄	

A mockup of the tool arrangement for a wall cabinet on a sheet of plywood, with temporary supports and partition indicators in place. Planes have been grouped in the interior above the drawer area, and layout tools are on the back of the door. Photo by Craig Wester.

When you are satisfied with the drawing, assign labels to each of the various components. (I generally begin labeling the largest pieces first, working my way down to the smallest.) Measure the components, and record their dimensions on a cut list (see the drawing at right on the facing page). Be sure to place a check mark next to the label symbol on the drawing when you record that piece on the list. As a final check, compare the count of the recorded pieces against the number of pieces on the drawing.

Finally, before you begin constructing the box from your drawings and cut lists, a word of caution: Like it or not, your toolbox or cabinet will probably become a focal point of your shop. There, amidst the landscape of tools, machines and materials, will be the fruits of your cabinetmaking skills for all to see. I'm not saying you should be nervous about doing this project. After all, what woodworking project could be more fun to design and build than one's own tool chest or cabinet? Instead, I'm encouraging you to see the project as an opportunity to do your best work. This is one example of your work that you actually get to keep and use every day that you spend in the shop.

5
WALL CABINETS

$\mathbf{A}$side from practical considerations, there is historical precedent for wall-hung tool cabinets. By the turn of this century, some woodworkers had given up the traditional cabinetmaker's tool chest in favor of tool storage on the wall. These boxes are generally tall and shallow—a practical shape for a toolbox that is to be hung on a shop wall. The demand for wall-hung cabinets in the early 1900s was apparently great enough to inspire a number of commercial toolbox makers (such as W. Marples & Sons of England and C. E. Jennings of New York) to offer wall-mounted toolboxes in their catalogs. As you can see in the photos on pp. 79-80, the offerings even included an unusual corner-mounted version.

One of the most magnificent examples of a wall-hung toolbox is that of H. O. Studley, a gifted joiner and patternmaker. Because the cabinet was built from the same materials with which one of his

H. O. Studley's wall-hung tool cabinet, built around the turn of the century, contains nearly 300 tools. Photo by Eric Long, Smithsonian Institution.

In this turn-of-the-century photo of the workshop of the Steinway Piano Co., wall-mounted tool cabinets hang at the head of each workbench. Photo courtesy of the Smithsonian Institution.

employers constructed pianos (mahogany, ebony, and rosewood with inlays of ivory and mother-of-pearl), it is thought that Studley built the box during his tenure with the Poole Piano Co. of Boston. That would place its construction between 1890 and 1920.

As you can see in the photo on p. 76, Studley managed to fit a remarkable number of tools into a small case (only 19½ in. wide by 39 in. high by 9½ in. deep when closed). There were nearly 300 tools inside the case when it was disassembled by the Smithsonian Institution for cleaning and restoration. Studley achieved this feat with equal measures of artistry and ingenuity. Using motifs from classical architecture, he constructed arched enclosures, Gothic-style swinging doors and intricate lift-up trays. These holding strategies nestled the tools as closely together as possible without compromising their accessibility. Most of the tools can be removed without having to move another tool out of the way.

Design Considerations

I can only speculate as to the reason traditional tool chests evolved into wall-hung cabinets in some shops. Perhaps they were crowded out by the addition of bulky machinery to shop floors already burgeoning with workbenches and assembly areas. Or perhaps it was the coming of poured concrete floors—an uncomfortable but often necessary flooring material for shops outfitted with heavy machinery. Concrete's tendency to rot any wood set against it may have been inspiration enough to get craftsmen to redesign their toolboxes.

While we may never know for certain why turn-of-the-century craftsmen

By the early 1900s, some commercial toolbox manufacturers offered wall-hung cabinets, such as this Marples tool cabinet, along with their usual line of traditional joiner's and cabinetmaker's chests. Photo courtesy of the Smithsonian Institution.

This unusual cabinet, offered by C. E. Jennings & Co. in a catalog of around 1910, was designed to fit into a corner of the shop, making use of a typically wasted space.

Left: A carriagemaker's wall-hung tool cabinet, c. 1880. Although a craftsman of this era and trade might have worked for a large company, his toolbox was apparently still his own, as evidenced by the "pin-ups." Photo courtesy of The Museums at Stony Brook.

Above: A rear view of the Studley cabinet, shown open on p. 76. Two mounting rails are fitted to the back panel. Mating ledger strips would have been attached to the shop's wall studs. Photo courtesy of the Smithsonian Institution.

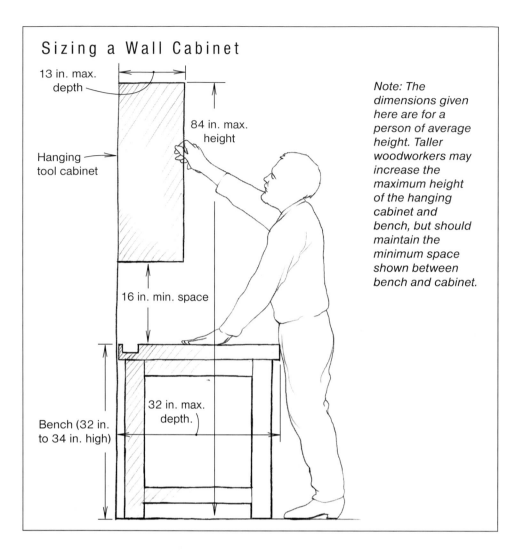

Sizing a Wall Cabinet

13 in. max. depth

84 in. max. height

Hanging tool cabinet

16 in. min. space

Bench (32 in. to 34 in. high)

32 in. max. depth.

Note: The dimensions given here are for a person of average height. Taller woodworkers may increase the maximum height of the hanging cabinet and bench, but should maintain the minimum space shown between bench and cabinet.

chose to mount their tool chests on the wall, I know why I have done so: It was a simple matter of space. Having done woodworking for many years out of a two-car garage, I became convinced that keeping the shop floor clear of storage, especially at the perimeter, is one of the best ways to maximize the precious open space. It is open space, possibly more than any other factor, that endows my small shop with the efficiency and flexibility I need to do woodworking comfortably, safely, and at the commercial pace necessary to make a living.

LOCATION

When looking for wall space to hang a tool cabinet, the first location to consider is the area over your primary workbench. That is where you'll likely want to keep most of your hand bench tools and where your floor space is already committed. Of course, this location may not work for you if your bench is so wide and deep that you would have trouble reaching into the cabinet. Note in the drawing above how the useful height and depth of a wall cabinet relate to the depth of a workbench underneath.

You can, however, reorient a workbench so that its narrow end butts against the wall, thereby allowing you to get at the tool cabinet from either side.

That is how the benches were arranged in the Steinway Piano Co. (see the top photo on p. 78). You may, in fact, discover some additional advantages to this orientation, especially if you use the bench surface for assembly as well as joinery work. For instance, since you can easily get at three sides of the project, you minimize the need to move the assembly around to work on it. In addition, if you attach additional vises, you can accommodate another worker along the other side of the bench. This is a highly suitable arrangement for school shops, where space and the need for versatility are at a premium.

Your shop may have other wall-mounting areas you'd like to consider, but when searching for that perfect location, there are some other factors to keep in mind. For energy conservation (yours), hang the tool cabinet as close as possible to the place you'll be using most of the tools. In addition, make sure that the box won't block any window light when its doors are fully opened. Also make sure that there is room to swing the cabinet doors flat against the wall (see the top drawing on the facing page). If swing-out doors pose a problem, you might want to build doors that disappear into the cabinet; see the bottom drawing on the facing page for some suggestions.

The final consideration is traffic flow—the cabinet should not interfere with it in any way. If the cabinet isn't hung over a bench or other fixed object, there will always be the risk that you or someone else will walk into it or stand up underneath it. You can minimize this hazard by placing the cabinet in an area where you normally do not walk. If you have little choice but to situate the cabinet in the traffic pattern, plan to make the box as shallow as possible.

Locating Wall Cabinets

LIGHT AND ACCESSIBILITY

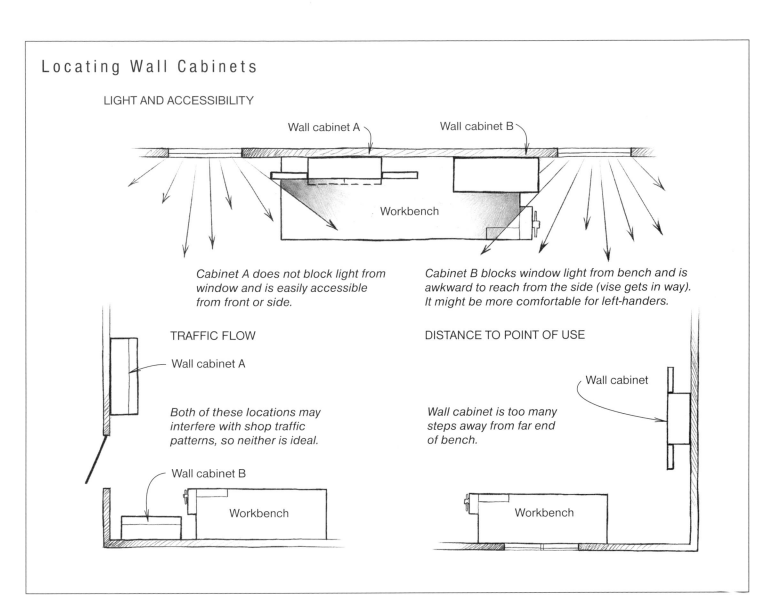

Wall cabinet A

Wall cabinet B

Workbench

Cabinet A does not block light from window and is easily accessible from front or side.

Cabinet B blocks window light from bench and is awkward to reach from the side (vise gets in way). It might be more comfortable for left-handers.

TRAFFIC FLOW

Wall cabinet A

Both of these locations may interfere with shop traffic patterns, so neither is ideal.

Wall cabinet B

Workbench

DISTANCE TO POINT OF USE

Wall cabinet

Wall cabinet is too many steps away from far end of bench.

Workbench

Doors that Disappear

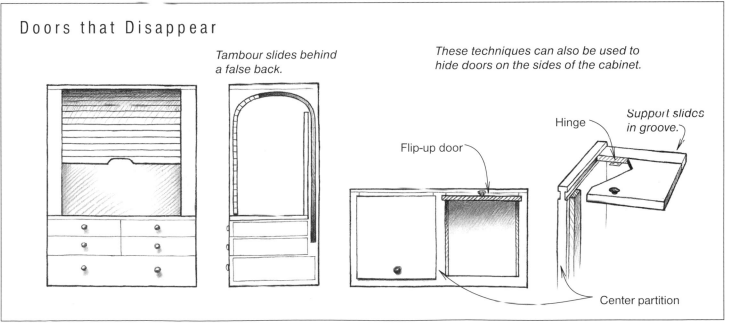

Tambour slides behind a false back.

These techniques can also be used to hide doors on the sides of the cabinet.

Flip-up door

Hinge

Support slides in groove.

Center partition

This bow-front wall-hung tool cabinet, designed and built by Garrett Hack, of Thetford Center, Vt., makes excellent use of space. Small items are in drawers at the middle of the cabinet; molding planes fill the lowermost bin, where their profiles are clearly in view; and handled tools are near the top of the cabinet on pegs or ledges. Photo by Vincent Laurence.

INTERIOR LAYOUT

Laying out the interior of a wall cabinet presents some challenges not encountered when designing a tool chest that sits on the floor. Because the wall cabinet is generally hung with its lowest point at chest height (either to fit over a bench or to make the most of the available space beneath it), you must carefully consider the weight of each tool you plan to keep there. Because your larger back muscles can't provide much support to your arms at chest height and above, it isn't comfortable or safe to store tools in a wall cabinet that weigh more than about 10 lb. This problem is exacerbated if a bench runs in front of the cabinet, forcing you to lean over to gain access to it. You may need to find another place, then, to store your plunge router or circular saw.

To make the most of interior space, you'll probably want your cabinet to be as tall as your reach allows. But bear in mind that the height of the cabinet will affect the design of the interior partitions. For example, you'll find that locating deep compartments near the top of a wall cabinet just doesn't work. Besides having to force your hands into an unnatural angle to grab anything—making it hard to get a good grip on certain items—you'll need to jump or stand on something to see what you have stored.

Instead of compartments, it's generally better to outfit the topmost part of a wall cabinet with pegs or brackets from which you can hang long-handled tools such as Japanese saws, squares, drill braces and planes (you'll have to pierce the soles of metal-soled planes or add eyebolts to the ends of wood-bodied planes). Since you can grab these tools low along their length, it works to hang them in the upper areas of the box.

The storage capacity and versatility of a wall-hung cabinet are much enhanced by drawers. Drawers can contain all manner of small tools and accessories that otherwise would be difficult to store. However, it is often difficult to see into the drawers of a wall cabinet—in typical installations, only the lowest areas of the box are below eye level. For this reason, relatively small, easily removable drawers work best. If the box is located near or over a bench, you'll have the option of setting the drawers down on the bench to get at their contents. If there is no bench nearby, you might consider (as I did in the cabinet described below) adding a slide-out support tray to the bottom of the cabinet (see the photo at top right).

Building a Wall-Hung Tool Cabinet

When I sat down to design a wall-hung tool cabinet, my intent was to create a box that would contain an ample selection of hand tools for both layout and joinery—enough to allow me to do most of my typical work without having to look elsewhere for a tool. I planned to locate these tools as close as possible to my work area at the vise end of my workbench, where they would be accessible, yet out of my way. As it turned out, this cabinet was an ideal solution. Because the tool-laden door swings out to the left over the open end of the bench, I can get at the tools stored there almost without taking a step—I just stretch out my left hand. This is especially convenient because I naturally want most layout tools in my left hand. I use my right hand to remove the drawer bins and to grab the hand planes stored on the right side of the cabinet.

Because I'm one of those restless people who like to try out new shop

Jim Tolpin's wall-hung tool cabinet features removable drawers and a slide-out support tray. Photo by Craig Wester.

Tolpin's wall-hung tool cabinet houses tools for layout and joinery. In its location close to the vise end of the workbench, the cabinet blocks no floor space yet is only a step away from where the tools are used. Photo by Craig Wester.

Because this cabinet hangs on angled cleats, it can easily be taken down and moved to another area of the shop. Photo by Craig Wester.

arrangements (not to mention new shop buildings) every few years, I design most of my cabinetry and other shop fixtures to be relatively easy to move. This wall-hung cabinet is no exception. I designed and built this cabinet to hang on a pair of full-length wooden cleats whose edges I'd cut to a 45° angle (see the photo at left). When I want to try out a different cabinet location in the shop, I screw a cleat to the studs at the new location, lift the box off the wall (I don't even have to empty it if I have a willing helper) and set it in its new home. I leave the old cleat in place in case I decide to move the cabinet back. For security, I can attach the cabinet permanently to the wall by driving screws from inside the cabinet into the wall-mounted cleat.

DESIGN NOTES

To make the box suitably strong yet relatively easy and quick to build, the case and door components are joined with biscuits. The door is made from $\frac{1}{2}$-in. maple plywood; edgebanding of $\frac{5}{8}$-in. thick solid maple enhances the appearance and protects the plywood edges from deteriorating (and possibly eventually splintering) in use. To strengthen the door so it would carry the weight of my tools without distorting, I "boxed" the door by making this banding $2\frac{3}{4}$ in. wide. The case and interior partitions are built from $\frac{5}{8}$-in. hard maple boards and the drawers from $\frac{5}{16}$-in. Honduras mahogany. The drawer and sliding shelf pulls are carved from ebony.

Since the faces of the drawers are visible even with the door closed, and because extractable drawers should have strong joints, I opted for finger joints. While a number of other joints might serve as well, I particularly enjoy the visual interest that finger joints lend to the face of a drawer box, and there is no question that they have tremendous

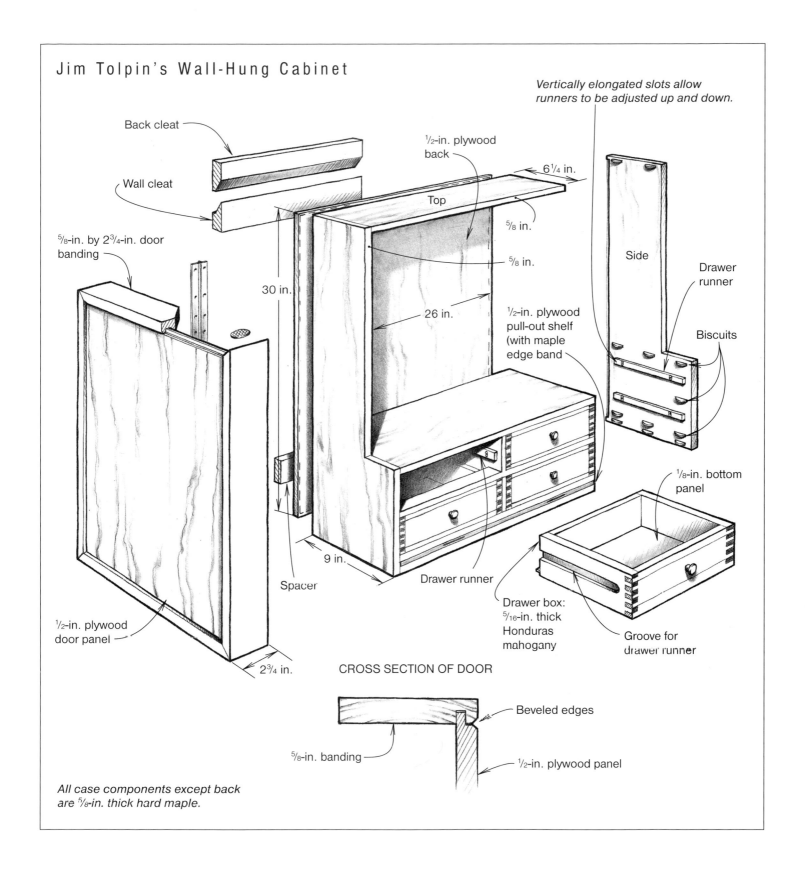

Jim Tolpin's Wall-Hung Cabinet

Back cleat

Wall cleat

⅝-in. by 2¾-in. door banding

Vertically elongated slots allow runners to be adjusted up and down.

½-in. plywood back

Top

6¼ in.

⅝ in.

⅝ in.

30 in.

26 in.

½-in. plywood pull-out shelf (with maple edge band

Side

Drawer runner

Biscuits

½-in. plywood door panel

2¾ in.

Spacer

9 in.

Drawer runner

⅛-in. bottom panel

Drawer box: 5/16-in. thick Honduras mahogany

Groove for drawer runner

CROSS SECTION OF DOOR

⅝-in. banding

Beveled edges

½-in. plywood panel

All case components except back are ⅝-in. thick hard maple.

Face-slotting the side board with a biscuit joiner. The bottom board is clamped over the side board, as the scrap piece at right helps support the machine. Photo by Craig Wester.

strength because of their extensive gluing surface.

I created drawer slides by making runners for the case from mahogany and cutting a matching stopped dado in the side of the drawer boxes. The bottom panel of the drawers extends past the sides to serve as an adjustable drawer stop. This simple system provides positive sliding action with little wobble or binding. The pull-out shelf (made from ½-in. maple plywood with a facing of solid maple) fits into its own compartment beneath the drawers.

To keep the toolbox from getting grimy under my work-soiled hands, I finished it inside and out with several coats of clear shellac—one of my favorite finishes. Shellac is low in toxicity, extremely easy to apply, self-leveling and quick-drying. It also buffs easily to a high sheen. However, shellac will not stand up well to many solvents or to standing water, but neither is much of a problem with a wall-hung tool cabinet.

CONSTRUCTION PROCEDURES

Once you have drawn a full-size rendering of your tool cabinet and used it to develop a cut list for all the components (see pp. 72-75), you are ready to assemble your materials and begin construction.

Preparing the parts

With your cut list in hand, lay out the solid-stock components on the boards and then cut them out to rough dimension (add ½ in. to the specified lengths and at least ⅛ in. to the widths). Next finish-plane the oversized components to their final thickness (⅝ in. for the case components and 5⁄16 in. for the drawer stock).

Now cut the components to final width and length, with this exception: Cut the drawer sides, face and back 1⁄16 in. over length. That way, when you cut the finger joints they will protrude 1⁄32 in. past the corners. You'll trim these joints flush after the boxes are assembled. Also wait to cut the door banding and its plywood panel to final size until after the case is assembled, in order to ensure a precise fit. Do, however, cut the plywood for the case back and the drawer bottoms to their finished dimension, taking diagonal measurements to be sure that these components are perfectly square.

End slotting the bottom board with the biscuit joiner. Photo by Craig Wester.

Making the case

To speed up the work and to increase the accuracy of making the slots for the biscuits, I have developed a method of using the case components themselves as a tool jig. This trick does two things: It provides a convenient, solid bearing surface against which to set the baseplate of the machine, and it shows you where to center the slots for both the face and end cuts.

Begin by clamping the bottom of the case on top of one side, holding the former in from the end of the side at exactly the thickness of the bottom board. Use a scrap of stock both to space the board the exact distance in from the end and to act as an additional support for the joiner's baseplate during the machining process. Having marked the biscuit centerlines on the bottom board, hold the joiner upright and align its baseplate centerline to the layout mark.

After making the slots in the face of the underlying side board at the centerline marks (see the photo on the facing page), hold the machine horizontally and run it into the end of the bottom board (see the photo above). Again, be careful to align the machine's baseplate to the centerline layout marks. To continue the slotting process, unclamp the bottom board and clamp another horizontal component at its layout mark on the side board. Repeat the process until you've made all the slots for this side of the case.

After cutting the slots for the entire case, install the drawer runners (note the vertically elongated pilot holes for the attachment screws) and then dry-fit the components. There should be no gaps at the butt joints, and all the components should meet at their layout marks. If necessary, make fine adjustments by trimming the shape of the biscuits. When you are satisfied with the fit, break the case down and remove the biscuits (keep track of the orientation of any biscuits you've had to modify). Now you are ready to assemble the case.

Begin by injecting glue into the slots and spreading a film of glue on the biscuits. Then insert the biscuits and tap the components together. Lift the assembly onto a pair of leveled supports and apply the clamps. To ensure that the

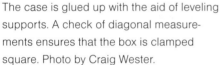

The case is glued up with the aid of leveling supports. A check of diagonal measurements ensures that the box is clamped square. Photo by Craig Wester.

The mitered ends of the door banding are slotted with a biscuit joiner. Photo by Craig Wester.

assembly is square, check for uniform diagonal measurements across the corners of the case (see the photo above left). If you need to make a correction, adjust the angle of clamping pressure. Once the glue has dried, remove the clamps and cut the rabbet to receive the ½-in. maple plywood back panel. (I used a router fitted with a rabbeting bit to make the cut, then squared the rounded corners with a chisel.) Finally, glue and tack the back panel in place.

Building the door

After cutting the door banding to rough length, mill a dado along its inside faces to receive the door panel. Next, cut the banding's ends with miter joints at the finished length after checking the size of the door opening in the assembled case. To join the miter with a biscuit, run the joiner into the face of the miter as shown in the photo above right. After cutting the ½-in. plywood door panel to size, make a rabbet around its perimeter to fit the dado cut into the banding. Bevel the

exposed edge of the rabbet for looks. After dry-assembling the door to check the fit, break it down and reassemble it with glue and clamps.

Building the drawers and slide-out shelf

The key to making tight-fitting finger joints on the table saw is to use a jig that will index the cuts precisely while carrying the parts smoothly by the dado blade without any noticeable side play. Once such a fixture is set up for a certain finger spacing, it will produce row after row of the joints with micrometer-like precision.

After some experimentation I came up with a jig that meets these two requirements (see the top drawing at right). To index the cut with precision, I made the index block from a piece of ebony—a dense wood highly resistant to wear. If it should eventually wear, I can easily replace it by unscrewing it from its notch in the fence. To ensure that the jig would run smoothly and without side play, I made its runners (which slide in the table saw's miter grooves) from straight-grained lengths of teak, a wood that is hard, stable and self-lubricating. I made the runners slightly oversized, then scraped them down until they had just the right amount of resistance with no side play whatsoever.

Since the distance between the block and the dado blade is critical, I made the jig with a double fence. The inside fence carrying the index block slides back and forth against the outside fence, locking in place with C- clamps. (Someday perhaps I'll clean up the design by replacing the clamps with through bolts run through slotted holes.) For details on how to use the jig, see the sidebar on p. 90.

After cutting the fingers for all the box corners, cut the dado for the bottom panel into the face and sides (I used a slotting cutter on my table-mounted router). Then dry-assemble the box. The fingers should protrude slightly ($1/32$ in. if you cut the pieces a total of $1/16$ in. oversize). After checking to see if the joints are tight and that the box is square and free of warp, proceed to glue the box up around its bottom panel. When the assembly is dry, chisel back the protruding fingers and lightly round over all the exposed edges (I used a $1/8$-in. roundover bit installed in a trim router).

Finger-Joint Jig

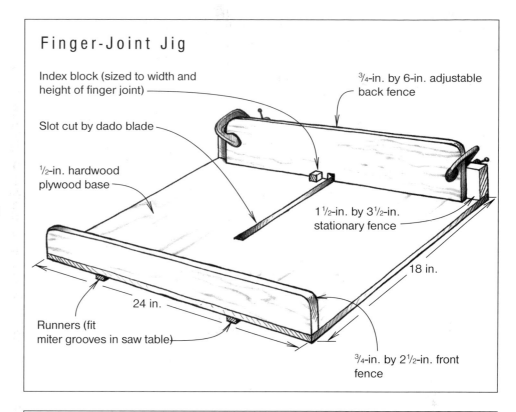

Index block (sized to width and height of finger joint)

$3/4$-in. by 6-in. adjustable back fence

Slot cut by dado blade

$1/2$-in. hardwood plywood base

$1\,1/2$-in. by $3\,1/2$-in. stationary fence

18 in.

24 in.

Runners (fit miter grooves in saw table)

$3/4$-in. by $2\,1/2$-in. front fence

Routing Drawer-Runner Grooves

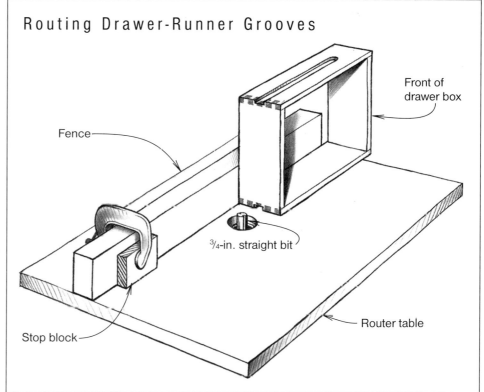

Front of drawer box

Fence

$3/4$-in. straight bit

Router table

Stop block

Begin by carefully preparing the stock to be finger-joined. The pieces should be of exactly the same thickness and width or the joints will not come out even. Make extra pieces to be used as scrap stock for setting up the jig. As an aesthetic rule of thumb (and to make setup a bit easier), plan to make the width of the finger joints equal to the thickness of the stock. After cutting the stock to length (I usually make the parts exactly $\frac{1}{16}$ in. oversize so I can later trim the $\frac{1}{32}$-in. protruding fingers at each corner flush), separate the components into two piles: ends (fronts and backs) and sides.

Install a dado blade set up to cut the desired finger width. Now place the jig on the saw table and begin the setup process. First, set the sawblade height equal to the

thickness of the stock plus $\frac{1}{32}$ in. for trimming. Next, by loosening the C-clamps and moving the back fence, set the index-block spacing. The block should be fixed at a distance away from the side of the dado blade exactly equal to the width of the cut.

Now make a test cut, using one piece of scrap to represent a box side and another to represent an end. For the cleanest cut, lift the stock from the jig after pushing it through the sawblade—do not bring it backward through the spinning blade. If the joints are too tight (you want the pieces to fit easily together without any forcing), move the block closer to the dado blade. If the joint is so loose you can see hairline gaps between the fingers, move the block away. Note that the adjustment range here is very small—you need only change

the block-to-blade spacing a few thousandths of an inch to affect the fit of the joint.

When you are happy with the look and feel of the joint between the two scrap pieces, you are ready to cut the real thing. First, though, check to be sure that the C-clamps holding the adjustable fence to

the back fence of the jig are secure and that the blade-height adjustment on the table saw is locked down tight. Now run all the sides through the saw, aligning the edge of the stock to the side of the dado cut as shown in the drawing at right. Finally, run all the fronts and backs.

Finger-Joint-Jig Setup

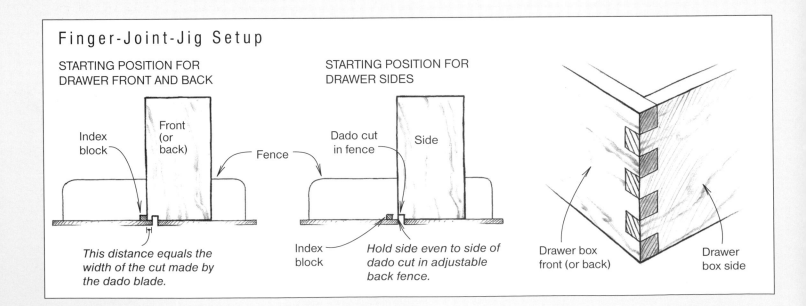

STARTING POSITION FOR DRAWER FRONT AND BACK

Index block

Front (or back)

Fence

This distance equals the width of the cut made by the dado blade.

STARTING POSITION FOR DRAWER SIDES

Dado cut in fence

Side

Index block

Hold side even to side of dado cut in adjustable back fence.

Drawer box front (or back)

Drawer box side

Using a table-mounted router fitted with a ¾-in. straight bit, cut the groove for the drawer runners along the sides of each drawer (see the bottom drawing on p. 89). Be sure to test the depth and the location of the cut on a scrap piece of stock first. Notice that the stop block prevents the groove from running through the face of the drawer. Also, because the groove is centered on the drawer side, you can flip the drawer to groove the other side of the box without changing any settings.

Finishing up

Slide the drawers into their runners in the case and check to see how smoothly they operate. You can trim the edge of the runners with a small scraper blade to fine-tune the motion of the drawer. To align the drawer box to the case, slide the runners up or down along their slotted screw holes. If the drawers protrude from the case, the back of the bottom panel is hitting the back of the case too soon—trim it back slightly with a plane. Rub candle wax into the groove on the drawer side to ensure a smooth sliding action. Next, install and then trim the edges of the slide-out shelf for ease of operation and fit. Finally, apply the finish of your choice to all the exposed wood surfaces.

To complete the tool chest, cut out the pieces for the hanging cleat and spacer and screw them to the back of the case. Then, with the case lying on its back on the bench, set the door next to it on some support blocks. Holding the door temporarily in place with clamps, proceed to screw on the piano hinge (see the photo above). With the box still lying on the bench, install the locking catch and add the interior partitions, ledges and holding fixtures. Finally, pick up the box and carry it to where you've installed the receiving cleat on your shop wall. With the cabinet now hanging in place, it's time for the most enjoyable part of the job: installing your cherished tools in their new home.

Cabinetmaker Martha Collins, of Sequim, Wash., installed this expansive standing cabinet near her workbench. Photo by Richard Schneider.

6
STANDING TOOL
CABINETS

The standing chest is one of the most efficient (and some would say most attractive) ways to store a collection of hand tools. It is not, however, necessarily everybody's best solution. A standing tool cabinet, though relatively narrow, still demands a chunk of floor space—usually at the juncture of the floor and the wall. In a small shop, this is a particularly valuable area, as it is one of the few places where parts can be collated and stacked out of the way, or where clamped assemblies can be leaned to dry without being disturbed. The decision to take away even a little of this prime, in-shop real estate should not be made lightly.

A standing cabinet, in order to contain a decent number of tools at a comfortable working height, must be a rather imposing piece of work—as high as the top of your head (or higher) and as wide (with the doors opened) as your outstretched arms. This requirement is

not, of course, necessarily a problem—tool storage is as good a use for wall space as any. But it does mean you must find a place for this sizable chunk of cabinetry close by your main workbench, yet not so close that it could interfere with your activities there. And once set in this location, the cabinet (with or without its doors open) should not block any natural light available to your work area. Nor should the opened doors block access to other tools or materials stored on the walls to either side. If you are lucky enough to be designing your own shop space, it would be wise to consider the placement of your standing tool cabinet as well as your major workbenches and stationary machines when developing the floor and window plan.

A Cabinet that Departs from Tradition

Several decades ago, furniture maker David Powell, now of Easthampton, Massachusetts, went to work in the renowned workshops of Edward Barnsley in Froxfield, England. Surrounded by master woodworkers who had learned and refined their skills in the Arts and Crafts era that flowered in the early years of this century, Powell received a rich, inspiring education that left him with a lifelong dedication to fine woodworking. Yet when it came time for him to build a chest for his hand tools, he passed over the traditional cabinetmaker's chests that surrounded him. Instead, he struck out on his own to design and build a box uniquely suited to his needs. For Powell, the classic chest wouldn't do—he felt the layered storage

tills opening into an empty well wasted space and made access to many tools more difficult and time-consuming than necessary. He also could not see building a box that would sit on the floor, forcing him to bend or crouch down every time he wanted to get at a tool.

Starting with a blank piece of paper and an idea of what he didn't want, Powell began designing his toolbox. Having designed and built a number of tall furniture pieces, he wasn't surprised to discover that an upright standing cabinet seemed to offer the ideal solution. In the upper half of the cabinet Powell drew in drawers to organize a multitude of small tools. In the remaining space, he created a variety of pigeonholes to contain his collection of planes and other assorted tools. To hold bulky items such as panel saws, Yankee screwdrivers, squares and other layout tools in plain view and ready for instant use, he designed a pair of sturdy

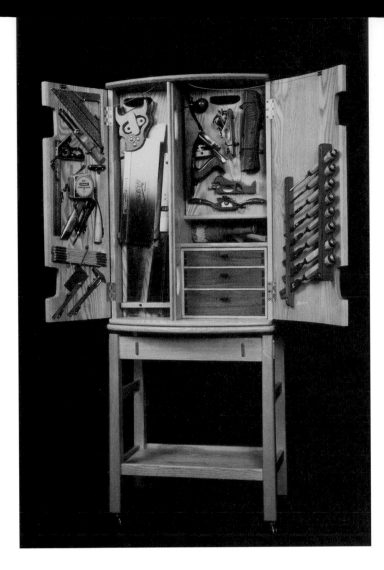 

swing-out doors and a lift-up top lid. To avoid creating difficult-to-reach storage areas near floor level, while at the same time bringing the rest of the case to a comfortable working height, Powell decided to support the case on a simple, open-base frame.

Now, years later and many thousands of miles away from Barnsley's shop, Powell still works daily out of this standing toolbox. Created in a place and time where the traditional cabinetmaker's chest reigned supreme, his standing cabinet has proven to be as easy and efficient to use as he had hoped. And now, having himself become a master craftsman who has overseen the education of many aspiring woodworkers, his tool-storage solution has inspired and engendered the creations of countless offspring.

A Standing Cabinet for Shop and Site

If the type of woodworking you do demands that you be versatile (perhaps you spend half your time building fine furniture in your shop and the other half installing doors and trim in new homes), then you may want to design your primary tool-storage system to be versatile as well. When Sheldon Perry, of Tamworth, New Hampshire, set out to build himself a toolbox, he was in just this situation. Appreciating the ease of access and voluminous storage area a standing cabinet would provide his shop, he was unwilling to do with less when he worked on site. The challenge was to find a way to make the cabinet serve both facets of his work situation equally well.

Sheldon Perry decided that his standing cabinet had to serve him in his shop and on building sites. His design features removable tool boards, drawer till and support stand, and a bowed front that maintains ample interior volume while giving the box a more manageable shape. Photo by Brooks Dodge.

significantly reduced. To provide carry points, Perry created hand grips by cutting elongated holes into the center partition. Notches cut along the edges of the door provide an attractive, yet entirely functional, access to these grips. To keep the tools in place on their support pegs or brackets while the case is being transported, Perry added miniature bungee cords to the tool supports. He removes the cords once the box is set up—either in the shop or on a job site.

An Outstanding Standing Chest

For ten years, furniture maker Andy Rae, of Lenhartsville, Pennsylvania, ruminated on the idea of building a standing tool chest that would be large and complex enough to contain the bulk of his hand tools. Finally, with the acquisition of five beautiful matched flitches of Honduras mahogany and a few prize tiger-maple boards, the time had arrived. Gathering together the tools to be stored, he arranged them in various groupings, measuring them until he finally got the design down on paper. Then the fun began.

Rae began construction by making the case framework from mahogany, joining it together with hefty mortise-and-tenon joints. He used sliding dovetails to attach the dividers and shelves to the frame. To build the upper box-type doors, he surrounded a solid-wood panel with four boards joined at

The solution came when Perry happened on the idea of creating removable "tool boards." These boards—one fitted to carry saws and the other a selection of planes and spokeshaves—would perform equally well whether fixed into the cabinet for shop work or installed on a job site. The till of drawers is also removable, allowing it to be independent of the mother case.

To make the case itself easily transportable, Perry had to limit its weight and bulk as much as possible. The gentle bow designed into the face of the cabinet both enhances the looks of the box and reduces its mass, yet sacrifices only a minimum amount of volume. And because the open base support is independent of the case, the the cabinet's overall size and weight are

Rae's cabinet features holly and ebony inlay and ebony handles (left).The Honduras mahogany veneer on the doors is thick enough to create raised panels; the coved drawer face (above) mimics waist molding in traditional furniture designs. Photo by John Hamel.

their corners with spline miter joints. The lower doors featured a mortise-and-tenon framework joined around a floating raised panel. Rae made up his own string inlay from ebony, holly and fiddleback maple, oversizing it in thickness to create a distinct border between the bevels and the flat fielded areas of the door panels.

To create an efficient work triangle within his shop, Rae teamed up his new toolbox with his workbench and low assembly table. Having outfitted the standing chest with an ample number of drawers and a pair of large tool-bearing doors, he brought the bulk of his hand tools close to the two work areas where they would most often be needed. Within the chest itself, he situated the

most frequently used tools, such as hand planes, chisels and layout tools, where they would be clearly visible and easy to grab. He tucked away lesser-used items behind doors or within the divided drawers. Because this toolbox was ten years in the making—at least in his head—Rae has found little that he would change or modify in the design.

For the doors, Faeth created his own three-ply plywood by gluing a thin veneer to either side of an edge-laminated core of solid wood. Photo by Reinhold Faeth.

Two Designs for Stacking Tool Chests

Another effective way to build versatility and mobility into a standing tool cabinet is to center the design around the concept of modular construction. In this scheme a large cabinet can be built up from a series of integrated, stacking modules. Remembering how in centuries past, Europeans kept their valuables in stackable "fire boxes" so they could be instantly carried out of a burning house, cabinetmaker Reinhold Faeth, of Heiligenberg-Steigen, Germany, created this tall standing tool cabinet from a set of four relatively small chests. To ensure the stability of the stacked assembly, he successively reduced the width of the boxes and angled back their faces. These angled faces take advantage of the force of gravity to hold the doors open at a full 180°.

Reinhold Faeth's modular stacking tool chests are based on the traditional European fire box. Each module holds a job-specific array of tools and can be removed from the stack for transportation to a job site. Photos by Reinhold Faeth.

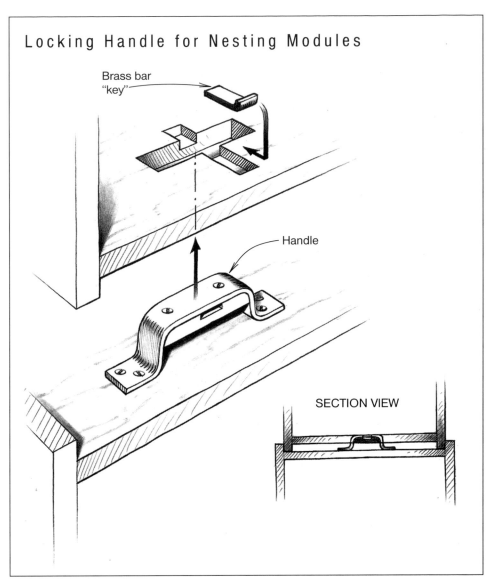

Locking Handle for Nesting Modules

Brass bar "key"

Handle

SECTION VIEW

The bar-stock handle on the lower module protrudes through the floor of the upper module. A brass bar "key" slides into the recess in the floor of the upper module, locking the two modules together. Photo by Reinhold Faeth.

Not wanting to have to tote the entire stack of cabinets with him every time he worked away from the shop, Faeth carefully organized his tools on a module-to-module basis. One chest contains only sketching and drafting tools, another holds tools specific to cabinet installation. To provide a convenient way to carry the chests, Faeth created and installed brass handles. With the units stacked, the handles protrude through the floor of the overlying module, where a brass bar locks the units together (see the drawing above). With the doors locked, it's impossible to remove these keys and unstack the modules.

Harold Purcell, of Port Townsend, Washington, also drew upon some old European memories when he set out to design a tool chest for his growing collection of hand woodworking tools and accessories: the 18th-century campaign chest. These chests, originally designed to accompany British military officers on their pursuit of Napoleon, were sturdily built of hardwood and often reinforced with metal strapping. To make them easier to carry on the campaign, the chests were made to

Inspired by 18th-century campaign chests, furniture maker Harold Purcell designed a large, but portable, tool cabinet composed of three units on a removable support base. Each component weighs less than 30 lb. when unloaded. Photo by Vincent Laurence.

A locking dovetail key links the bottom and middle units together. Photo by Craig Wester.

A shopmade brass cam locks the doors shut. Photo by Craig Wester.

separate from their base frames. Side handles provided lifting and tie-down points. Knowing how much a fully stocked tool cabinet might weigh and that a helping hand might not always be available when he needed to move his tools, Purcell was drawn to the idea of a campaign-style tool chest.

To ensure that he would be able to lift the chest by himself, Purcell broke it into three parts: a base featuring two deep drawers to contain power tools and accessories; a middle unit of 18 slide-out trays for small hand tools and miscellaneous items; and a lidded top

bin to hold bulkier tools such as jointer planes and a 24-in. straightedge. Wanting to be sure that these components would form a rigid structure when assembled onto the support base, Purcell devised a locking dovetail key between the bottom and middle units (see the photo at top right). To lock the top unit in place, he designed the sides of the bin to lip over the underlying unit. A simple, shopmade brass cam (see the photo above right) acts as a lock to hold the doors shut.

Building a Standing Cabinet

When Greg Radley, of Ventura, California, set out to design a tool cabinet for his shop, he did not worry about portability—he had no intention of ever moving this particular toolbox. Instead of designing for versatility and mobility, Radley's challenge was to create a box of a reasonable size that would not only hold his large collection of tools, but would hold them in a way that allowed those most commonly used to be visible and easily accessible. In addition to his hand tools, Radley also hoped to store a good assortment of power tools in the cabinet, creating a one-stop tool station for perhaps 90% of his day-to-day tool needs. As if this weren't challenge enough, Radley was also faced with having to live up to his hard-won reputation as a fine furniture maker—this tool cabinet was going to have to be finely made and be good-looking to boot.

How did the concept of this particular cabinet come about? In Radley's own words: "In the beginning, my tools fit neatly in a cardboard box. In short order I outgrew the box so I bought a small mechanic's-type toolbox. Soon I outgrew that one, too, so I built and fit my tools in a portable folding chest that was much like a suitcase. I found that I seldom carried my tools around so I hung it up on the wall. I eventually outgrew this, too, and had tools all over the shop. This was a problem that had to be solved, so I began looking at every tool chest and article on tool chests that I could find. I was inspired to build my tool chest from several sources, one of which was the Studley toolbox (see the photo on p. 76). I am a very visual person and I like to have my tools where I can see them. I don't like searching through drawers. When I'm in a hurry (which is most of the time), I quite often open the wrong drawer first and then realize that the drawer next to it was the one I wanted. I had to have an orderly layout where the tools could be easily seen and accessed as I needed them.

"When I finally decided on the configuration of the tool chest, I decided to make it beautiful as well as functional. This tool chest was going to be mine and I was planning to look at it every day for a long time. I also wanted to impress future clients so they would know without a doubt that I could build their furniture."

Greg Radley's standing tool cabinet, of Honduras mahogany, ash and curly and stained ash veneers, was designed with both beauty and function in mind. Photo by Vincent Laurence.

To my mind, Radley's cabinet is the epitome of a good toolbox. The chest itself is certainly attractive, and the joinery impeccable. But even more important, I give this tool chest top grades for practicality and function. By devoting the utility cabinet in the base of the chest to his collection of power tools, Radley left the rest of the cabinet free to carry an impressive selection of hand tools. To some extent, the function of the case followed its form.

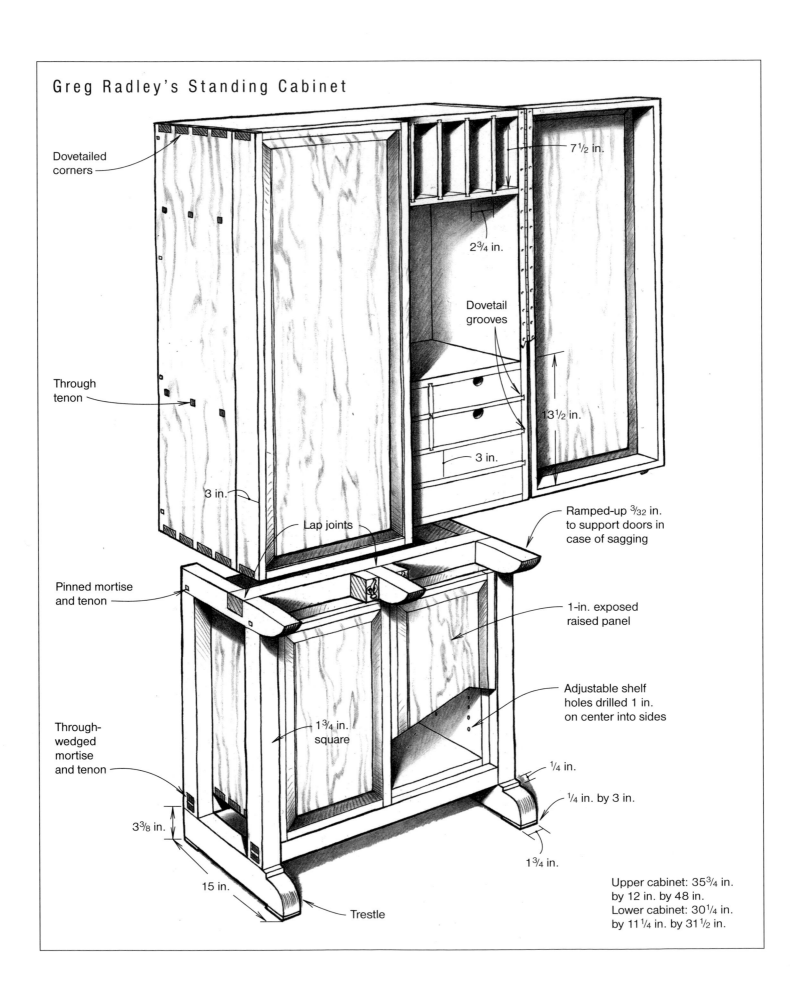

Greg Radley's Standing Cabinet

Dovetailed corners

7½ in.

2¾ in.

Dovetail grooves

13½ in.

3 in.

Through tenon

3 in.

Lap joints

Ramped-up ³⁄₃₂ in. to support doors in case of sagging

Pinned mortise and tenon

1-in. exposed raised panel

Adjustable shelf holes drilled 1 in. on center into sides

1¾ in. square

¼ in.

¼ in. by 3 in.

Through-wedged mortise and tenon

1¾ in.

3³⁄₈ in.

15 in.

Trestle

Upper cabinet: 35¾ in. by 12 in. by 48 in.
Lower cabinet: 30¼ in. by 11¼ in. by 31½ in.

DESIGN NOTES

Radley built the cabinet out of Honduras mahogany, ash, and curly and stained ash veneers. He determined the overall width of the cabinet by the size of the pieces of veneer he had, calculating the maximum size of the door from the width of one piece of veneer. Two doors equaled the width of the cabinet. He determined the maximum practical height of the tool chest by the length of his outstreched arm, and the depth by the length of the hand planes he wanted to store in the top of the chest. He set the depth of the doors to the width of the widest tool he wanted to hang on the door, and made the lowest measurement of the chest correspond to how far he was willing to bend over to get tools out of the bottom drawer.

The interior layout was developed through a series of thumbnail sketches, but the final layout wasn't established until after the cabinet was assembled. Like tools are grouped together: layout tools in one area, saws in the next. Radley lay the chest on its back with the doors supported in the open position and then started placing the tools inside. Gravity held them in place while he shuffled them around until he had them all organized in the least possible amount of space.

Clustering the eight small tool drawers at elbow level makes them easy to see into, and to remove for sifting through at a bench. (Note that the finger-pull holes are drilled large enough to accommodate a gloved hand.) To ensure that bulky tools would be easy to get at, Radley arranged them on quick-release brackets in the boxed upper-cabinet panel doors. His clever arrangement maximizes the number of tools fixed to the doors without interfering with access to them. No tool need be moved in order to get at another. Radley also carefully thought out the placement of his planes, setting the heaviest at the mid-height of the cabinet while sliding the rest into pigeonholes marching across the top of the case. Stops prevent the shorter planes from getting lost toward the back of their holes. Finally, note how Radley placed up to 18 chisels in a stepped bracket arrangement—though crowded, each handle is visible and readily accessible.

Decisions about joinery were next. When planning the construction methods for the tool cabinet, Radley was after sturdiness, and he also wanted to show off the effort that would go into the project. Thus he decided on through dovetails and through-wedged tenons.

CONSTRUCTION PROCEDURES

Now let's go through the building of the upper and lower cases of the standing chest, then discuss the building and fitting of the doors and drawers. Next comes the construction of the trestle, which encloses the lower utility cabinet and supports the upper cabinet. Finally comes a discussion of the design and fit of the upper-cabinet tool supports. But be forewarned: Before attempting to build a complex project such as this one, I highly recommend that you create a full-scale rendering from the scaled drawings, as discussed on pp. 72-75. The time it takes you to generate this drawing will be more than repaid with greater overall accuracy and easier layout and measuring. Overall construction details for this cabinet are shown in the drawing on the facing page.

Building the case

Begin by edge-gluing straight-grained, warp-free stock for the sides, top, floor and interior partitions of both cases. Be sure to leave the parts ⅛ in. long so you can trim them to their finished dimension after you've joined them. (The pins and tails of the dovetailed box components, and the through tenons of the horizontal partitions, will thus protrude 1⁄16 in.) Please take note: Wait to cut and join the parts of the lower utility case until after you have assembled the

The stopped dovetail grooves in the case side are routed with the aid of a shopmade fixture. Photo by Greg Radley.

Cut the tenon cheeks with a backsaw (far left), then remove the waste between tenons with a bandsaw (below left). Chisel the outside tenon shoulders square (left), and from the tenons, lay out the mortises (below). Photos by Greg Radley.

trestle. The inside dimensions of the trestle (into which this case must fit), may turn out differently after the final trimming of the trestle frame's joints than the dimensions—even in the full-scale rendering—might suggest.

Lay out and hand-cut the dovetails. Radley suggests cutting the tails first, and then using these as a template to lay out the pins. As long as you are careful to make the tail cuts perpendicular to the face of the board, this method produces quick and accurate results. After cutting and testing the fit of the dovetails, rabbet the edges (Radley uses a router) to receive the ¾-in. plywood back panel. Stop the rabbet before it exits the ends of the boards; you can cut the corners square with a chisel.

Now, on the two sides, top and two horizontal partitions of the upper case, lay out the position of the dovetail grooves. (If you made a full-scale rendering, you can hold a stick to the drawing, tick off the locations, carry the stick to the component, and transfer the layout lines from the stick to the stock.) Cut these grooves with a router guided by a shop-made fixture (see the photo on p. 103). Note that the cross support on the jig acts as a stop for the router—and thus for the groove. Cut the matching sliding dovetails on the ends of the horizontal and vertical partitions. Radley does this on the router table.

Create a ⅛-in. deep shoulder to a length equal to the depth of the case sides (plus ⅟₁₆ in.) at the ends of the two

main horizontal partitions. Then lay out the cutlines of the through tenons. Cut the tenons out with a backsaw followed by a bandsaw. Use a chisel to trim the tenon shoulders. Now lay out the mortises to the outside of the case side by holding the cut tenons directly to the case sides and marking their outlines. Cut the mortises out by roughing the hole with a drill bit and then chiseling to the lines from the outside.

Now comes the magic moment: Dry-fit the entire upper-case assembly together, checking to be sure that all the joints are snug as the case sits flat and square. Make any necessary adjustments with a chisel or file. When satisfied, disassemble the case, cut kerfs for the wedges in the ends of the through tenons

Saw kerfs in the through tenons for wedges (left). Then assemble the case and glue in the wedges (below). Photos by Greg Radley.

(see the photo at top), and reassemble the case with glue. Install the back panel into the rabbet—Radley uses ¼-in. square mahogany pegs driven into squared ¼-in. holes. Drive wedges into the through tenons to hold the panel in place (see the photo above) and then trim the protruding portion flush with the outside of the case. Also trim the protruding through dovetails flush.

Follow the same procedure for the lower case unit after putting together the trestle as detailed on p. 106. There will not be any dovetail grooves or through mortises to deal with here. However, don't forget to dry-assemble the case to test it in the trestle, or to predrill holes along the case sides for the shelf clips to support the adjustable shelves. Apply your choice of finish to the cases after

final assembly. (Radley used penetrating oil, followed by wax.) Be sure the finish is completely dry before assembling the case to the trestle.

Building the doors

Make the panels for the doors by first edge-gluing a panel of solid mahogany to size. Then apply a shop-made ¹⁄₃₂ in. thick veneer of ash to both sides with either a vacuum press or a weighted panel. (If you choose to use commercial veneer, which is thinner, you can use contact cement and rollers to apply it to the mahogany substrate.) When the veneer is dry, square up the panel and shape the profile on the router table— this exposes the underlying mahogany.

Select the straightest stock for the door frames, then cut the pieces to rough

length. Mill the rabbets for the raised panel, and then cut the pieces to exact length (plus ⅛ in. for the upper door components). Make the through-dovetail joints for the upper door frames and the stepped rabbet for the lower door frames. Try the joints dry with the panel installed in its rabbet. If the fit looks good, proceed to glue-up. Be sure to keep glue out of the panel rabbet—you want the panel to float with changes in ambient moisture levels. To keep the panel centered, Radley inserted a ³⁄₁₆-in. peg through the top and bottom rails at the centerline of the panel. Apply the finish.

Building the drawers

Cut all the parts to size—the sides and back from ½-in. thick stock and the fronts from ¾-in. stock (see the drawing on p. 106). Make the faces oversize for now. Note that the ¼-in. plywood bottom panels are cut ¼ in. longer than the drawer sides. This allows the back of the panel to act as a drawer stop. Apply veneer to the faces and then, when the glue is dry, cut the faces to their final dimensions, being sure to maintain the alignment of the veneer grain across all the fronts. Cut the finger pull as shown in the drawing on p. 106.

Lay out and cut the tails on the sides, half-blind in the front (see the photo on p. 106) and through in the back. (Radley cut only two tails in the back corners to speed the process.) Use the cut tails to lay out the pins in the ends and faces. Cut the groove for the bottom panel on the table saw or rout it using a slotting bit.

Dry-fit each box before gluing it up. Be sure the boxes sit square and flat before setting them aside to dry. Finally, smooth the sides of the drawers, apply the finish, and then fit them into their compartments in the case. Make center guides for the two larger drawers to help keep them from binding. Wax the guides with a candle stub.

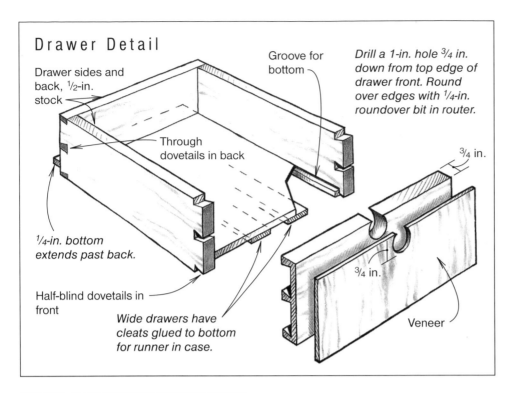

Drawer Detail

Drawer sides and back, 1/2-in. stock

Through dovetails in back

Groove for bottom

Drill a 1-in. hole 3/4 in. down from top edge of drawer front. Round over edges with 1/4-in. roundover bit in router.

1/4-in. bottom extends past back.

Half-blind dovetails in front

Wide drawers have cleats glued to bottom for runner in case.

3/4 in.

3/4 in.

Veneer

Dovetailed drawers have cut-out finger pulls. Photo by Greg Radley.

Making the trestle

Cut the pieces of the trestle to rough dimensions and then surface-plane and joint them to size. Leave the parts long for now. Lay out the through mortises for the two bottom rails (the mortises should be 1/8 in. less than the width and thickness of the rails, requiring the tenon to have a 1/8-in. shoulder.) Cut out the mortises with either a milling machine or a drill bit followed by a hand chisel. Then cut the rails to length—plus 1/8 in. to allow a 1/16-in. protrusion at either end—and lay out and cut the tenons. Trim the tenons with a chisel until you get a smooth, tight fit into the mortises. Make the kerf for the wedges.

Make the mortises in the two foot rails for the base of the four posts and then make the tenons in the posts to fit. Similarly, make the mortise-and-tenon joints for the two top supports. Lay out and cut the lap joints for the center top rail and the cross support. A crosscut box on the table saw makes these cuts go quickly and accurately.

Now dry-fit the entire trestle assembly. There will undoubtably be much trimming to do to get all the fits tight and the parts correctly aligned. When you are satisfied, go for the glue. First, however, radius all the sharp edges with a router fitted with a 1/8-in. roundover bit and then sand the surfaces smooth. After final assembly, drive wedges into the through tenons and to pin the blind mortise-and-tenon joints. Apply the finish.

Final assembly

Fit your tools to the upper case, playing with the layout to take the best advantage of the available space without making the tools cumbersome to remove. Holders can be made in various ways. For some, trace the outline of the tool on the stock and cut out the shape to fit; for others, slot a length of stock. Install the holders with screws and add rotating cleats where appropriate to secure the tools in place. Sometimes it takes a little imagination to come up with just the right holding strategy for a particular tool; some possible solutions are shown in the bottom drawing on the facing page.

With the upper cabinet on its back, install the piano hinges to both outside edges of the case—to get a close, dust-proof fit between the doors and the case, rout in a long mortise in which to recess the hinge. Prop the doors in position and screw the hinge to them. Install European-type cup hinges to the back of the utility cabinet doors (this requires drilling a 35mm hole in the back of the stiles) and the hinge plates to the inside walls of the case. As shown in the top drawings on the facing page, install elbow catches at the bottom of the upper doors and, for the lower doors, cut a small recess in the door frame where it joins the panel—just enough to get your fingertips in.

Elbow Catch on Upper Doors

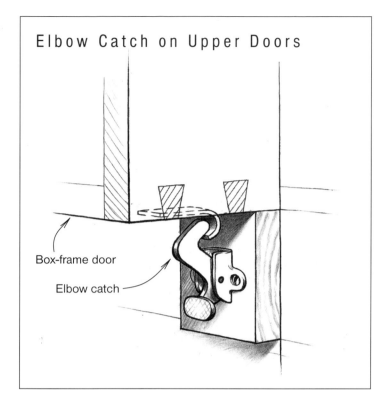

Box-frame door

Elbow catch

Finger Recess on Lower Doors

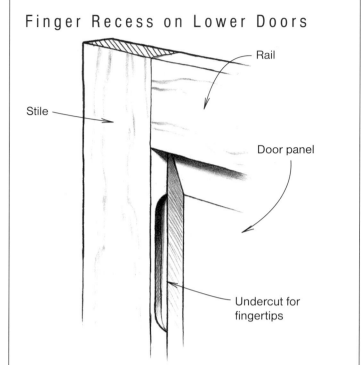

Stile

Rail

Door panel

Undercut for fingertips

Install the upper case onto the top of the trestle, drilling pilot holes and running screws through the underside of the top rails of the trestle into the bottom of the floor. Be sure to select a screw length that will not protrude.

Now install the lower case into the trestle. If you were careful to measure the finished trestle before final-cutting the parts for the utility cabinet and you dry-fit it before clamping up the case, it should now slip neatly into place. Some planing of the trestle, however, may be necessary. To secure the cabinet in place, run four screws through the bottom rails of the trestle into the underside of the case floor. Set pins into the shelf support holes, and set the shelves in place.

Finally, set the case upright and load it up with your tools. If you live in earthquake country, screw a pair of metal straps across the top of the upper chest and up the wall (over a stud). Unless the wall falls over, your chest will remain upright in the severest of shakers.

Tool Holders

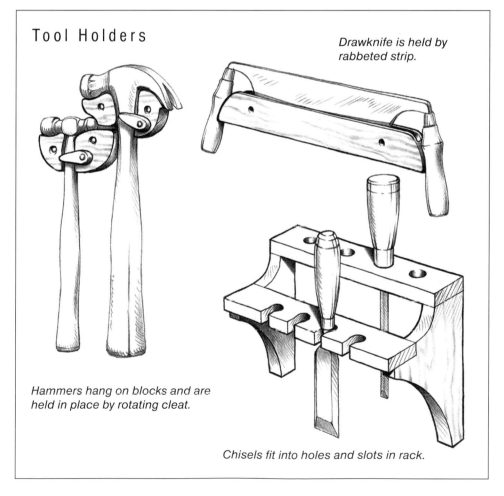

Drawknife is held by rabbeted strip.

Hammers hang on blocks and are held in place by rotating cleat.

Chisels fit into holes and slots in rack.

7
ROLLING TOOL CARTS

I have had a long, personal relationship with rolling tool carts, or "tool stooges," as I call them, since I began cabinetmaking many years ago. (You may have met my friends Larry, Curly and Moe in my first book, *Working at Woodworking*.) Having set up my business in a small two-car garage, I didn't have the luxury of leaving all my work stations set up at the same time. While the knock-down fixtures I designed and built helped me get around this limitation, I rarely had the right tools at hand when I needed them.

One operation, assembly, was particularly problematic. My assembly area was (and still is, for that matter) a flat 3-ft. by 7-ft. platform placed across a pair of leveled 12-in. high lifts. Unfortunately, the only space I could spare for this work station was at least four or more steps away from my workbench and its accompanying tool-storage units. At first I made do, trying to arrange

Rolling tool cart by Chris Wanlass. For other views of the cart, see p. 111. Photo by William Sampson.

Steve Johnson's mobile cart, shown at far left with a small machinist's chest (also by Johnson), features full-extension drawers. When they are extended, the light-colored maple drawer sides stand out against the darker walnut (left), warning that the drawers should be shut before the cart is moved . Photo by Jon Binzen.

all the tools I thought I would need on the platform before getting started. Invariably, of course, I would forget something—usually just the tool I needed while trying to hold a bunch of parts together with both hands and one foot.

Throughout the assembly process, I was constantly traipsing to and from my standing or wall-hung toolboxes; by the time I got to them, I couldn't always remember what I was looking for. Worse, I would occasionally knock a loose tool off the platform as I worked around the project (in accordance with Murphy's law, this would invariably be a freshly sharpened chisel). Like the woodworkers whose carts are featured in this chapter, I

realized that I needed to build some kind of tool stooge to furnish me with the tools I needed at this work station. I decided that a rolling tool cart would suit my needs perfectly. On pp. 114-123, I'll show you how I built it.

A Tool and Die Cart

When Steve Johnson, of Washington Court House, Ohio, decided to replace his old and rickety commercially made mechanic's cart, he had a long list of design criteria in hand. Johnson, a professional tool and die maker, wanted the cart to have a full bank of smooth-running, full-extension drawers. These

drawers would need interior partitions to encourage organization, a locking system that was easy to operate, and no protruding pull hardware (at least below the height of 30 in.). To contain his tools, the new cart would have to be at least as large as the biggest commercial mechanic's chest: 44 in. tall by 39 in. wide by 24 in. deep. Finally, and perhaps most important, Johnson insisted that the new cart be designed to withstand the rigors of everyday use in a busy commercial workshop.

To meet the last requirement, Johnson decided to build the case around an internal framework of 2-in. thick by 2½-in. wide walnut. This design element would make the fully loaded cart highly resistant to racking when being pushed. But the sudden braking of a wheel against an obstruction can also produce severe stresses on the structure of a rolling cart. Since the shop's floors were littered with everything from bottle caps to extension cords, Johnson installed 4-in. diameter soft rubber casters so the cart would roll over the debris rather than being stopped by it.

The cart also features a galley rail around the top to keep tools from rolling off, slide-out extension tables to either side, an inlaid granite surface plate (to provide a true flat surface for tool and die work) and replaceable corner protectors. Johnson chose maple for the drawer sides for one particular reason: The light-colored wood stands out sharply against the darker walnut drawer face, acting as a highly visible warning flag when a drawer is left open. Finally, to protect the walnut surfaces of the cart from the solvents commonly used in his work, Johnson used a three-step wipe-on polyurethane finish.

A Shop in a Box

Not satisfied with a straightforward rolling bank of drawers, sign maker Chris Wanlass, of Pleasant Grove, Utah, decided to add compartments for bulky tools such as panel saws, long planes and squares. To keep out dust and provide security, he enclosed the compartments behind ¾-in. hardwood-plywood doors. Although these compartments add length and depth to the cart, they also add considerable versatility, allowing Wanlass to transport a full range of hand tools throughout the shop. The metal rub rail that runs around the base of the cart would be a hazard around casework, but it isn't a problem for a sign maker, and it certainly ensures that the cart won't be damaged in its travels.

Chris Wanlass' cart is 42 in. wide by 25½ in. deep by 35½ in. high. Photos by William Sampson.

A Touch of Tansu

Furniture maker William Tandy Young, of Stow, Massachusetts, often finds himself away from his workbench and hand-tool storage when he builds large projects such as entry doors. Since these usually linger by the stationary machines grouped at one end of the shop, he was forever traipsing back and forth for tools. Finally tiring of this, he decided to design his new tool chest to roll.

Like Chris Wanlass, Young realized that a bank of drawers on wheels would not offer enough storage—there would have to be room in the box for larger tools such as jointer planes, framing squares and 24-in. layout rules. As seen in the bottom photo at left, Young provided storage for these in a full-height compartment on the back of the case. To keep dust out of this area and out of the drawers, he fit the cabinet with two sets of doors mounted on knife hinges. After rolling the box to the work area, he folds the doors back against the cabinet sides.

To organize the smaller hand tools and to make them easy to get at, Young decided that the drawers should each contain a specific grouping of tools. For example, one drawer is filled entirely with chisels, held in place by a notched divider (see the top photo at left). As a result, the drawers are all relatively small and lightweight—a good thing since they run on all-wood guides. At first finding hardware for the drawers was a problem. For appearance's sake, Young wanted pulls that would graduate in size from the small top drawer to the large bottom drawer. He also wanted them to protrude as little as possible, so the doors could close over them. Luckily he stumbled upon tansu-style pulls (tansu is the traditional storage cabinetry of Japan). Made in a variety of sizes, the pulls solved the design problem while adding a delicate Oriental flavor to the cart.

On William Tandy Young's cart, a slotted drawer insert that holds individual chisels in place. Tansu drawer pulls give an Oriental flavor to the cherry and bird's eye maple chest. A compartment at the back of the chest holds larger tools. Photos by Vincent Laurence.

Having used the cart in his workshop for several years, Young has been quite happy with its performance, though he would like to add a pair of grab handles and to replace the wood drawer guides with full-extension metal slides. Not surprisingly, the cart has also served him well as a silent salesman. No wonder: It is meticulously built of solid cherry and bird's-eye maple in a pleasing design. More than a few furniture commissions have been clinched after potential clients have seen the toolbox in use in his shop. And best of all, the box doesn't ask for a cent of commission.

From Hand Tote to Rolling Chest

While making the transition from hobbyist woodworker to full-time commercial furniture maker, Eric Smith, of Sacramento, California, set out to create a small, simple, one-hand tote for a selection of hand tools. Two hundred hours later, an impressive case built from Honduras mahogany and trimmed in pao ferro (see the photo above right) emerged from Smith's workshop.

Instead of the simple hand tote, Smith now has a 40-in. high by 30-in. wide by 19-in. deep rolling case that stylishly and securely houses nearly his entire inventory of hand tools. For strength and appearance, Smith made the case sides, top and floor from 1-in. thick stock, joining the corners with finger joints. He chose the dark, tough pao ferro wood for two reasons: to provide a visual accent and to protect the edges of the case. The through finger joints of the drawer faces add visual interest. One interesting feature of the drawers is that their bottoms double as runners—they slide along grooves worked into the sides and partitions (see the drawing at right).

Eric Smith's cart of Honduras mahogany houses most of his hand tools. Photo by Eric Smith.

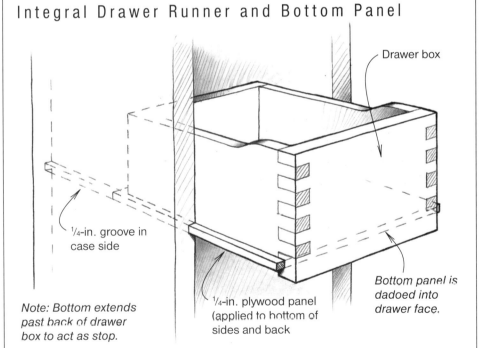

Integral Drawer Runner and Bottom Panel

Drawer box

¼-in. groove in case side

Note: Bottom extends past back of drawer box to act as stop.

¼-in. plywood panel (applied to bottom of sides and back

Bottom panel is dadoed into drawer face.

Jim Tolpin's small tool cart rolls on full swivel casters. Photo by Craig Wester.

Though the cart spends most of its time in its niche by his workbench, Smith does not regret adding an expensive set of casters to the design. Their presence give Smith the freedom to experiment with the cart's position in various locations throughout the shop. The casters will stay with the case at least until the day Smith discovers his ideal shop layout.

Building a Rolling Tool Cart

Size was a paramount concern even before sitting down to get the design of my rolling tool stooge on paper. While I wanted the cart to contain all the tools I needed for assembly work, it would have to be small enough to maneuver between my 3-ft. by 7-ft. assembly platform and some stationary tools—a rather tight squeeze in some places. I decided to limit the width of the cart's base to 24 in. and its depth to suit 18-in. long drawers. To maintain a stable footprint, I dared not go smaller. I fixed the overall height of

the cart at 35 in., slightly below the surface of my table saw. Sized this way, the cart could then also serve as a support for my sliding crosscut box or as an outfeed table for supporting large sheet materials or long boards. The fold-down extensions I added to the table surface provide extra support when the cart is used for these purposes (see the photo on the facing page).

To make the cart easy to maneuver within the tight confines of my shop, I installed a set of four full-swivel casters, which allow the cart to turn a full 360° in its own footprint. The casters have a locking feature, which I use only when the cart acts as an outfeed table . Because of the cart's weight and the smooth, low-friction operation of the drawer slides, the cart generally stays in one place even when I pull out the heaviest drawer at the bottom.

Since most cutting and planing operations would already be completed by the time I began work at my assembly station, I didn't need to design the cart with large enclosed spaces for panel saws or long planes. I could hang my only awkward-to-store tools, a 24-in. framing square and a 30-in. level, on cleats fastened to the outside of the back panel. Following the train of thought that prompted Steve Johnson to build his all-drawer cart (see the photos on p. 110), I made the most of my cart's limited volume by designing the cabinet with a full bank of drawers, which I mounted on full-extension slides.

Finally, I opted not to enclose the drawers behind a door (or pair of doors) as Eric Smith had done (see the photo on p. 113). Admittedly, doors do offer advantages: They nearly eliminate dust infiltration into the drawers; they hold the drawers shut while the cart rolls about; and the broad expanse of the door panels can beautify the cart. But I decided that doors would only get in the way when my cart was in use, especially in my limited space. I could live with a little dust infiltration, and I would solve the locking problem by adding a file-cabinet-type gang lock.

DESIGN NOTES

As I developed the concept of my mobile tool cart, I incorporated a number of features that would add stability and durability to the design. Safety was also a concern. For a dimensioned drawing of my cart, see p. 116.

Case and face frame

The back, floor, and sides of the case are of ¾-in. maple plywood joined together with biscuits. I chose this material for its dimensional stability, relatively low cost and ease of milling. Biscuit joinery is quick and easy to execute yet also strong. To reinforce the cart against racking, I decided on a face frame with relatively wide top and bottom rails. Though the presence of a face frame necessarily reduces the size of the drawers, it does not take up more space than an internal framework would—and it is much easier and cheaper to make. I made the face frame from maple and the drawer fronts from cherry for durability and appearance.

Top and bottom structural framing

Instead of forming the bottom of the cart from a single sheet of plywood, I constructed a heavy, solid-wood external framework. This does three things: It adds weight to the bottom of the cart (which increases stability by lowering the cart's center of gravity); it protrudes to act as a rub rail; and it evenly distributes the loads from the individual casters to the entire cart, reducing racking stresses. I made the frame from 1⅜-in. thick hard maple and joined the corners with splined miters, adding glue

Tolpin's cart in use as outfeed table. Photo by Craig Wester.

blocks for additional rigidity and support for the casters.

To strengthen the top of the cart and to provide support for the table, I made up an external top frame similar in construction to the bottom frame. But to keep the cart's center of gravity low, I reduced the size of the components and made them from lightweight alder. I

attached the table to the top frame using figure-eight desk-top fasteners. This hardware allows the top boards to move, preventing both the table and frame from distorting with seasonal fluctuations in humidity.

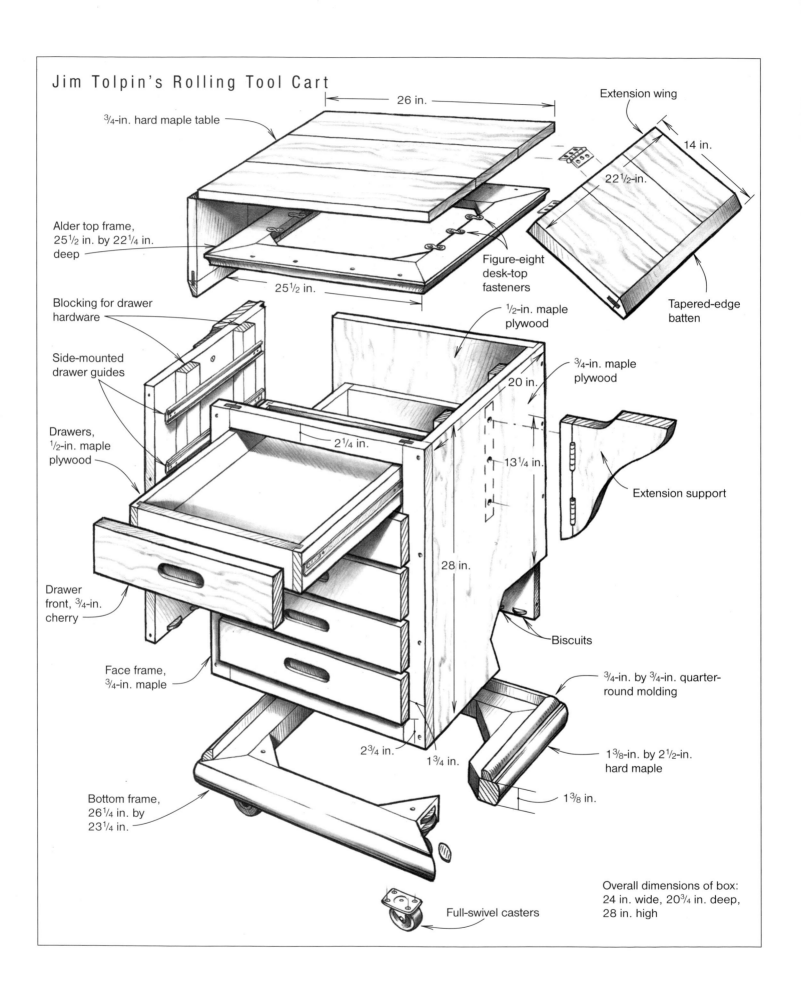

Jim Tolpin's Rolling Tool Cart

¾-in. hard maple table

26 in.

Extension wing

14 in.

22½-in.

Alder top frame, 25½ in. by 22¼ in. deep

25½ in.

Figure-eight desk-top fasteners

Tapered-edge batten

Blocking for drawer hardware

½-in. maple plywood

¾-in. maple plywood

Side-mounted drawer guides

20 in.

2¼ in.

13¼ in.

Drawers, ½-in. maple plywood

Extension support

28 in.

Drawer front, ¾-in. cherry

Biscuits

Face frame, ¾-in. maple

¾-in. by ¾-in. quarter-round molding

2¾ in.

1¾ in.

1⅜-in. by 2½-in. hard maple

1⅜ in.

Bottom frame, 26¼ in. by 23¼ in.

Full-swivel casters

Overall dimensions of box: 24 in. wide, 20¾ in. deep, 28 in. high

Drawers

I happened to have some ½-in. maple plywood on hand, so I used that for the drawer boxes, joining the corners with a shaper-made lock-rabbet joint. Dividers of ¼-in. plywood create interior compartments to help organize the tools and to reduce their shifting about as I move the cart around the shop. Remembering how the sliding trays of traditional chests made such efficient use of limited space, I added such a tray in one of the deeper drawers (see the photo on p. 70), and I use it to hold my collection of files. I decided to line some drawers with felt to reduce the tendency of certain tools to roll about, as well as to protect their cutting edges.

To avoid using protruding pull hardware (which tends to catch on work aprons), I cut finger grips into the ¾-in. cherry drawer faces. I cut them considerably wider than a single hand width, which make the grasps easy to find by touch alone.

Table surface

I decided to go with ¾-in. thick hard maple for the cart's table, edge-gluing up several boards to reach the required width. While I could have used laminate-covered plywood, I like the look and feel of solid wood. Finished in shellac or polyurethane, the hardwood surface would be just as slick as plastic laminate when pressed into use as an outfeed table for the table saw.

Finish

To protect the top, sides, and drawer faces of the cart from impact and from the occasional drippings of finish materials and solvents, I applied several coats of polyurethane. Except for the underside of the table surface, I left the interior of the cart unfinished.

To cut the slots for biscuits in the miter faces, index the machine base to the marked surface of the component. Photo by Craig Wester.

CONSTRUCTION PROCEDURES

I approached the construction of my rolling tool cart by dividing the process into several stages. First I cut out, milled and assembled the top, bottom and face frameworks. Next I cut out and milled the case panel components and assembled them with the three frames to create the carcase, which I then finished with polyurethane. While waiting for the finish to dry, I laminated the top and its side extensions, smoothed them and applied finish to all their surfaces. The drawers were next: I cut out and milled their components and assembled the boxes. After installing the hardware for the drawers, table top and extension supports I attached the latter two items and then slid the drawers into the case. Finally, I attached the drawer faces and the swivel casters.

Making the frames

Lay out, then cut out (oversized in width and length), the stock for the top and bottom frames from your choice of hardwood. Plane the stock to finished thickness, join the edges square and profile one edge to the shape of your choice (I used a 1⅜-in. bullnose bit on my table-mounted router). Now miter-cut the pieces to finished length, orienting the jointed edge to the inside of the frame. Make the slots for the biscuits in the face of the miter-joint meeting surfaces. Be careful to index the base plate of the biscuit joiner to the same surface of the frame components (mark symbols on the stock to help you keep everything correctly oriented).

Dry-assemble the frames to ensure that the joints meet tightly with the frame sitting flat and square (check the corner-to-corner diagonal measurements). Make any necessary adjustments to the face of the miter

Plane the miter joint to fit by trimming its face on a shooting board. Photo by Craig Wester.

Cauls help distribute the clamping force and protect edges. To glue up the frames (left), use notched cauls. Use diagonally cut cauls when gluing up corner blocks (above). Photos by Craig Wester.

joints with a hand plane and shooting board (see the photo at top left). When satisfied with the fit, apply glue in the biscuit slots and on the miter faces, then clamp the frames together. I made up special notched cauls to place across the outside corners—these distribute the clamping forces, forcing the frame miter joints firmly together (see the photo above). If you are working alone, use double-stick tape to hold the cauls in place while you position the clamps. Set

the assembly aside to dry on a flat, level surface. When ready, remove the clamps, scrape off any glue residue and install the corner blocks (I glue and screw them in place, but you could use biscuits instead). Diagonally cut cauls allow you to clamp them firmly into the corner.

Follow this procedure for making up the face frame: Lay out and then cut out the components oversize; surface-plane and join the stock to final thickness and width; and then cut the two rails and

two stiles to their finished length. Slot the butt joints for biscuits where the rails meet the stiles; run a dry test to check for tightness of fit and that the frame sits square and flat; and then glue and clamp up the frame. Round over the inside edges of the frame with a router and an $\frac{1}{8}$-in. roundover bit.

Making the case

Cut the sides, floor, and back panel of the case from ¾-in. hardwood plywood, then cut the full-length rabbet to receive the back panel in both side pieces. Make the slots for the biscuits where the sides join the floor by folding—and clamping in place—the floor panel over each of the side panels in turn. This technique does two things: It allows the floor to act as a stop for the base of the joiner when slotting into the face of the sides, and it places the floor in a good position to be end-slotted at the same layout marks. See the drawing below for details.

Dry-fit the case parts together. When you're satisfied with the fit, proceed with wet assembly. If you wish, you can save the trouble of clamping up the assembly by screwing the components together. (For appearance's sake, you can countersink the screws and insert wood plugs to hide the heads.) Glue and screw the assembled face frame to the front edge of the case. To improve the appearance of the joint between the frame and case, I bevel the edges of the joint. I use a dual-purpose flush and V-groove router bit designed especially for this application. It trims the face frame flush to the case side while at the

A flush and V-groove router bit trims the face frame to the case side. Photo by Craig Wester.

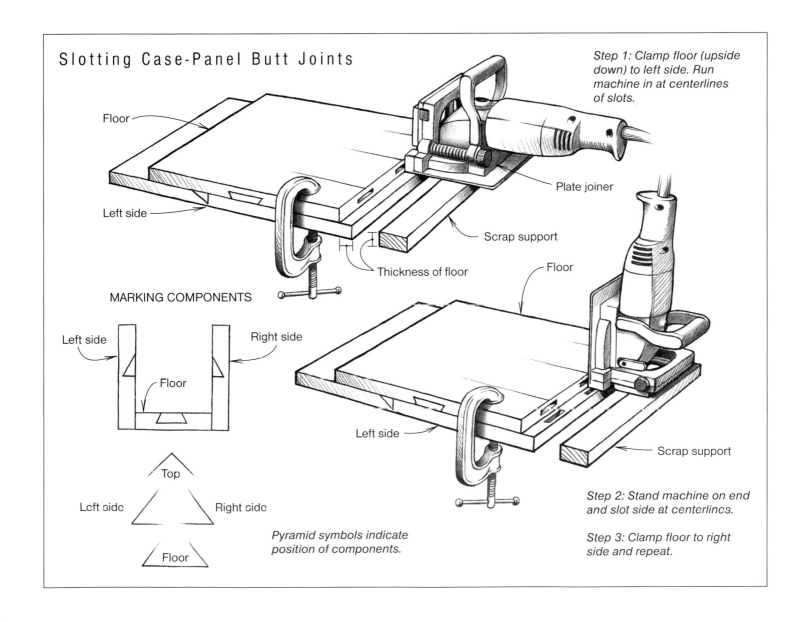

Slotting Case-Panel Butt Joints

Floor

Left side

MARKING COMPONENTS

Left side

Right side

Floor

Pyramid symbols indicate position of components.

Top

Left side

Right side

Floor

Plate joiner

Scrap support

Thickness of floor

Step 1: Clamp floor (upside down) to left side. Run machine in at centerlines of slots.

Floor

Left side

Scrap support

Step 2: Stand machine on end and slot side at centerlines.

Step 3: Clamp floor to right side and repeat.

same time cutting in a beveled groove. Install the blocking for the drawer-slide hardware. Note that the blocks should be of a thickness to match the inside overhang of the face frame.

Making the table top and extension wings

Lay out and cut the stock for the table and the pair of extension wings (leave the stock long enough to accommodate both the table and the two extensions). Edge-glue the boards together to achieve the desired width—be sure to keep the lamination as flat as possible. When the assembly is dry, surface the boards through a planer or wide belt sander, then cut the table and wings to their final finished width and length. I "breadboard" the ends of the wings with a tapered-edge batten. This helps to keep their surface flat and to ease the stock feeding off the table saw up onto the table. To attach the batten, rout a groove along the edge of both the table and the batten stock, then glue in a spline. To allow the boards to move in relation to the batten, glue only the middle third of the spline. Apply finish to both sides of the table and extension wings.

Making the drawers

For this cart, the drawer boxes are joined with a lock-rabbet joint (see the drawing above right). I find this joint to be good looking, fast to execute on my table-mounted router, and quite strong. For the fastest construction, cut all the drawer stock to finished width and length, then run all the sides by the bit. Then run all the ends. (Be sure the end cuts are perfectly square or you will end up with a warped box.) It's a good idea to test-cut the joint in scraps before committing the stock to the bit.

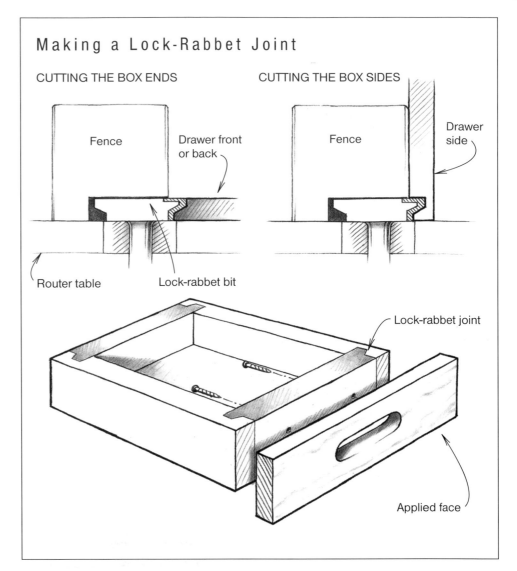

Making a Lock-Rabbet Joint

CUTTING THE BOX ENDS

Fence

Drawer front or back

Router table

Lock-rabbet bit

CUTTING THE BOX SIDES

Fence

Drawer side

Lock-rabbet joint

Applied face

Clamp up the drawer; shown here are Bessey system case clamps. Photo by Craig Wester.

Decide on the width and length of the finger pull for the drawer faces and then lay it out in the center of a 6-in. wide by 16-in. long scrap of void-free ½-in. plywood, which will become a template. Drill holes at both ends of the pull slot, and then carefully cut between the holes with a jigsaw. While you can use files to straighten up the saw cuts, I find it faster to use a router. I fit the router with a pattern-following bit, clamp a board with a perfectly straight edge along the cut line (I cut to within ¹⁄₁₆ in. of this line with the jigsaw) and then trim to the line. The cut line will be as straight as my guide board.

Using the template as a guide, lay out the pull slots on the drawer faces. Orient the template to centerlines drawn on the drawer faces, and then trace the outline of the pull slot. To mark the drill centers of the end holes, use a template insert. (To make it, use the first template to trace the outline of the insert, then cut it out with a jigsaw. Make the centering holes just large enough to accommodate the point of a marking awl.)

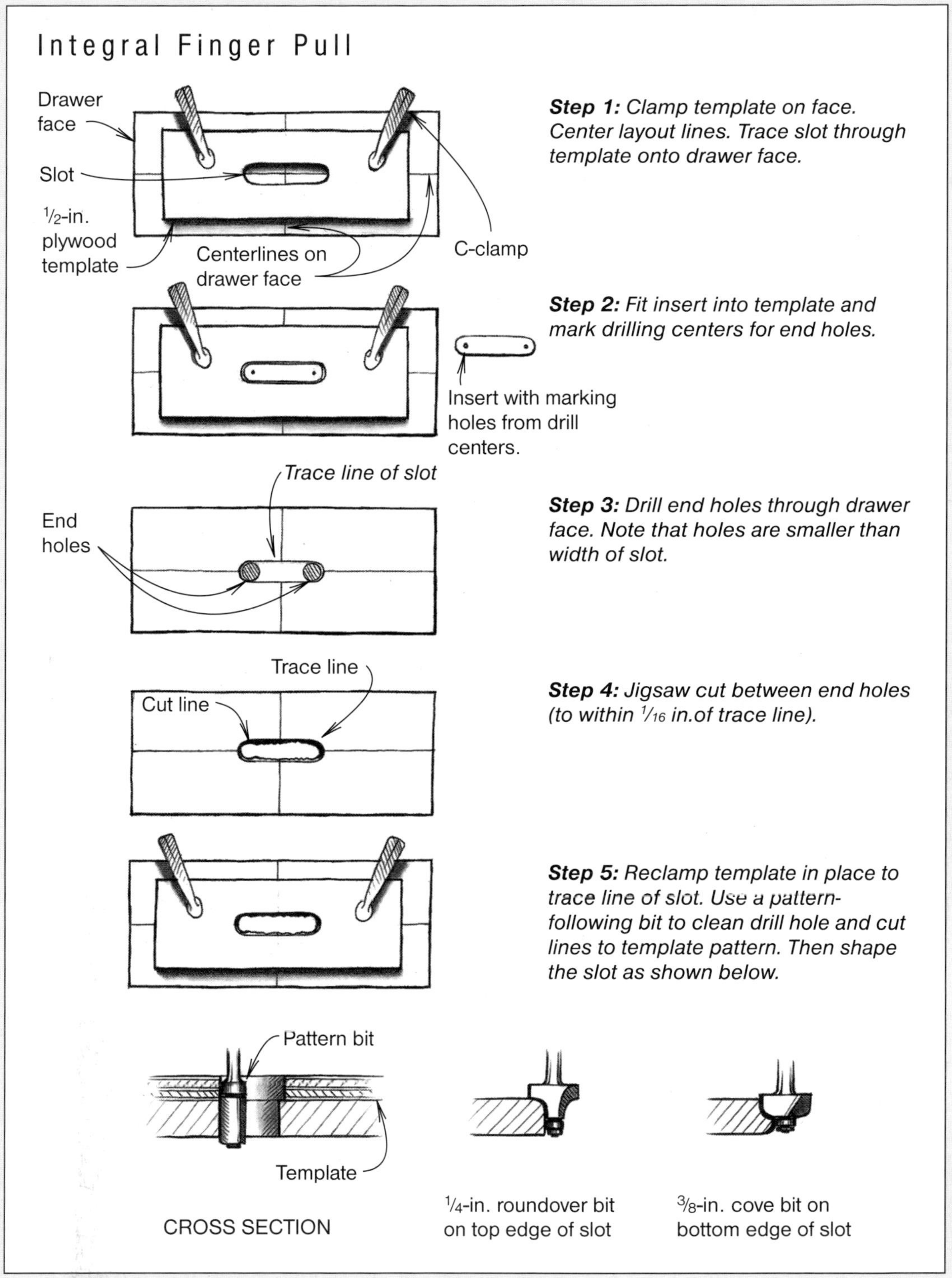

To cut the pull slot, remove the templates, drill the end holes at the two center points (use a bit ⅛ in. less in diameter than the width of the slot), and then cut to the inside of the remaining lines with a jigsaw. Then clamp the template back in place on the

trace lines and use the pattern following bit on the router to clean up the cut. To shape the pull, first round over the outside edge of the slot with

the router (using a ¼-in. roundover bit), then form the undercut with a ⅜-in. cove bit. Hand-sand the cut edges with fine sandpaper.

Integral Finger Pull

Drawer face
Slot
½-in. plywood template
Centerlines on drawer face
C-clamp

Step 1: Clamp template on face. Center layout lines. Trace slot through template onto drawer face.

Insert with marking holes from drill centers.

Step 2: Fit insert into template and mark drilling centers for end holes.

Trace line of slot
End holes

Step 3: Drill end holes through drawer face. Note that holes are smaller than width of slot.

Trace line
Cut line

Step 4: Jigsaw cut between end holes (to within ¹⁄₁₆ in. of trace line).

Step 5: Reclamp template in place to trace line of slot. Use a pattern-following bit to clean drill hole and cut lines to template pattern. Then shape the slot as shown below.

Pattern bit
Template
CROSS SECTION

¼-in. roundover bit on top edge of slot

⅜-in. cove bit on bottom edge of slot

Using a story stick, mark the position of the drawer hardware along the case blocking. Photo by Craig Wester.

After cutting all the joints, fit a slotting bit into the table-mounted router and cut the grooves for the ¼-in. plywood bottom panels. Cut the bottom panels to size, checking to be sure they are square, and then dry-assemble each drawer. If the joints are tight and the box sits square and flat, proceed to glue up the boxes. You can use nails to hold the joints together while the glue dries, or case clamps if you find nail holes offensive.

Cut the drawer faces out of a length of solid stock. You can either cut each face from the board individually, or, to reduce waste, you can edge-glue a panel the width of all the drawer faces together (plus saw kerfs) and then rip out the individual faces. The finger pulls can be made quickly and precisely with the aid of a router template, as explained in the sidebar on p. 121.

Final assembly and adjustments

Screw the top frame to the case from above, attach the figure-eight desk-top fasteners, and then turn the case over on top of the table. Screw through the fasteners into the table. Turn the case back over, this time on top of the base frame. Screw through the floor of the case into the frame.

Now install the drawer hardware to the blocking along the case sides and to the sides of the drawers, using a layout stick along the blocks to ensure accuracy in locating the attachment holes. You can use the same layout stick to mark the position of the hardware on the drawer sides. Slide the drawers into the case, adjusting the position of the hardware if necessary to allow the drawers to run smoothly and sit level in the opening.

Now you can install the faces (see the drawing at right). First, hammer a pair of brads partway into the back of the faces where the attachment screws will be fitted, and then clip off the heads to form a point. Next, starting at the bottom, press the bottom drawer face against its box after carefully aligning the edges of the face with the bottom and sides of the case. Drill shank holes for the attachment screws at the marks left by the brads. Then remove the brads from the back of the face and drill pilot holes for these same screws. Install the face to the box. Repeat the process with the next drawer face, this time aligning it to the face below. Use even-sized shims (laminate sample chips work well) to hold an even gap with the drawer face below.

Finally, attach the casters to the base frame by drilling pilot holes for, and installing, machine screws. (Tapered wood screws have a tendency to work loose in this high-stress situation.) Attach a pair of loose leaf hinges to the parts of the extension-wing supports. Install the ¾-in. spacer to the case side and then install the swing-out supports by engaging the hinges. Finally, attach the wings to the table with a pair of butt hinges (or a length of piano hinge).

Marking Attachment Points for Drawer Face

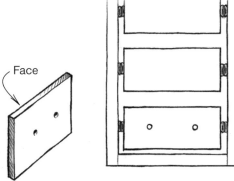

Step 1: *Hammer brads into back of face and clip off heads.*

Step 2: *Align face to edges of case, then press face against drawer box to imprint brads.*

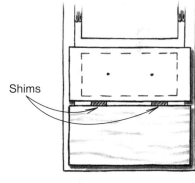

Step 3: *Drill shank holes in drawer box at brad marks and pilot holes (for threads) at location of removed brads in drawer face.*

Step 4: *Install bottom drawer face with screws, then hold next face (with clipped brads) against next drawer box. Use shims to maintain even gap. Repeat steps.*

8

DESIGNING SITE BOXES

Why spend a lot of time designing and building a box to carry tools to the job site? After all, you can always throw them in a motley—and dirt-cheap—assortment of 5-gal. plastic buckets and cardboard boxes to get them where they need to go. I know, because that's how I lugged my tools from job to job when I first started doing residential finish work. But I also know how tired I got of losing track of my tools and of damaging them in transit, and I remember how it feels to pour rusty water out of the bottom of a tool bucket left out in the rain, or to pick up a sodden cardboard box and have all my tools spill onto my feet.

My shabby collection of tool carriers did little to enhance my reputation as a fine craftsman. I'll never forget the first time I walked onto a job site teeming with hot-shot finish carpenters. To a man (and one woman), they proudly carried their tools in finely crafted totes

Jim Tolpin built this small tote 25 years ago from scraps of pine found on the job site. All the cuts were made at the site with a circular saw. Photo by Craig Wester.

Boatbuilder and physician Bertram Levy, of Port Townsend, Wash., built this diminutive open shoulder tote to carry a task-specific selection of hand tools to his boat. The curved handle, which is wrapped in leather, helps to center the grip on the box and allows easy access to the tools Photo by Craig Wester.

that they had designed and made themselves. I went home that evening with my tail between my legs, determined to come up with a decent way to carry my tools onto the job site.

Types of Site Boxes

The size and shape of your site box will be determined by what you will carry in it. A small one-hand tote is fine for a limited number of task-specific tools; my touchup box (see the photo on p. 124) was dedicated to the tools I needed to complete cabinet and architectural molding installations. A large box can be designed to contain a number of smaller

boxes plus power tools and accessories— add wheels and you can roll it right out of your truck onto the construction site. Finally, you could go the whole nine yards and turn a truck, van or trailer into one massive, rolling toolbox.

OPEN SHOULDER TOTES

You can plan to carry a group of tools weighing less than about 50 lb. in a single-hand tote as long as you keep the shape of the box relatively narrow (see p. 134). The simplest, and probably the most efficient, design is the open shoulder tote (see the photo above). Here most of the tools—even bulky ones—are visible and instantly accessible, even when the box is surrounded by other equipment. This accessibility, of course,

has its price: The contents are not particularly well protected from damage during transport; there is no protection from rain (unless you make a waterproof slipcover); and the tools are easy to steal.

An open shoulder tote need not be restricted to the 50-lb. weight limit. If you have a willing partner and design a carrying system for two people, you can make a larger box with greater capacity. Nor must you make your tote of wood. You can also make practical and easy-to-use totes from canvas and leather (see pp. 136-139). Open shoulder totes are discussed more fully in Chapter 9.

This lidded tote by furniture maker David Bevan of Gloucester, Ontario, Canada, features two movable lids—a top lid containing a pair of saws, a tape and a level, and a drop-front lid that opens to reveal a small open tool well and banks of pivoting drawers. Photo by David Bevan.

Carpenter Jeff Olson of Montara, Calif., wanted his toolbox to contain both a framing square and a 24-in. level, so he designed a briefcase-style tote. When the tote is open, all the tools within the case are easy to see and to get at. When closed, the narrow case is easily carried and stowed. Photo by Jeff Olson.

LIDDED TOTES

Adding a tight-fitting, locking lid to a single-hand tote makes the box more secure in shipping and protects the contents from the weather, dust, debris and theft (although a scoundrel can always make off with the whole box). Equally important, a lid provides extra tool-storage area, making the box more versatile. There are, however, a few drawbacks to adding a lid to an open shoulder box. If you want the tote to enclose bulky tools such as a framing square or some panel saws, you'll find you have to design it to be somewhat larger—or at least taller if you go with a briefcase-type design—than it might otherwise be as an open box. The box will consequently be heavier and will take up a bit more room in your vehicle. And access to a lidded tote is often impossible until it is unloaded it from its position in the truck. Lidded totes are discussed more fully in Chapter 10.

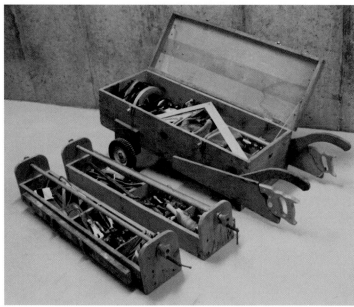

A "tool barrow" by Linden Frederick of Belfast, Maine. Two open shoulder totes hitch a lift on the lid of the box; scabbards carry panel saws. Photos by Chuck Lockhart.

TRUCKS, VANS AND TRAILERS

If your work demands that you regularly haul a wide variety of tools and supplies to the job site, you need the last word in luxury: a vehicle outfitted with well-organized, easily accessed storage units for supplies as well as removable totes that can be carried onto the site as needed. With a truck, van or trailer, no matter where you are or how long you must stay there, nearly everything you need is close at hand.

With such convenience, it's not surprising that there are significant drawbacks. You must accept that the vehicle is committed to your work life—no way will you want to be piling in the cub-scout troup for a camping trip to the beach. And if you must bring stock to your job sites, a fully outfitted vehicle is a poor substitute for a pickup truck with a rack. With such a dedicated rig, you will probably have to own—and pay for and maintain—at least one more vehicle for private use and a truck or a trailer to get materials to the job site. Vehicles as toolboxes are discussed more fully in Chapter 12.

Design Considerations

Whatever type of site box you decide to build, pay attention to the following points when developing your design. (You'll notice they are much the same as the guidelines for in-shop tool storage, discussed on pp. 69-71).

• Give each tool its own place. That way tools will be easy to find, and you'll see at a glance if any are missing. (See pp. 71-75 for how to develop working drawings.)

WHEELED SITE BOXES

If the weight of the tools you need to carry exceeds 60 lb. to 70 lb., lifting the box becomes a lot less appealing. Here's a solution dating back to antiquity: Build the box on wheels. Big wheels. For unlike their shop-bound cousins, site boxes roll over extension cords, chunks of 2x4s and other construction rubble, all in a day's work. You can plan to carry a wide variety of tools and smaller boxes within (and on) these "tool barrows," since weight and shape are nowhere near as

restrictive as they are with a hand-carried tote. But you do need to make sure the box will fit in the bed of your truck with other commonly carried tools and that it can pass through standard door openings. And you must, of course, provide some way to get the box off your truck, whether it's an offloading ramp built from two scaffolding boards or a commercially manufactured hydraulic tailgate. Wheeled site boxes are discussed more fully in Chapter 11.

The tool trailer of timber framer George Nesbitt, of Berkeley, Calif., contains all the tools and supplies he needs throughout the workday, leaving his truck free to carry materials to and from the job site. Photo by George Nesbitt.

• Arrange the tools so you will be able to reach them easily. Avoid layering tools over one another. Instead, use lift-out trays, drawers or racks to make the most of the space without compromising accessibility.

• Make sure that the tools are held securely, but avoid complex holding mechanisms that require two hands or a lot of attention to manipulate. Sometimes the simplest solutions—like using a leather holding strip for chisels or a pair of slotted partitions for saws—are the most effective.

BUILDING FOR DURABILITY

Unlike tool boxes that remain cloistered within the shop, site boxes must withstand the rigors of life on the road. At some time, your box will probably be exposed to extreme weather conditions, rough rides and less than courteous treatment from site gorillas ("sorry, was that your toolbox we used to jack up the loading ramp?"). In your design you should strive for great durability while maintaining the lightest weight possible.

Plan to build a site box from rugged, stable, but lightweight materials using strong joinery (see the drawing on p. 130 for general design parameters). I would build boxes larger than 2 cu. ft. from ½-in. hardwood plywood, reinforced at the corners with an internal metal or wood framework. Boxes smaller than this can be built from lightweight solid stock—even pine—as long as you use durable joints (such as the dovetail or wedged through mortise and tenon) and metal guard plates at the outside corners. Any glues or adhesive caulking used in construction must be rated waterproof for exterior applications. Fasteners and hardware should be chosen for weather resistance—in other words, no uncoated ferrous metal. Instead, choose from stainless steel, bronze or hot-dipped galvanized steel.

Toolboxes on construction sites can be put to any number of uses, and must be strong enough to take the abuse. Photo by Craig Wester.

A Site Box Designed for Durability

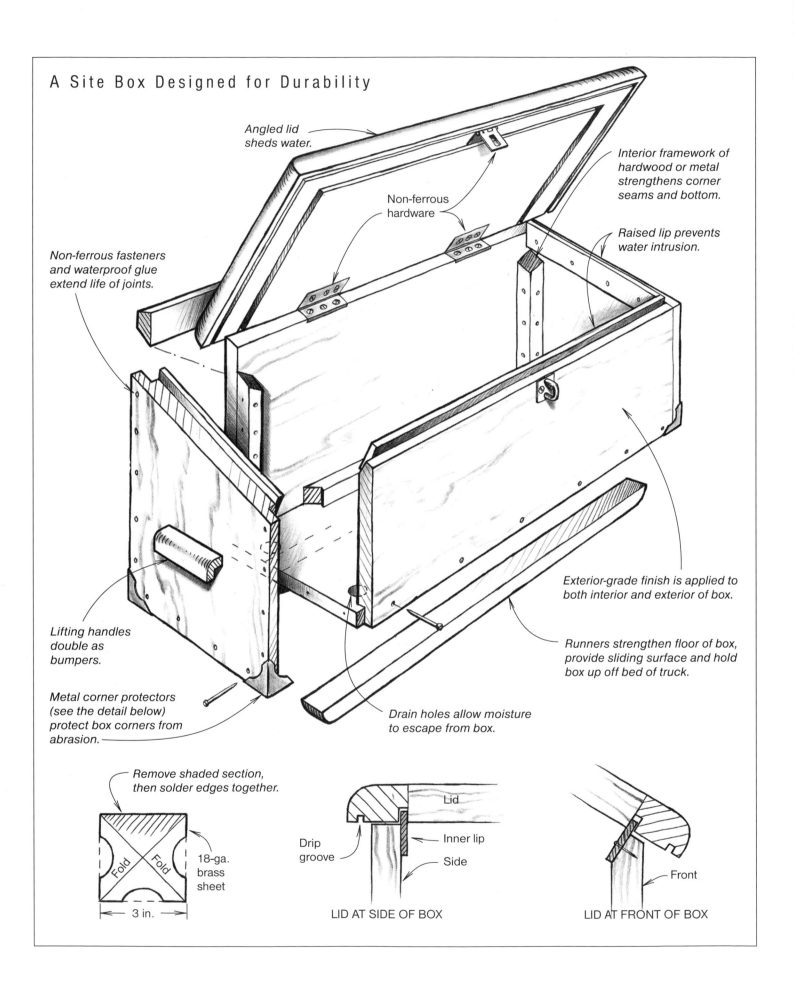

Angled lid sheds water.

Non-ferrous hardware

Interior framework of hardwood or metal strengthens corner seams and bottom.

Raised lip prevents water intrusion.

Non-ferrous fasteners and waterproof glue extend life of joints.

Lifting handles double as bumpers.

Metal corner protectors (see the detail below) protect box corners from abrasion.

Exterior-grade finish is applied to both interior and exterior of box.

Runners strengthen floor of box, provide sliding surface and hold box up off bed of truck.

Drain holes allow moisture to escape from box.

Remove shaded section, then solder edges together.

Fold   Fold

18-ga. brass sheet

3 in.

Drip groove

Lid

Inner lip

Side

LID AT SIDE OF BOX

Front

LID AT FRONT OF BOX

To make efficient use of the limited space in the bed of his pickup truck, carpenter and magazine editor Kevin Ireton, of New Milford, Conn., sized his tool totes to fit around other metal tool boxes. Because all the boxes fit on a sheet of plywood placed between the wheel wells, Ireton can slide the entire lot forward and behind the swing-down lid, creating a secure enclosure and providing room to carry materials. Photos by Kevin Ireton.

Even small hand totes that are designed to carry tools used only for interior work should be designed to resist water penetration—there's always a chance your box will get rained on going to and from the site. One solution, especially effective for small open totes, is to fit the box with a waterproof fabric cover (see the photo at right). For lidded truck boxes, you can cut the lids at a water-shedding angle and install a raised inner lip. Feet or runners fixed to the underside will raise the box above the puddles. To rid the box of any moisture that might find its way into a box left open in a sudden downpour, drill drain holes in the lower corners. Boxes destined for use outdoors should have fully waterproof lids with overhangs and drip edges.

Any site box benefits from the application of a durable finish—from a polyurethane varnish on hand totes to a deck- or marine-grade paint (or perhaps a fiberglass and epoxy) finish on the larger boxes. To ensure stability, apply an equal amount of finish to both the inside and outside of the box. This strategy minimizes the variation of moisture exchange—and thus movement of the wood fibers—between the inside and outside surfaces. Applying a light color to the box's interior will brighten the inner recesses, making it easier to see the contents.

SIZE AND SHAPE

One last design consideration is how the box will fit around other tools and storage containers when loaded for transportation (see the photos above). You may have to size larger boxes to fit a specific truck bed, and you'll want to size any site box to fit through standard doorways (I never make a site box more than 28 in. wide.) As I will explain in the next chapter, totes designed to be carried by one hand must be of a certain size and shape or they can be difficult and uncomfortable to carry. And because of the rugged nature of many job sites, I design my site boxes with a relatively low (and thus stable) profile.

Louis Plourd of Edmonton, Alberta, Canada, covers his site boxes with custom-fitted tarps for transporting in his open-bed pickup. Photo by Forfar Products.

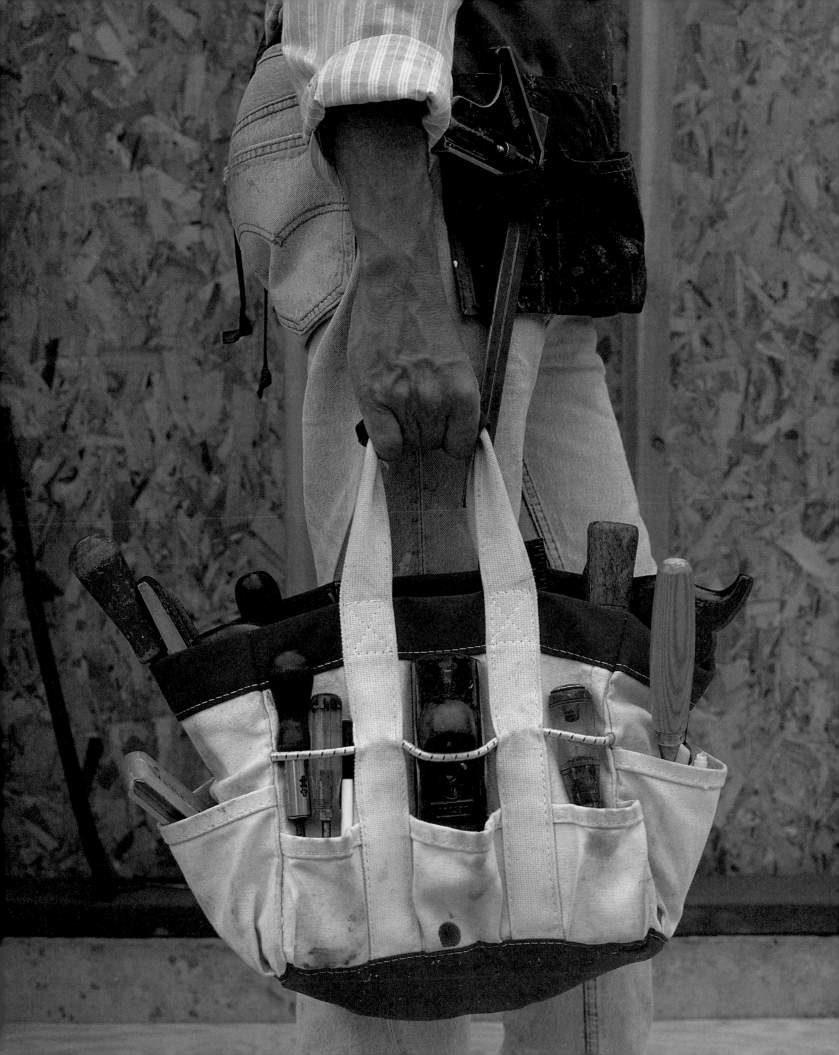

9

OPEN SHOULDER TOTES

At the end of the 1960s and fresh out of college, I decided that
rather than adding yet another suit to the corporate world, I would
instead move to the woods of coastal New Hampshire and add
another pair of overalls to the world of woodworking. With little
knowledge and even less skill, I was hoping to find employment with
either a timber framer or a boat carpenter—I had been told that both
were plentiful in this area. After much searching, and stooping to
offering my meager services for next to nothing (it was nothing, come
to think of it), a timber-frame house builder finally took me on.

Heeding my new employer's advice, I gathered together the tools
I would need to make other woodworkers think I belonged among
them. My employer assumed—correctly, it turned out—that hunger, if
not the raw enthusiasm of youth, would soon drive me to learn how
to use the tools. Indeed, the realization that I would need to create

Inger Olsen's soft and pliable canvas hand
tote, described on pp. 136-137, can hold as
many tools as a comparably sized wooden
tote. Photo by Craig Wester.

133

Jim Tolpin's toolbox for timber-framing tools. The side compartments contain chisels and other small carpentry tools; a slotted partition holds panel saws. A canvas cover provides a measure of protection from the elements. The original closet-pole handle has been replaced with a pipe clamp. Photo by Craig Wester.

a device to carry and store my new tools initiated my first real woodworking project: the making of an open shoulder tote of ¾-in. plywood. Nearly 25 years and two handles later, this box is still with me. It sits in a corner of my shop in semi-retirement, holding a set of rough carpentry tools in readiness for occasional shop repairs.

During a three-day period of very intense woodworking, I worked on the toolbox project, building a series of three prototype toolboxes (although I didn't realize at the time that I was making prototypes). As I remember, I made the first box about 16 in. square and rather shallow. It lasted only as long as it took for me to fill it with some tools, pick it up, and then set it down again, at which point I pried the box apart. I realized immediately that its shape would be a serious problem. I could not carry the box at my side without literally walking

into it. A square tote larger than about 12 in. wide was not a good solution.

I decided to build the second box long and narrow—as long as the 48-in. width of a sheet of plywood (how clever of me, I thought, to make such efficient use of materials). I figured that a tote of this shape would keep out of the way of my legs, fit through doors easily, and, best of all, hold virtually my entire collection of tools. This box in fact met all my design criteria; the only problem was that I couldn't pick it up. Loaded with tools, it weighed over 75 lb., far too much for me to lift with one arm. At first I thought the problem was the sheer weight of the load. But after unloading some tools, I still found the box difficult to carry—my wrist quickly tired and begged my other hand to come around to help. With my other hand now in the game, the box ended up in front of me, putting a tremendous strain on my back and making the box even more awkward and troublesome to carry.

I realize now that the problem was one of leverage: With some tools up to 2 ft. away from my hand on the handle, their weight exerted a tremendous amount of torque on my wrist. The remedy was either to concentrate as much weight as possible directly below my hand (which is not very practical with woodworking tools) or to shorten the box. I opted for the latter, cutting the box down to 3 ft. in length. So much for efficient use of materials. The size reduction reduced the carrying capacity to about 50 lb. worth of tools—a manageable load. The result is the third box, shown in the photo above left. Its sides and floor are ¾-in. fir plywood, rabbeted at the corners with glue and fastened with threaded nails. Two levels of side compartments contain chisels and other small tools. A slotted partition holds panel saws; ledge strips contain a 30-in. level and a 24-in. framing square.

Tote Baskets and Rigging Buckets

When you conjure up images of old-time cabinetmakers or joiners trundling about with their tools, you most likely think of them as carrying a heavy wooden chest or a handled open box. But this was not always the case. There is much evidence that these tradesmen often used soft, bag-like baskets when transporting tools to a job site (much like the carry bags of contemporary plumbers). In fact, it's likely that many, if not most, itinerant woodworkers carried their complete tool collections in a basket hung from the shoulder on a carrying stick.

While the baskets of the Middle Ages (called "frails" or "tool basses" in England) were probably made from rush or willow shoots and fitted with a rope handle, versions appearing by the 18th century were often made from sail canvas with leather handles and linings. Linings were needed to reinforce the baskets against the increasing presence of metal tools.

In the marine trades, another version of the carpenter's tool basket was in common usage: the rigging bucket. Featuring numerous internal pockets and carrying straps that automatically close the bag into the shape of a cylinder, rigging buckets were designed to carry many different hand tools and various supplies aloft into the ship's rigging. The pockets made tool access quick and easy—a welcome blessing in a situation where often only one hand is available "for the ship" (the other hand hanging on for dear life).

The rigging bucket is particularly suited to the nautical environment: First, it is pliable. Unlike a wood tote with its rigid external structure, the soft cylindrical bag can be fit into the smallest amount of shipboard space possible—the shape of the fabric tote

A tool tote basket from C. Lasinio's engraving of the late 1300s fresco entitled "Building of Noah's Ark" by Piero di Puccio. The joiners who modeled for this fresco carried their tools to the work site in baskets. Engraving courtesy of Norman Muller.

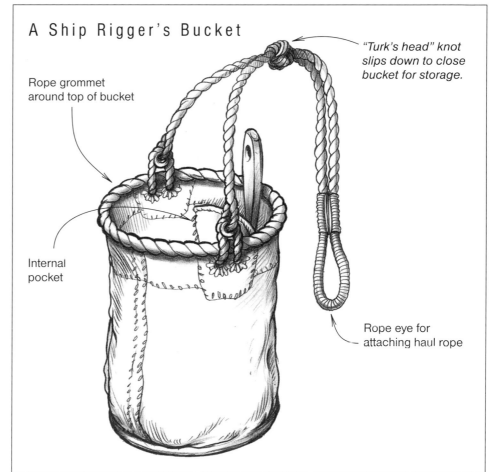

A Ship Rigger's Bucket

Rope grommet around top of bucket

Internal pocket

"Turk's head" knot slips down to close bucket for storage.

Rope eye for attaching haul rope

conforms closely to that of the tools contained within. Second, the soft, non-abrasive bottom makes the bag safe to set down upon varnished decks and to carry around delicate topside brightwork.

A Canvas Tool Tote

Inger Olsen, an awning- and sail-maker in Port Townsend, Washington, has made her share of rigging buckets over the years. So when her husband, Sean, needed a tote to carry his tools down to their sailboat in the marina, she naturally thought of making the tote from canvas. Because the tote would not be used much for working aloft and because she wanted to provide plenty of room for a wide assortment of tools, Olsen decided to give the tote more of a box shape than a cylindrical one. (A box shape tends to catch on things when hauled up into the rigging.)

To determine the exact size and shape of the bag, Olsen laid out all of the tools she knew her husband wanted to carry, arranging them to take up a minimum amount of space. She ended up with a box shape 9 in. wide by 12 in. long by 10 in. high. By using a double layer of 14-oz. canvas to create the bag, she was able to form outside pockets on the ends and sides to help organize the tools. Olsen added bungee cords to hold the tools upright, and a strap handle fitted with a leather sleeve at the carry point. To stiffen the bottom of the bag and to make it more resistant to water, she sewed on a third layer of synthetic water-repellent fabric. The sidebar at right gives step-by-step instructions on making a canvas tote; the tote Olsen made is shown in the photo on p. 132.

CONSTRUCTING A CANVAS TOTE

First, determine the overall size of the bag by the number and size of the tools to be carried, then draw and cut out the patterns for the three major components of the bag (labeled A, B and C in the drawing on the facing page) from a sheet of clear Mylar or paper. Pin the patterns to the canvas, aligning them parallel to the weave in the fabric, and trace the pattern onto the canvas with a soft pencil. Then cut out the pieces.

Fold over the last ½ in. of the fabric to eliminate raw edges (to keep the weave from unraveling). Hold the fold in place by flattening it down with a piece of wood. Pushing down hard, run the edge of the board (round the edge so it won't cut the fabric) back and forth along the seam, creating a sharp crease. Sew the hem down with a zigzag stitch using a heavy-duty sewing machine or by hand. If you wish, you can sew a leather edging over these seams to add beauty and to extend the life of the bag.

If you don't have access to a heavy-duty sewing machine and you don't want to strain your home machine, consider having the cut pieces sewn at a local tent and awning shop (or a sail-maker's loft, if you are lucky enough to live in the kind of town that has such a place). If you are stitching the canvas by hand, use a #13 or #14 needle and waxed thread. You will need a hefty thimble or a sail-maker's sewing palm to help you push the needle through the canvas, especially when sewing through three layers.

Needles, thread, thimbles and other supplies can be purchased at awning shops.

Now lay the pocket layer (piece A) over the larger layer (piece B) and sew it in place at the corners. On the longer sides of piece B, lay down a length of bungee cord about 1 in. in from the edge. Sew the ends to hold the cord in place.

Make the strap from a piece of 2-in. wide webbing or a strip of canvas folded over on itself. Cut it to length and lay it down over pieces A and B as shown in the drawing. If you wish, you can add leather sleeves at the carry points to make the bag more comfortable to carry. Sew the webbing strap to the two canvas layers. Note that you also sew through the bungee cords.

Next, sew the water-repellent fabric bottom (piece C) to pieces A and B. This forms a tool pocket between the canvas layers in the area between the straps. Then, folding the bag inside out, sew up the corners, running the machine up and down the seam several times. When you fold the bag right side out, the stitches disappear inside. Finally, if the canvas is untreated, brush it with several coats of canvas sealant, available at most building-supply or awning shops, to keep moisture from working its way into the seams and weakening the bag.

A Canvas Tote Bag, Step by Step

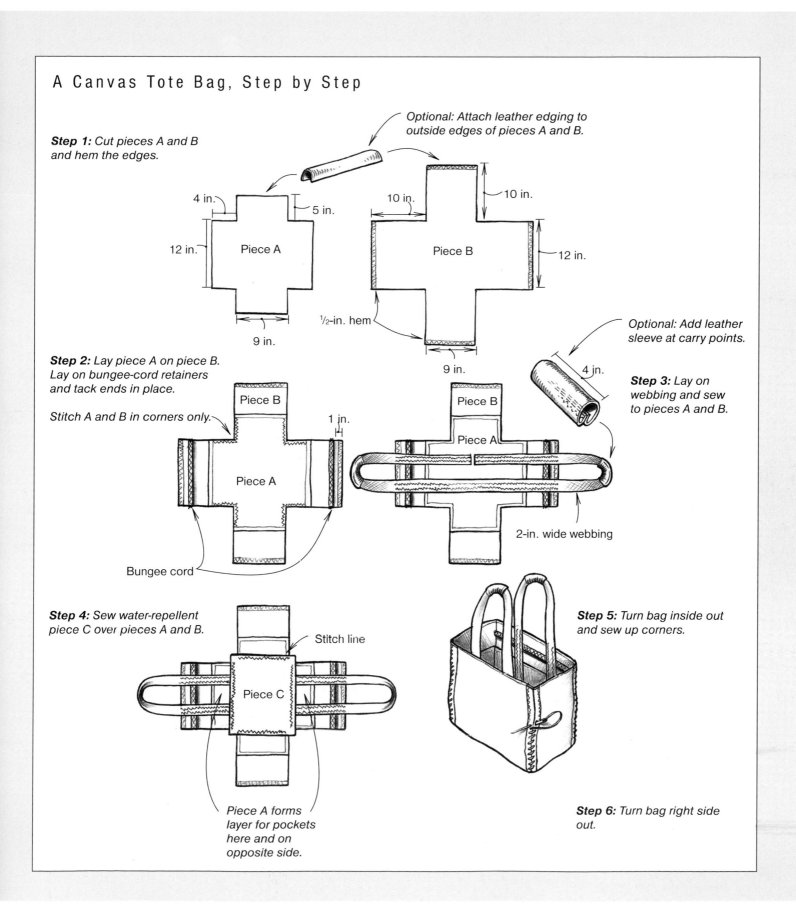

Step 1: Cut pieces A and B and hem the edges.

Optional: Attach leather edging to outside edges of pieces A and B.

4 in.

5 in.

10 in.

10 in.

12 in.

Piece A

Piece B

12 in.

9 in.

½-in. hem

9 in.

Optional: Add leather sleeve at carry points.

4 in.

Step 3: Lay on webbing and sew to pieces A and B.

Step 2: Lay piece A on piece B. Lay on bungee-cord retainers and tack ends in place.

Stitch A and B in corners only.

Piece B

Piece A

Piece A

1 in.

Piece B

Piece A

2-in. wide webbing

Bungee cord

Step 4: Sew water-repellent piece C over pieces A and B.

Stitch line

Piece C

Piece A forms layer for pockets here and on opposite side.

Step 5: Turn bag inside out and sew up corners.

Step 6: Turn bag right side out.

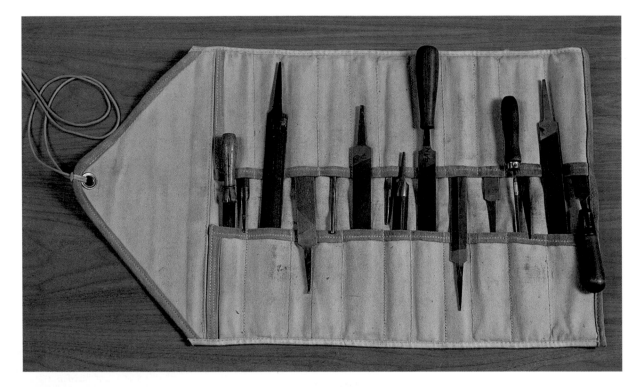

A small canvas tool roll is ideal for holding tools such as files or drill bits. The tools within are easy to get at if the roll is designed to hang on a wall. Photo by Craig Wester.

CANVAS TOOL ROLLS

To contain smaller tools such as chisels, files and drill bits, Inger Olsen also made some canvas tool rolls. A tool rool protects the tools in transport while offering easy access, especially if you hang the roll up on a wall. And compared to the rigger's bags, tool rolls are also quite easy to make.

Olsen starts her tool rolls by sizing a Mylar or paper pattern to the particular tools, then cutting the fabric to size. To keep the roll from getting too bulky when rolled up, she generally restricts the opened length to under 2 ft. She adds stiffness and strength to the top of the roll, which bears the burden of hanging, by cutting and sewing a second layer to the triangular tongue.

With this done, Olsen then hems the raw edges of the fabric. To make the roll look nice and to increase durability, she sometimes adds a leather edging. She also often adds a leather reinforcement to what will become the outside edges of the roll, centering a 3-in. wide leather strip over the fold line and sewing it in

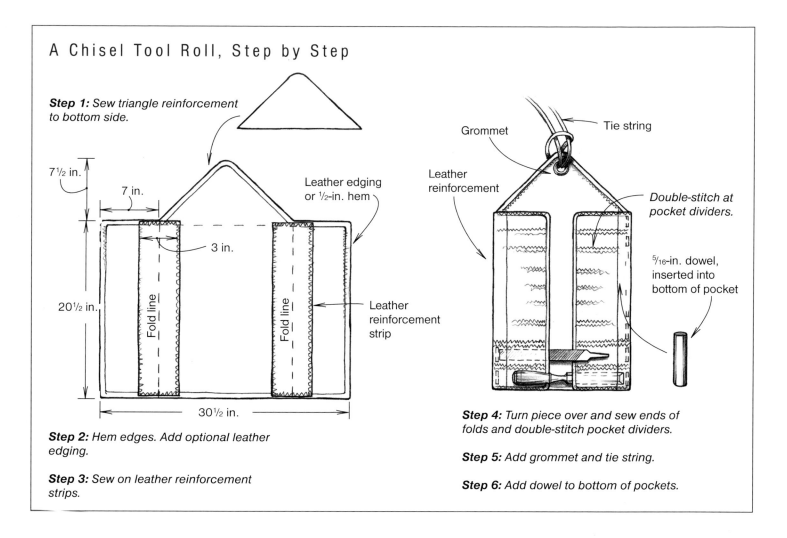

A Chisel Tool Roll, Step by Step

Step 1: Sew triangle reinforcement to bottom side.

7½ in.

7 in.

3 in.

20½ in.

Fold line

Fold line

Leather edging or ½-in. hem

Leather reinforcement strip

30½ in.

Step 2: Hem edges. Add optional leather edging.

Step 3: Sew on leather reinforcement strips.

Grommet

Tie string

Leather reinforcement

Double-stitch at pocket dividers.

5/16-in. dowel, inserted into bottom of pocket

Step 4: Turn piece over and sew ends of folds and double-stitch pocket dividers.

Step 5: Add grommet and tie string.

Step 6: Add dowel to bottom of pockets.

place at the ends. These reinforcement strips help to strengthen the fold line and prevent tools such as screwdrivers and files from wearing through the bottom of their compartment pockets. If the tool roll is to contain chisels, short lengths of $5/16$-in. dowel are added to the bottom of the pockets for the blades to bear against. These dowels prevent the sharp edges from cutting through the canvas and into the leather reinforcement strip.

Next Olsen folds over the sides of the roll and stitches down the ends. She double-stitches dividers to form pockets after checking the spacing with the tools. Finally, she presses in a metal grommet near the top of the triangle and attaches the tie-down string.

Building a Tackle-Box Tool Tote

When Wayne Law, of Canton, New York, set out to make an open shoulder tote to carry a selection of hand tools and small fittings for electrical work around the shop, his goal was to create a "no-rummage" toolbox. It would be a challenge: Law wanted the box to be as small as practical, yet contain plenty of compartments. Tired of searching through catch-all bins of small parts, he knew that the more he could compartmentalize the design, the happier he would be with the result. The finished toolbox is shown on p. 140.

DESIGN NOTES

While working up the design, Law hit upon the idea of using the configuration of a fisherman's tackle box. The stacking trays and swing-out design maximized the number and accessibility of the compartments while minimizing the footprint of the box when closed. The handle folds down, increasing accessibility even more. To prevent the box from rolling from side to side on the handle's pivot point, Law cleverly slotted the handle and added a locking peg that engages when the box is lifted.

Law designed his box to fit his particular assortment of tools and supplies, laying them all out on a table to establish the sizes of the various compartments. He kept the size

manageable: 12¾ in. wide by 18¾ in. long by 10½ in. high. While you can make your box larger, be careful to make it no wider than Law's 12¾ in. or it will be awkward to carry. Remember, too, that the bigger you make your box, the more stuff you will be tempted to stow, and the heavier the box will be to haul around.

To keep both cost and weight down, Law used ⅜-in. A-C fir plywood and pine. You could go to ½-in. maple plywood for a nicer looking, though admittedly somewhat heavier (and definitely more expensive), box. For increased durability, use hardwood for the handle arms.

CONSTRUCTION PROCEDURES

Lay out the tools to establish the configuration of the box. Then make a full-size drawing (see pp. 72-75), make up a cut list and gather the materials you will need.

Constructing the lower box

Cut the plywood parts to size and lay out and drill the holes for the swing arms and the swing-arm pivot bolts, as shown in the drawing on p. 142. Also drill for the pivot bolt and the stop dowel for the swing-down handle. Dado the sides and ends for the bottom panel, then glue and screw these components to the four pine corner blocks. Apply glue to the dadoes, then slide the bottom panel in place before screwing in the last end piece. Make sure that the box is square by checking its diagonal measurements, then set it aside to dry.

Wayne Law's tool tote carries small hand tools and electrical fittings around his shop. Modeled on a fisherman's tackle box, the tote features straightforward joinery and lightweight materials. When the box is open, the handle folds down out of the way, making the contents of the box more accessible. Photos by Craig Wester.

Wayne Law's Tackle-Box Tool Tote

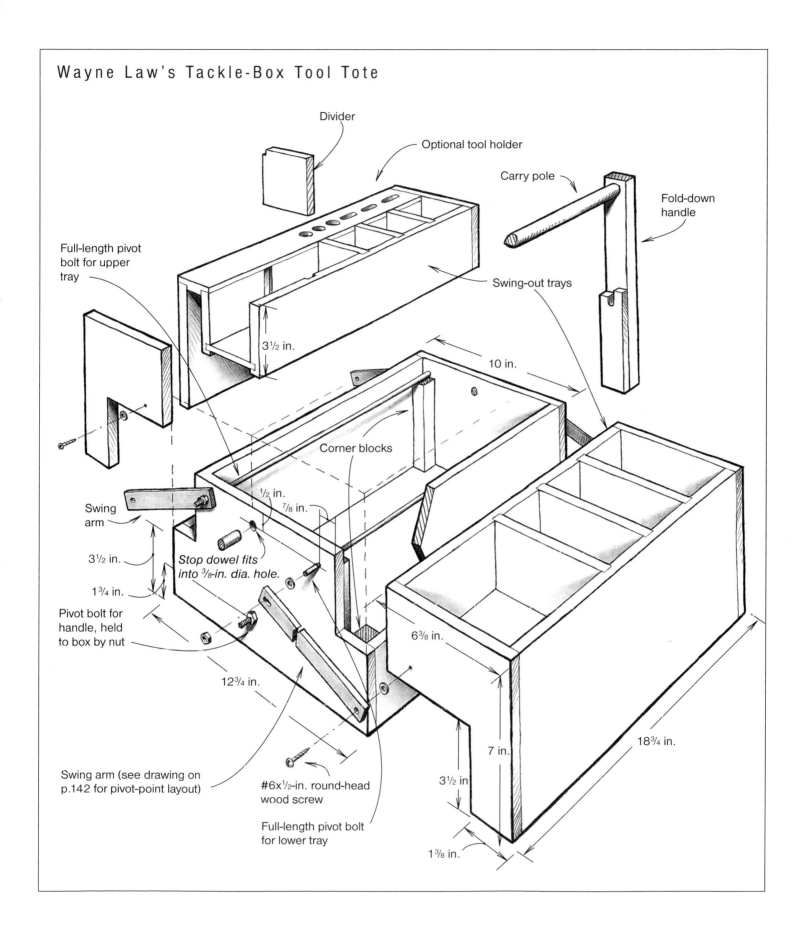

Divider

Optional tool holder

Carry pole

Fold-down handle

Full-length pivot bolt for upper tray

Swing-out trays

3½ in.

10 in.

Corner blocks

Swing arm

½ in.

⅞ in.

3½ in.

Stop dowel fits into ⅜-in. dia. hole.

1¾ in.

6⅜ in.

Pivot bolt for handle, held to box by nut

12¾ in.

7 in.

18¾ in.

3½ in

1⅜ in.

Swing arm (see drawing on p.142 for pivot-point layout)

#6x½-in. round-head wood screw

Full-length pivot bolt for lower tray

Pivot Points and Pivot-Arm Length

END VIEW OF BOX

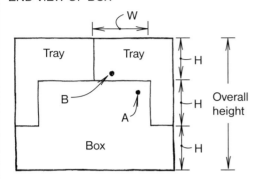

Each tray has two pivot points, one on the box (A) and one on the tray (B). First, choose a convenient location for point A where the pivot rod will not interfere with items stored in the box. The distance from the top of the box to point A must be less than ½ H.

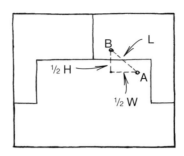

Locate point B ½ H higher than point A and ½ W to the side, as shown. The length of the swing arm (L) between the pivot points can be calculated using the Pythagorean theorem:

$$L^2 = (\tfrac{1}{2}H)^2 + (\tfrac{1}{2}W)^2$$

$$L = \sqrt{(\tfrac{1}{2}H)^2 + (\tfrac{1}{2}W)^2}$$

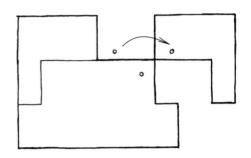

When the points are correctly located, the tray will just clear the corner of the box if it is held level as it pivots open.

Constructing the swing-out trays

Cut the parts to size, using gang-cutting methods on the dividers to ensure uniformity. Dado the sides and ends for the bottom panel and dividers, then glue and nail the parts together. If you leave some dividers loose, you can change the arrangement of compartments later. Rabbet and install the tool holder, if you want one in your box. You can use the assembled lower box as a jig to hold the tray assemblies square while they dry.

Making the handle

Rather than trying to shape the handle arms from 1⅛-in. thick stock, it is easier to cut the notch for the stop dowel in a separate piece of wood and then laminate it to the longer section (see the top drawing on the facing page). Law used ¾-in. stock for the notched piece,

planing it down to ⅜ in. after the pieces were joined. Cut the counterbore for the pole at the top end of the arm (it need only be about ⅛ in. deep), and cut the slotted hole for the through bolt toward the bottom of the arm. You need to step-cut the slot as shown, to fit it around the nut holding the bolt to the box.

Making the swing-arm fittings

Cut the four swing arms to length (at least ½ in. longer than the distance between the two pivot points, as shown in the bottom drawing on the facing page) from a ⅛-in. by ½-in. aluminum bar. In each arm, drill a 9/64-in. hole for a #6x½-in. round-head wood screw at one end and then drill and file a ⅛-in. wide by ¼-in. long slot for the pivot bolt at the other. Now cut the ¼-in. steel rods to length (be sure to allow enough length to accommodate lock nuts over the arms at either end), and thread the ends to receive the ¼-20 lock nuts. File the threaded ends of the rods passing through the base of the box until they fit snugly into the slots you cut in the arms. File the flats at either end of the rod parallel to one another so that the arms will also sit parallel to each other once installed. To be sure that the flats are parallel, final-fit the arms to the rod with the assembly laid across a large flat surface.

Final assembly

Slide the pivot rods into the lower box and install the arms at either end. Set the swing-out trays on the box and attach the swing arm to the trays at each point B using a #6x½-in. round-head wood screw through each ⁹⁄₆₄-in. hole in the swing arms. Use a flat washer between the swing arm and the tray. Test the operation—the inside corner of the tray should just brush the outside corner of the box as the tray swings down to the side. You can plane a light roundover into the corners to prevent binding.

Set the handle arms in place over the pivot bolts, fixing them loosely in place with lock nuts. Then insert the pole into the recess cut for it at the top ends of the handle arms, securing it with screws. Test the operation of the swing handle as you tighten down the lock nuts: It should easily swing down to one side (the side opposite the pine tool holder, to avoid catching on any tool handles), and pull up to engage the stop dowel. If the upper arm catches on the swing-arm lock nuts, file them down until it clears.

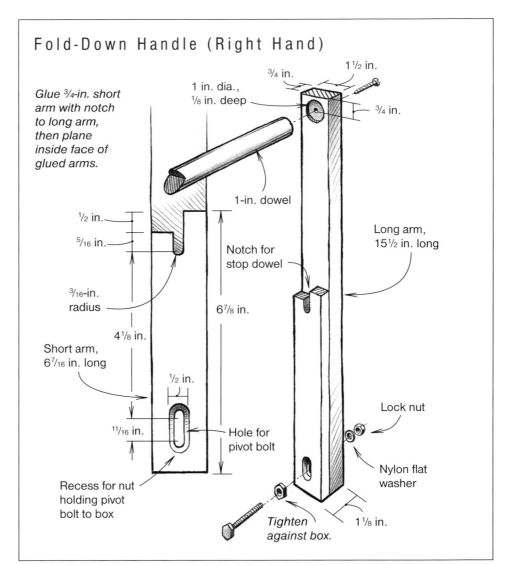

Fold-Down Handle (Right Hand)

Glue ¾-in. short arm with notch to long arm, then plane inside face of glued arms.

1 in. dia., ⅛ in. deep

¾ in.

1½ in.

¾ in.

1-in. dowel

½ in.

⁵⁄₁₆ in.

Notch for stop dowel

Long arm, 15½ in. long

³⁄₁₆-in. radius

6⅞ in.

4⅛ in.

Short arm, 6⁷⁄₁₆ in. long

½ in.

¹¹⁄₁₆ in.

Hole for pivot bolt

Lock nut

Nylon flat washer

Recess for nut holding pivot bolt to box

Tighten against box.

1⅛ in.

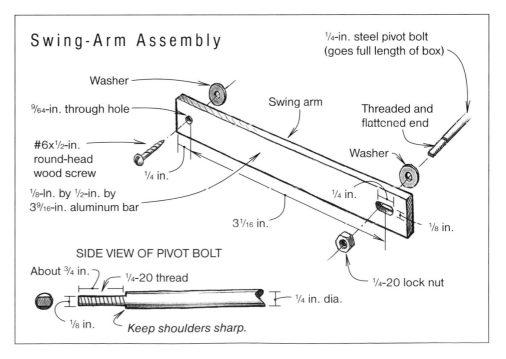

Swing-Arm Assembly

Washer

⁹⁄₆₄-in. through hole

#6x½-in. round-head wood screw

⅛-in. by ½-in. by 3⁹⁄₁₆-in. aluminum bar

¼ in.

¼ in.

Swing arm

3¹⁄₁₆ in.

¼ in.

¼-in. steel pivot bolt (goes full length of box)

Threaded and flattened end

Washer

⅛ in.

SIDE VIEW OF PIVOT BOLT

About ¾ in.

¼-20 thread

⅛ in.

Keep shoulders sharp.

¼-20 lock nut

¼ in. dia.

Stephen Freund built this open shoulder tote from pine, using router-made dovetail joints in the corners. Sized to fit behind the seat of his pickup truck, the box holds an impressive number of hand tools and accessories. Photo by Alec Waters.

A Remodeler's Pine Tote

Stephen Freund, a remodeling and architectural woodworking contractor in Laguna Hills, California, explains why he took the time to build his open shoulder tote: "It doesn't do you any good to have a collection of quality tools if you don't know where they are." While this statement may ring true for most woodworkers, it is doubly significant for those who spend most of their time out on a job site, where, finding tools quickly is critical for making the most of each day. Having a spot to put a tool when you're done with it is also essential, since a tool lost on a job site often sprouts legs and walks away. As they say in New England, "It turns up missing."

Freund approached the design with three important things in mind. First, he wanted the box to be long enough to hold his panel saws, yet not so long or wide that it wouldn't fit behind the seat of his pickup truck. Second, he wanted as many hand tools as possible to have a safe, yet visible (so he could see instantly

if they were missing) and easily accessible niche. Realizing that he would acquire new tools and replace others over time, he wanted some of the compartments and tool-holding strategies to be temporary, rather than fixed.

Finally, Freund wanted to be able to carry a multitude of small tools (such as drill and router bits) and accessories (such as stop collars, trammel points and tweezers). For these he designed three drawers to run along the base of the tote. Dividers within the drawers helped organize and protect the items. Lift-out divided trays sized to hold the smallest items maximized the holding capacity of one drawer. As it turned out, locating the set of drawers along the base lowered the tote's center of gravity, making the box easier to carry and more stable. Since a protruding drawer pull would most certainly catch on things, and a cut-out pull could allow small items to escape, Freund chose instead to use marine-type recessed ring pulls for handles (see the photo on the facing page).

Knowing that he was going to shoehorn many tools into this box (68 in all, as it turned out), Freund opted to build most of it from pine to keep the overall weight down. To make the box as durable as possible, he chose sturdy joints—routed blind dovetails, which are as attractive as they are strong. Several clients, hesitant to hire Freund because of his youth (he was 25 when he built this tote), were won over when they learned that he made this impressive toolbox from scratch.

Freund's major design concerns centered on size—the box had to hold panel saws and a 24-in. level, and it had to fit behind the seat of his pickup truck. After drawing out the final design in a scaled three-view drawing, Freund went on to make up the materials and cut lists.

After cutting the sides, ends, and floors to size, Freund used a dovetail template to rout the joints that would tie them together. (The dovetailed stiles between the drawers were cut by hand.) He then cut the dadoes in the sides and end boards to receive the interior floor, and cut the through mortises in the end pieces to accept the handle. Satisfied

Divided drawers and lift-out trays organize items in a small space. Marine-type recessed ring pulls are used as handles. Photo by Alec Waters.

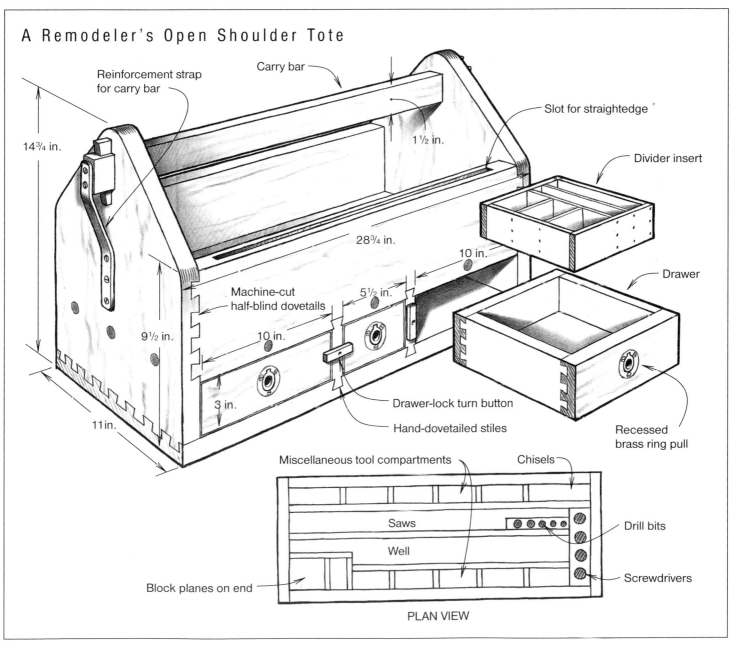

A Remodeler's Open Shoulder Tote

Reinforcement strap for carry bar

Carry bar

Slot for straightedge

14³⁄₄ in.

1¹⁄₂ in.

Divider insert

28³⁄₄ in.

10 in.

Drawer

Machine-cut half-blind dovetails

5¹⁄₂ in.

9¹⁄₂ in.

10 in.

Recessed brass ring pull

3 in.

Drawer-lock turn button

Hand-dovetailed stiles

11 in.

Miscellaneous tool compartments

Chisels

Saws

Drill bits

Well

Block planes on end

Screwdrivers

PLAN VIEW

with a dry-fit test of all the components, Freund then glued and clamped the assembly together.

With the box assembled, Freund continued to build and fit the drawers, tool racks, and ledges. Finally, he slid the handle through the mortises, locking it in place with wedges.

A Tote without a Handle

Over the last ten years or so, remodeling carpenter Doug Warren, of Port Townsend, Washington, has built a considerable number of open shoulder totes—and found every one of them lacking. Even after experimenting a bit with their sizes and shapes, he found them all uncomfortable to carry when fully loaded. Finally, Warren realized that he just didn't like to carry anything heavier than about 30 lb. with one arm, no matter how it was shaped or balanced. Warren consequently decided that the next box he would build—the one shown in the photos above—would eliminate the typical carry pole running the length of the box, allowing him to carry the box in two hands, like a tray.

Warren soon discovered other benefits of this design. For one, the new tote would weigh less than its predecessors even without a reduction in volume, because eliminating the pole meant the ends of the box didn't have to extend upwards. Also, access to many tools and especially to the sliding trays—a favorite feature of his boxes—was greatly improved. In this box there would be no risk of lifting up a tray only to have it catch on the pole and spill its contents.

Warren added a strip of wood to either end of the box for a hand grab; he was pleased to discover that these strips did double duty as bumpers when the box was being pushed into the bed of his truck. To lift the box, Warren bends his

legs, wraps his fingers around the strips at either end and stands up, letting the box bear against his stomach.

A Tall Tote for a Boat

Rather than designing around a long, horizontal box enclosure, as remodelers Freund and Warren did, yacht carpenter Bill Slaby, of Hazel Park, Michigan, took an entirely different tack with the open shoulder tote he built for carrying hand tools to the boatyard. Slaby configured the storage systems of his tote as tall, exposed, vertical surfaces. Though it can't carry as much as a typical open shoulder tote of the same volume, the box offers vertical storage that is easy to

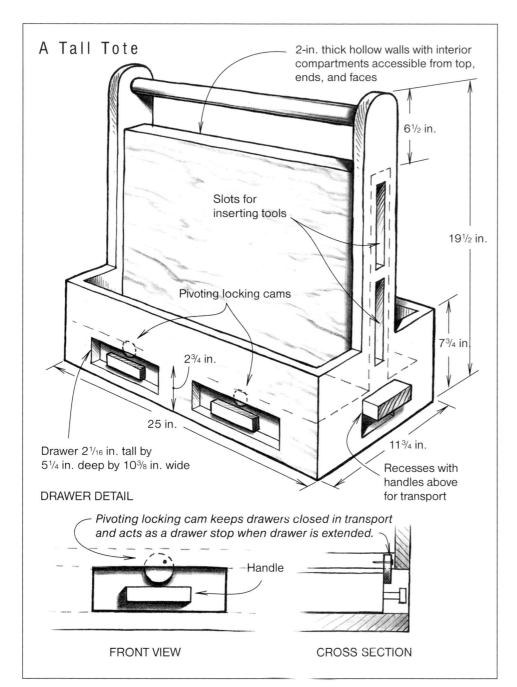

A Tall Tote

2-in. thick hollow walls with interior compartments accessible from top, ends, and faces

Slots for inserting tools

Pivoting locking cams

6½ in.

19½ in.

7¾ in.

2¾ in.

25 in.

11¾ in.

Drawer 2¹⁄₁₆ in. tall by 5¼ in. deep by 10⅜ in. wide

Recesses with handles above for transport

DRAWER DETAIL

Pivoting locking cam keeps drawers closed in transport and acts as a drawer stop when drawer is extended.

Handle

FRONT VIEW

CROSS SECTION

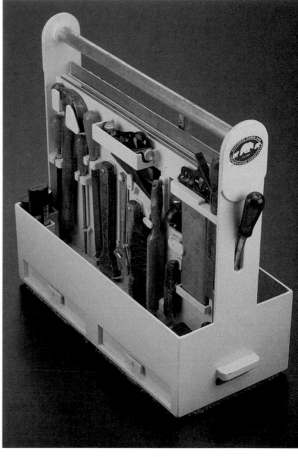

Yacht carpenter Bill Slaby designed his tool tote along a vertical plane. This strategy produced a box whose contents are in clear view and readily accessible. However, the box has somewhat less carrying capacity than a typical long, rectangular, open shoulder tote of the same volume. Photo by Eric Smith.

get at. As you can see in the photo above right, the tools that hang on either side of the tall central wall are plainly visible almost in their entirety. You can tell at a glance if they are in place, and your hands meet no interference from other tools (or from a carrying handle) when reaching for them.

To organize small tools, Slaby added four divided drawers to the base of the box. Because the drawers have recessed faces, the pulls can neither cause nor suffer damage (though a little storage space is sacrificed). In addition, the recess allows the installation of a positive-acting, but easily manipulated, pivoting locking cam, which prevents the drawers from opening in transit. The locking cam also acts as a stop against the

back of the drawer box to prevent the drawer from accidentally being pulled all the way out of the tote.

The hollow central vertical wall of the tote houses a couple of saws, a 24-in. level and a long Yankee screwdriver. The saws are stored upside-down to protect the cutting teeth; like the level, they rest at a downward angle, which keeps them securely in place.

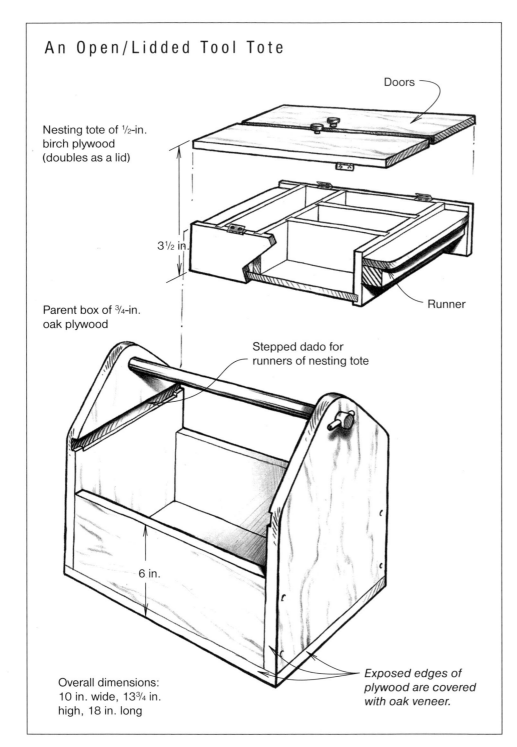

An Open/Lidded Tool Tote

Doors

Nesting tote of ½-in. birch plywood (doubles as a lid)

3½ in.

Runner

Parent box of ¾-in. oak plywood

Stepped dado for runners of nesting tote

6 in.

Overall dimensions: 10 in. wide, 13¾ in. high, 18 in. long

Exposed edges of plywood are covered with oak veneer.

A Hybrid Open/Lidded Tote

When finish carpenter and architect Tetsuo Shibata, of Temple City, California, went out to buy a site box for his hand tools, he couldn't find what he was looking for. Of course, he was asking for a lot: The box had to keep Shibata's tools secure and protected from the elements, yet allow immediate access to the contents as needed. Moreover, Shibata wanted the box to break down into small independent modules so that he wouldn't always have to carry the whole kit. The box he eventually designed and built turned out to be an open shoulder tote with a nesting tote that doubles as a lid.

Shibata built his box from scraps of ¾- in. oak plywood, applying veneer tape to the edges to cover the laminations. He built the nesting tote from ½-in. birch plywood to reduce the overall weight of the box. Because the runners of the nesting tote are captured in a stepped dado, the tote automatically locks itself into the open box—it can't slide out even if the unit is tipped over on its side. The interior of the main box can be accessed by either lifting and sliding the nesting tote to one side or by removing it entirely, as shown in the photos on the facing page. The nesting tote can be accessed without removing it from its parent box.

Building an Arts and Crafts Tote

As you can see in the photo on p. 150, the two open shoulder totes build by furniture designer and builder David Sellery, of Santa Cruz, California, are extraordinary. The lighter-colored one, which contains saws, hand planes and a

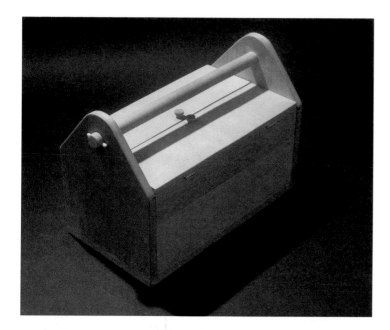

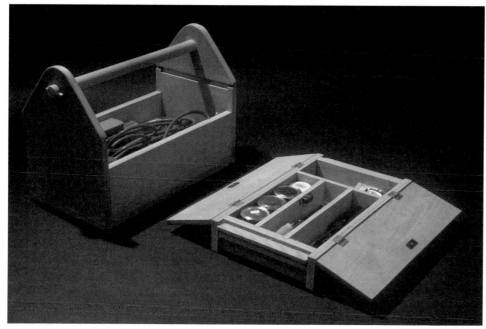

When the nesting tote is slid over and removed, Tetsuo Shibata's toolbox transforms from a lidded tote to an open shoulder tote. Photos by Tetsuo Shibata.

set of chisels, is made from bird's-eye maple and bubinga. Koa is the primary material for the other tote, which holds a framing square, clamps and various hand tools. This tote also features a drawer running the full length of the box. Brimming with tools, an appealing Arts and Crafts era design and fine joinery (note the meticulously executed dovetail, through-mortise-and-tenon, and bridle joints), these totes are works of art in themselves.

Where did the inspiration come from? In the words of the maker: "I decided to make these two toolboxes because I missed designing and building something with care—I missed handwork and unstained wood—and I missed being around work that I thought was beautiful. I was working as a finish carpenter at that time, and I longed for the work of a designer/craftsman of interiors and furniture—the job I had left behind in Los Angeles. I needed to make

something I felt good about, and that I could take with me to those jobs that I didn't have much interest in. And I wanted to feel reconnected to why I had chosen to be a woodworker in the first place."

Despite their beauty and high level of craftsmanship, the boxes are very practical. Sellery spent a lot of design time deciding how to fit as many tools as possible into the available space without reducing access or throwing the boxes

out of balance. He also wanted the overall shape and size of the totes to make them easy to transport and to hand-carry over a considerable distance. The boxes succeeded on both counts, They accompany Sellery to every job site—carrying the tools of his trade and symbolizing his love of woodworking.

DESIGN NOTES

Before you begin this project, a hybrid of the two totes designed by Sellery specifically for inclusion in this book, note that it is not for the faint of heart—the profusion of complex, and highly visible, joints demands close attention and a steady, skilled hand. Right from the outset, the layout of the components and their joint lines must be accurate and your cutting to these lines precise.

If you want to build an exact copy of this box, I suggest that you first develop a full-size rendering of each view from the scaled three-view drawing presented. (For instructions on how to create full-scale drawings, refer to pp. 72-75.) This exercise will not only help you visualize how the box will go together, but the drawing will provide you with a fail-safe way to lay out the exact locations and dimensions of the joints. If you have specific tools that you wish to carry in this tote, this is the time to decide where to place them and to design their support blocking or compartments.

CONSTRUCTION PROCEDURES

Although this tote is one of the most challenging projects in this book, the process should go smoothly if you take the time to study the drawings and to understand the sequence of steps. Like

many of the other projects, the basic steps after developing your cut list include getting out the materials to size, laying out and cutting the joints, dry assembling the pieces, applying finish to the interior surfaces, final assembling with glue, and then finishing the outside of the tote.

Getting out the stock

Make up a bill of materials and a cut list from your full-scale drawing. Procure the necessary stock and plane it to final thickness. (It is usually best to purchase stock at least $1/16$ in. oversize in thickness so you can surface it yourself—at most hardwood suppliers the planers are rarely sharp or clean enough to give a finished surface.) Next, referring to the cut list, rip out lengths of stock to make up the various components, adding about $1/2$ in. to each length. As you mark the pieces (in chalk) with their letter

David Sellery's Modified Arts and Crafts Tote

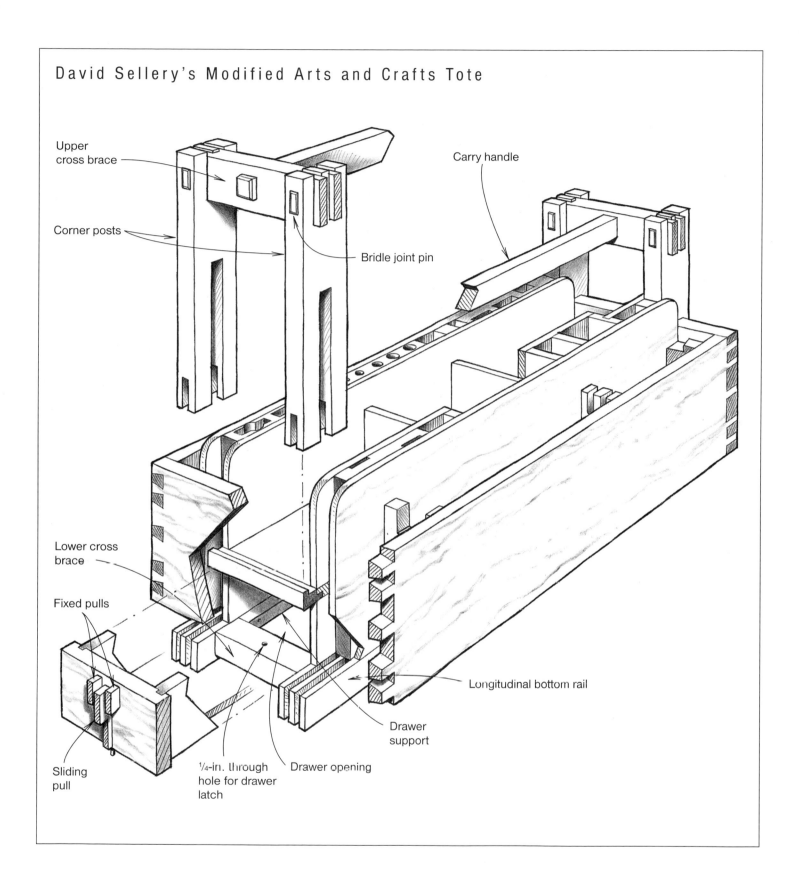

Upper cross brace

Corner posts

Carry handle

Bridle joint pin

Lower cross brace

Fixed pulls

Sliding pull

¼-in. through hole for drawer latch

Drawer opening

Drawer support

Longitudinal bottom rail

Tool Storage: Top View

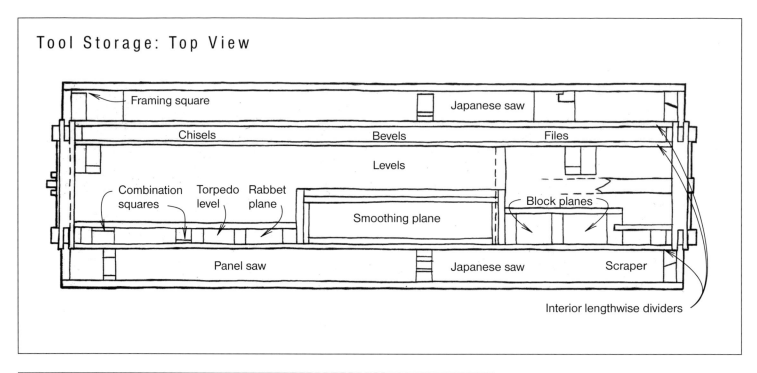

Framing square

Japanese saw

Chisels   Bevels   Files

Levels

Combination squares

Torpedo level

Rabbet plane

Smoothing plane

Block planes

Panel saw

Japanese saw

Scraper

Interior lengthwise dividers

Tool Storage: Section View

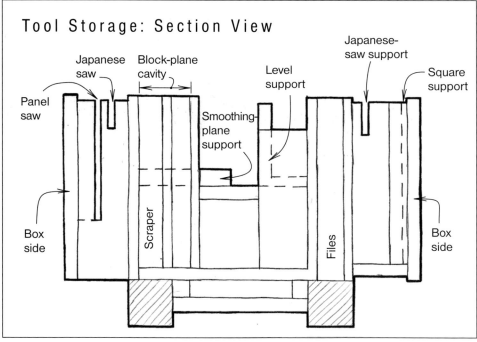

Japanese saw

Block-plane cavity

Level support

Japanese-saw support

Square support

Panel saw

Smoothing-plane support

Box side

Scraper

Files

Box side

---

symbols, check them off the cut list. Be sure to make up extra lengths of stock for the frame work: You'll need scrap when setting up to cut the mortise-and-tenon and bridle joints.

Making up the box

Sort out the various components of the box and then cut the parts to their final length as shown on the full-size rendering. (Exceptions are the box sides and ends: Cut these about ⅛ in. oversize, and trim them to their exact size after you have dovetailed them together at their corners.) To cut the dovetails, hold the pieces against the rendering and mark the location of the base line of the pins and tails. Remember to hold the stock so that it extends evenly past the finished size line at either end (¹⁄₁₆ in., assuming the pieces were cut ⅛ in. overlong). Extend the line around the board with a try square. Now cut the tails in the side boards and use them as templates for the pins in the end boards. After cutting the pins, dry-fit the box; when you are happy with the joinery, finish-sand the interior surfaces and glue up the box. Be sure it sits square and flat. Don't worry about the cutout for the drawer or the installation of the bottom boards—you'll take care of these later. But take the time now to finish all the interior components and the inside faces of the box while you can still get at them easily.

Making up the surround frame

Here's where you'll be glad you took the time to make that full-size drawing. To establish the exact locations of the shoulders of the bridle joints on the surround-frame components (see the

Bridle-Joint Layout

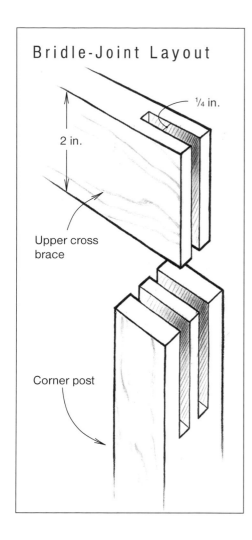

1/4 in.

2 in.

Upper cross brace

Corner post

Frame-Joint Layout

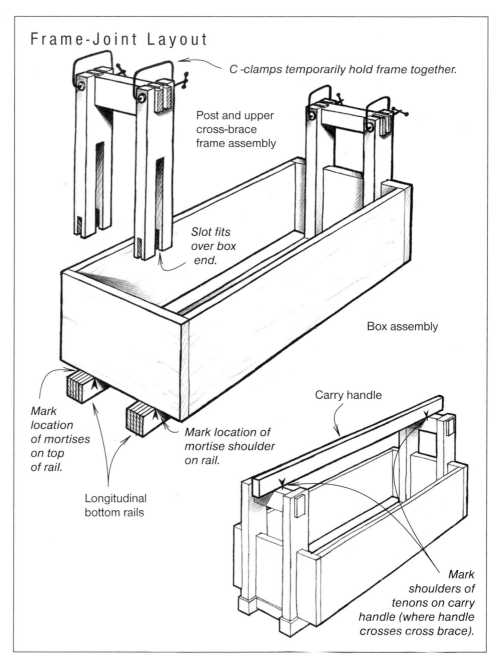

C-clamps temporarily hold frame together.

Post and upper cross-brace frame assembly

Slot fits over box end.

Box assembly

Mark location of mortises on top of rail.

Mark location of mortise shoulder on rail.

Longitudinal bottom rails

Carry handle

Mark shoulders of tenons on carry handle (where handle crosses cross brace).

drawing above), hold each part against the rendering and mark the shoulders of each joint with a penciled V tick mark. On the ends to be tenoned, extend the shoulder line around the stock with a sharp knife. Then mark the sides of the tenon with a marking gauge—set the gauge's points to the joint lines drawn on the rendering. Note that the tenons protrude past the corner post—and that the post protrudes past the top of the cross brace—by 3/32 in. when the joint is finally assembled. Mark the waste portions of the joint with an X. In a similiar fashion, lay out the cutlines of the mortises. To keep the parts oriented properly, assign numbers to the joints and write these on the stock.

Cut the mortises in the posts to the scribe line (either by hand or using a bandsaw or table saw). In most cases, you will need to use a chisel to square and flatten the bottom of the cut. Cut the tenons in the cross braces and the bottom of the posts and trim them precisely to the layout lines with a chisel. Dry-fit and adjust the surfaces of the tenon cheeks and the shoulder cuts until you achieve a tight, square joint between the top cross brace and the posts. But

don't glue up these joints yet. Instead, continue by laying out and cutting the slot in the posts that allows the frame to slip over the box ends. Now dry-assemble the frame pieces by clamping the joints temporarily together and slipping the assembly over the box. Hold the bottom of the posts to the longitudinal frame pieces to get an accurate layout of the bridle joint you will make here. In a similar fashion, lay the carry bar on the frame and mark where it crosses the

Mortising for Bridle-Joint Pins

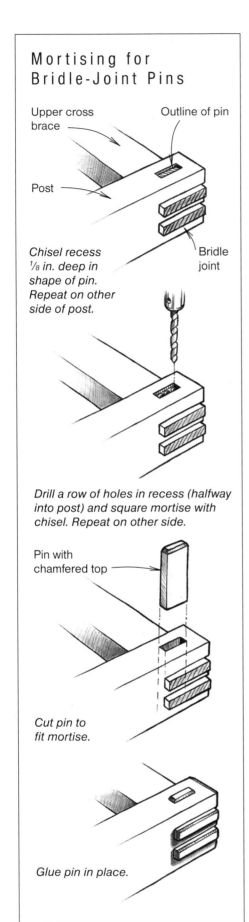

Upper cross brace

Outline of pin

Post

Bridle joint

Chisel recess 1/8 in. deep in shape of pin. Repeat on other side of post.

Drill a row of holes in recess (halfway into post) and square mortise with chisel. Repeat on other side.

Pin with chamfered top

Cut pin to fit mortise.

Glue pin in place.

Clamping the Frame

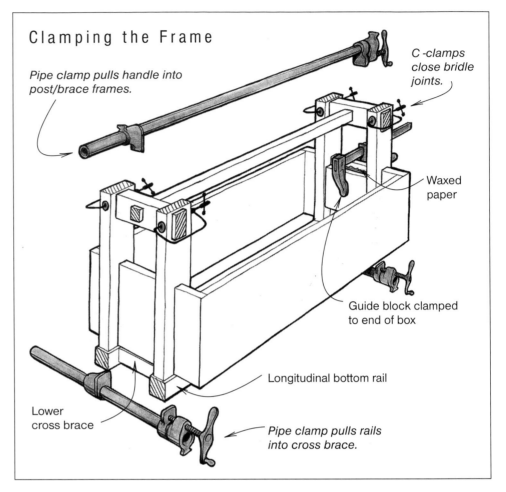

Pipe clamp pulls handle into post/brace frames.

C-clamps close bridle joints.

Waxed paper

Guide block clamped to end of box

Longitudinal bottom rail

Lower cross brace

Pipe clamp pulls rails into cross brace.

braces. These points represent the shoulder cut of the tenon you will cut in the ends of the bar.

Disassemble the frame and cut the mortises in the two longitudinal bottom rails. Cut the mortise and tenons of the carry handle. Also lay out and cut the mortise and tenons of the lower cross braces. Finish-sand the surfaces of the framework and chamfer the protruding tenons and the top of the corner posts.

Now you are ready to glue up the frame—in stages, to simplify the process. Begin by gluing the lower cross braces to the longitudinal rails. When you're sure the assembly is square, set it aside to dry. Now glue the top braces to the posts, clamping the bridle joint together with C-clamps (use protective pads). Slide the

bottom of the posts into the lower frame assembly to ensure proper alignment, but don't glue them yet.

When the two cross-brace/post assemblies are dry, remove them from the lower frame assembly and cut the mortises for the wood pins as shown in the drawing at left. Begin by outlining the rectangular hole with a chisel, creating shoulders about 1/8 in. deep. Now make the mortise itself with a drill followed by a chisel to square the cut. To prevent tearout, go in from either side of the post. Note that since the pins on either side of the post are independent, you don't have to worry about aligning the holes perfectly. Make a pair of pins for each bridle joint, trim them to fit, and then glue them in place.

For the last glue-up stage, slide the carry handle into its mortises in the cross braces and slip the entire assembly over the box and into the lower frame assssembly. To guide the posts over the box in their correct locations, cut scraps of wood to the width of the inside post spacing and clamp them to the ends of the box. Put waxed paper under the scrap blocks to prevent the glue squeeze-out from the post slots cementing them to the end boards. Clamp the bridle joints together with C-clamps, and pull the carry handle into the cross braces with a bar clamp (see the drawing at right on the facing page).

When the frame is dry, remove the clamps and scrap guide blocks and begin the installation of the interior components. Glue the interior walls to the sides of the posts, sandwiching support blocks for the various tools in between. Next create the cavity around the drawer by gluing the bottom boards in place.

Making up the drawer

Get out the pieces for the drawer, cutting them to size as indicated on the cut list. Refer to your full-scale rendering to locate the dadoes in the face to receive the sides. Cut these dadoes as well as those for the bottom panel and for the box end. Note that the drawer sides extend past the back end—these will act as stops, taking the stress away from the drawer face.

Make the lift-up locking pull as shown in the drawing at right. Dry-assemble the drawer, testing fits and alignments, then glue it up, being sure to keep the assembly flat and square. Test the action of the drawer when installed in the box. Apply candle wax to the sliding surfaces (including the pull) to reduce friction and eliminate sticking.

The drawer is opened and closed by means of pulls. Lifting the central sliding pull releases a retainer screw, as detailed in the drawing below. Photo by Dancing Man Imagery.

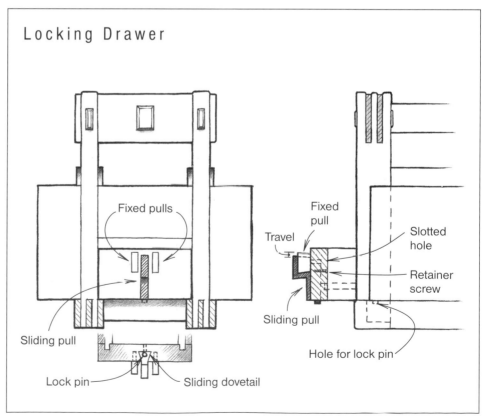

Locking Drawer

Fixed pulls

Sliding pull

Lock pin

Sliding dovetail

Travel

Fixed pull

Sliding pull

Slotted hole

Retainer screw

Hole for lock pin

10
LIDDED TOTES

Over the years, countless carpenters and other tradespeople have gotten along just fine with the traditional open shoulder totes featured in Chapter 9. So why build a lid, which adds complexity, not to mention extra weight? Perhaps the most important reason is security: A lid keeps the tools out of sight and out of the minds of co-workers who "borrow" tools. (They don't steal them, of course, but they don't put them back where you expect to find them, either.) It also protects the tools from dust and the onslaught of site debris. A well-fit lid can even offer some protection from a rain shower. Sometimes the lid itself can be used to hold additional tools. For the same amount of volume as an open shoulder tote, a lidded version might offer considerably more storage capacity.

Like other types of tool storage, lidded totes can be complex or simple, ranging in workmanship from impeccable to quick-and-

Michael Doiron, of Peabody, Mass., turned a plastic bucket into a tool tote, adding a lid so he could stand on it. A pair of jeans serves as a tool holder. Photo by Michael Doiron.

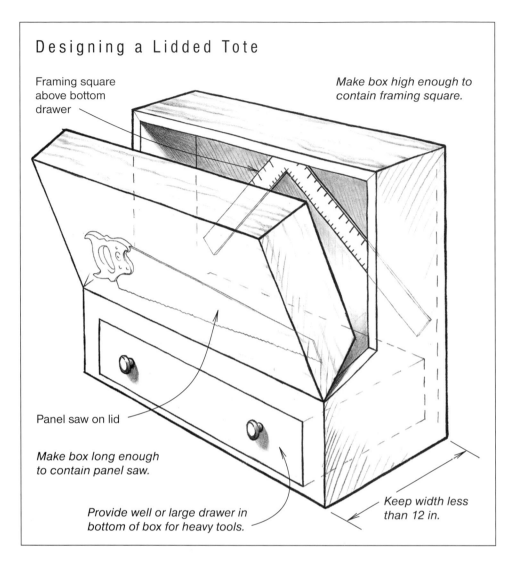

Designing a Lidded Tote

Framing square above bottom drawer

Make box high enough to contain framing square.

Panel saw on lid

Make box long enough to contain panel saw.

Provide well or large drawer in bottom of box for heavy tools.

Keep width less than 12 in.

INTERIOR LAYOUT

First, think about the interior design of the box. A long well running along the bottom of the box, perhaps with a few dividers to encourage organization, can be useful for storing heavy and bulky tools such as hammers, pry bars, planes and sharpening stones. You could also place these tools in a full-length drawer. Either way, plan to store your heaviest tools as low in the box as possible. A low center of gravity will make the box more stable when it is used—as it inevitably will be —as a stepstool or sawhorse.

To contain small tools such as drill bits, files, punches and pencils, consider fitting your tote with one or more divided drawers located toward the top of the box. Also think about giving larger, but delicate, tools such as calipers, marking gauges, and other precision layout tools either a drawer of their own or a lift-out tray fitted into the well.

HANDLES

Next, consider how you will carry the box. If the lid opens to sit on top of the box, you can plan to install handles at either end. To make the tote compact for transporting, choose campaign-style handles that recess into the sides. (Though they protrude more, you can substitute fold-down chest handles to save a little money.) If your box allows a top-mounted handle (because the lid folds down, not up), you can make one from a pole, running it from end to end like the handle of an open shoulder tote. Alternatively, you can buy a steel or brass handle from a builder's supply store. To make sure that the metal handle won't pull out under the load of a tote crammed full of tools, substitute through-bolts for the attachment screws typically supplied with this hardware. Although leather briefcase-type handles offer perhaps the most comfortable grip, most are not sturdy enough for a toolbox.

dirty. You are limited only by your ingenuity. As I discovered early on, wherever there is a craftsperson, there is innovation—and probably a unique toolbox as well.

Design Considerations

Because lidded totes can be jam-packed with tools, most builders make them smaller than open totes. A lidded tote the size of my open shoulder carpentry box shown on p. 134 (1 ft. wide by 3 ft. long), would probably weigh far in excess of 60 lb.—more than most people want

to carry with one hand. For totes designed to carry a typical selection of carpentry tools, it's a good idea to limit their size. Make them just long enough to hold a panel saw, and just high enough to enclose a 24-in. framing square. Of course, as for any hand-carried tote, keep the width around 12 in. or less so it will be comfortable to carry at your side.

To keep down the overall weight of the box, consider building it from either 3/8-in. or 1/2-in. plywood, or from a lightweight solid wood such as pine, alder or western maple. If you use a lightweight wood, be sure to take the time to make durable joints. Dovetails or finger joints would be good choices.

Lidded-Tote Handle Options

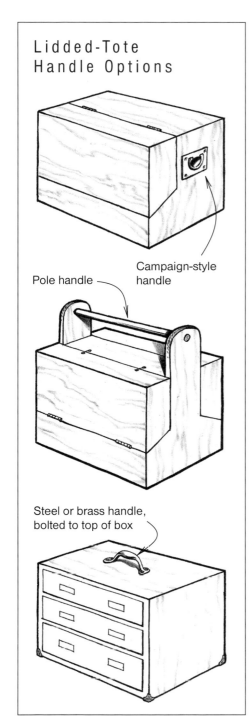

Campaign-style handle

Pole handle

Steel or brass handle, bolted to top of box

Tote with Drop-Down Lid

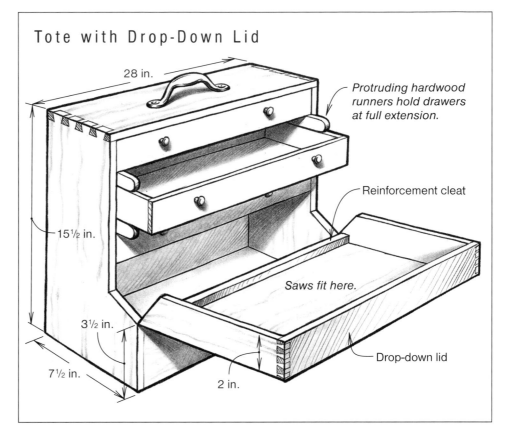

28 in.

Protruding hardwood runners hold drawers at full extension.

Reinforcement cleat

15½ in.

Saws fit here.

3½ in.

7½ in.

2 in.

Drop-down lid

LID PLACEMENT

There are several different ways to place a lid on a tool tote. You can make the lid drop down to one side. Or you can install it so it opens upward to rest on the top of the box. You can even design a version featuring two drop-down lids that open to either side of the tote. However you decide to orient the lid (or lids), remember that the inside of the lid provides excellent storage for tools, especially saws (secured with a combination of slotted dividers and a turnbutton through the handle hole) and sets of chisels (held in place with some sort of strap).

Single drop-down lid

When opened, the single drop-down lid reveals a bank of shallow drawers (see the drawing above). In a typical design, at least one of these drawers contains chisels, which are separated and held secure by dividers. The drawer runners,

which protrude beyond the face of the drawers, support the drawers when they are pulled out to nearly their full depth. Without these long runners—or a full-extension slide mechanism (see pp. 48-49)—you would have to remove the drawers from the tote to get full access. Below the drawers is a large open well designed to carry a wide assortment of tools.

Single lift-up lid

Lids that lift up may also carry saws, though they are generally too small to hold a framing square. The tote shown in the photo on p. 161, which was designed and built by Tom Law, of Smithsburg, Maryland, has a lift-up lid. In the open position the lid rests on top of the box and reveals a large, shallow tool well and the back wall of the tote. While the well contains the usual motley assortment of tools, the back wall holds layout tools where they are safe, yet immediately

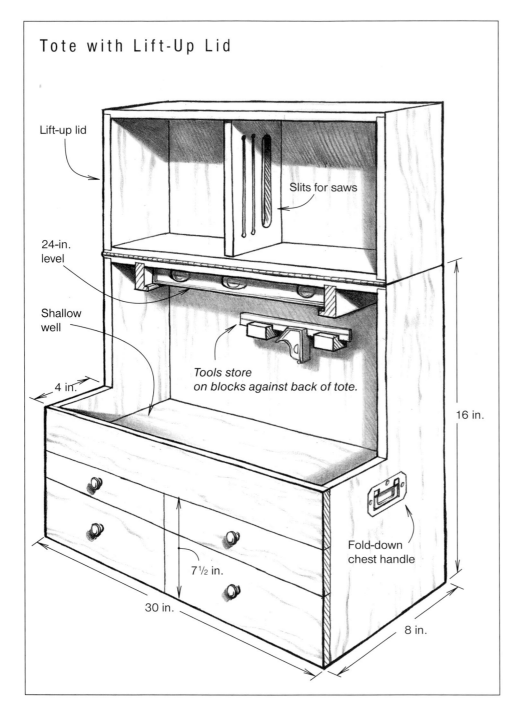

Tote with Lift-Up Lid

Lift-up lid

Slits for saws

24-in. level

Shallow well

Tools store on blocks against back of tote.

4 in.

16 in.

Fold-down chest handle

7½ in.

30 in.

8 in.

Double lid

A double lid provides a good deal more visible, accessible storage space than a single lid. You have another place to stow tools, and you also gain a second vertical surface (the center partition in the interior of the box) on which to hang tools. And because the two lids allow access to the well from either side of the box, tools carried there can be reached more quickly and easily than in a single-lidded tote.

A double-lidded tote often contains drawers, either substituted for the open well along the bottom of the box (which means, however, that you must close a lid to access them) or installed near the top of the box. Though drawers at the top of the box are necessarily narrow and not very deep, they usually open to either side, allowing full and easy access to their contents.

Building a Lidded Tool Roll

When boat builder and rigger Kit Africa, of Port Townsend, Washington, decided to create a lidded tote for his rigging and ship's carpentry tools, he set specific goals: The box had to be strong, durable and commodious, and hold his tools readily accessible. Yet, to be accommodated aboard ship, it also had to fit into the smallest possible space.

While mulling over—and rejecting—many typical lidded-tote designs, Africa realized that certain features of the canvas tool roll, which is most commonly used for carrying sets of chisels or auger bits (see pp. 138-139), might well meet his demanding criteria. When rolled up, the enclosed tools would form a cylinder, one of the most efficient shapes to stow on a crowded boat. When unrolled, the tools would become instantly accessible. The only

accessible. Resting just under the well is a bank of divided drawers—the larger, lower ones generally contain the heaviest tools. The nice thing about this design is that you don't have to open the lid to open the drawers. In addition, because the drawers are located at the widest part of the box, they can be deeper and hold more items. You carry this type of tote by

handles mounted at both ends of the box. If you like to keep one hand free to carry other gear, this design may not suit you. In that case, you can make a recessable handle in the top of the box like the one on Reinhold Faeth's tool cabinet (see pp. 98-99).

The lift-up lid on Tom Law's tool tote stores a selection of saws. Photo by Tim Snyder.

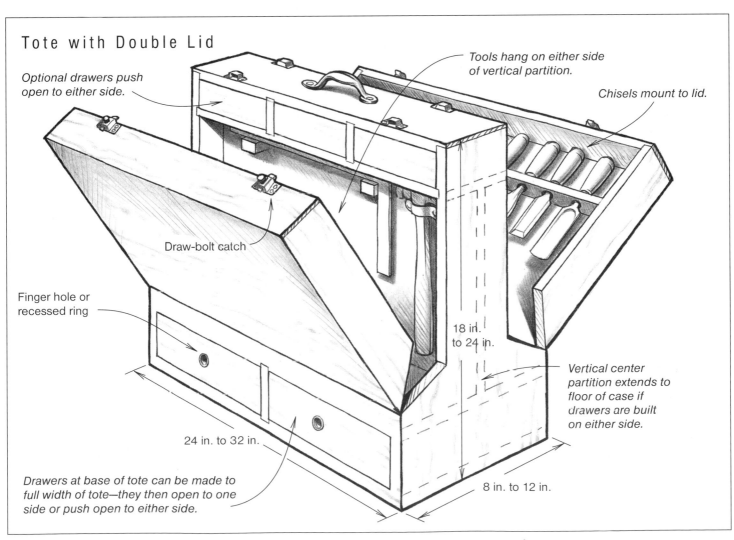

Tote with Double Lid

Optional drawers push open to either side.

Tools hang on either side of vertical partition.

Chisels mount to lid.

Draw-bolt catch

Finger hole or recessed ring

18 in. to 24 in.

Vertical center partition extends to floor of case if drawers are built on either side.

24 in. to 32 in.

8 in. to 12 in.

Drawers at base of tote can be made to full width of tote—they then open to one side or push open to either side.

shortcoming might be durability. A fabric wrapping, even of tough sailcloth, could not offer the same protection against impact or abrasion as a wooden box.

Thus was borne out of the mind of Africa this inspiration: Why not make a tool roll from wood? It would not have to be perfectly round, he realized—a hexagon would do just fine. This would make the box easy to build yet sacrifice few of the qualities afforded by the shape of a true cylinder. Over a cup of coffee, Africa showed me his design and offered suggestions on how to build the box. Unfortunately, he had no boxes of his own to show me. They had proven so successful that he ended up selling the ones he had to his shipmates and fellow boatbuilders. I had no choice but to scurry back to my shop and make one for myself, sizing it to contain my collection of carving chisels.

A hexagonal tool-roll tote designed by Kit Africa and built by Jim Tolpin to carry carving tools, mallets and sharpening stones. When the tote is "unrolled" by unstrapping the box's lid, the tools are easy to see and grasp. Note the lift-out lid, which holds the items set in the well tightly in place. Photo by Craig Wester.

DESIGN NOTES AND CONSTRUCTION PROCEDURES

I decided on the overall size of my box by laying out the tools I wanted it to contain and gauging the amount of space they would need. Then I made up a drawing—in this case the box is so simple I needed only to draw a rough sketch and a full-size end view. This view gave me the pattern for the end pieces of the box and the profile of the lift-out lid. I chose to make my box from cherry; a larger box should probably use a less heavy wood. The fixed side segments, the fold-out lid segments and the lift-out lid are all 3/8 in. thick; the hexagonal end pieces are 5/8 in. thick. If you know how long you want one side of your box to be, you can lay out the rest of the hexagon using only a ruler and a compass, as shown in the drawing on p. 164.

Kit Africa's Tool-Roll Tote

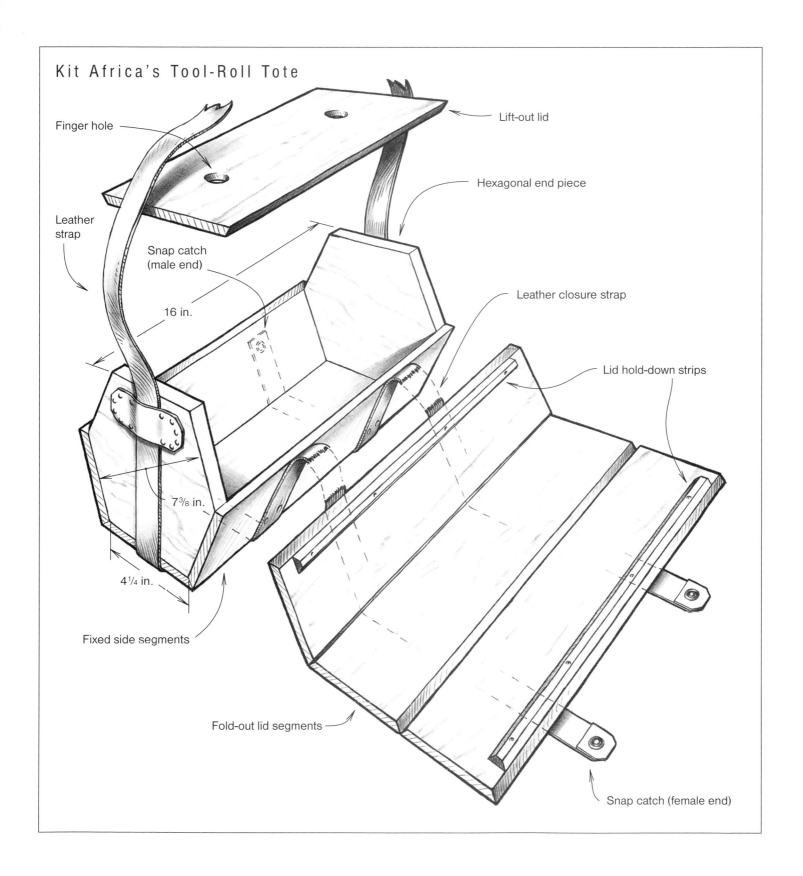

Finger hole

Leather strap

Snap catch (male end)

16 in.

7³⁄₈ in.

4¹⁄₄ in.

Fixed side segments

Lift-out lid

Hexagonal end piece

Leather closure strap

Lid hold-down strips

Fold-out lid segments

Snap catch (female end)

Laying Out a Hexagon

Step 1: *Set out points A and B to desired width of facet along a base line. Because a hexagon is composed of six equilateral triangles, it can be laid out from these two points using only a compass and a straightedge.*

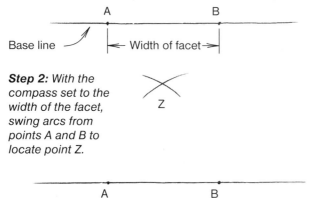

Step 2: *With the compass set to the width of the facet, swing arcs from points A and B to locate point Z.*

Step 3: *Without changing the compass setting, swing arcs from points B and Z to locate Point C. In similar fashion, lay out the three remaining points of the hexagon.*

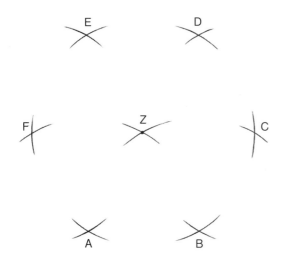

Step 4: *Connect the facet points with a straightedge.*

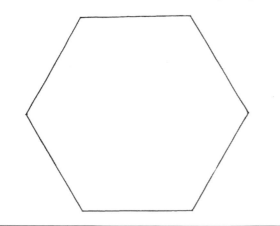

Copy the hexagonal end pattern onto the stock. Photo by Craig Wester.

Making the hexagonal end pieces

Make up a pattern for the end pieces of the box from your drawing, and affix it to the stock with double-stick tape. (I drew the full-scale end view on a piece of poster board and cut it out using a razor blade and a metal straightedge.) After copying the pattern onto the stock (see the photo above), cut the pieces to the outside of the lines on the bandsaw. To ensure that both end pieces are exactly the same, temporarily join them together with double-stick tape; then, holding them in a vise, plane the facet faces to the layout lines (see the top photo on the facing page). As you plane, frequently check the size of the facets with a small scrap of wood cut to the cross-sectional shape of a side segment (see the bottom photo on the facing page). Continue trimming until all the facets are the same length. Don't worry if the facets come out slightly shorter than the section of scrap in order to be equal—you will cut the segments to fit.

With the end patterns temporarily taped together, plane the facets (left), checking frequently against a test block (below). Photo by Craig Wester.

Making the side segments

Lay out and cut the six side segments of the box to rough width and length. (Note that the finished length is simply the overall length of the box.) Rip-cut a 30° angle into one edge of each segment on the table saw, and plane this edge smooth with a hand jointer plane set upside down in a vise. To guard against the joints opening up should the wood warp slightly in drying conditions, orient the boards heart side out. To ensure accuracy, rig up a fence at a 30° angle to the sole of the jointer plane to support the stock at the exact angle (see the top photo on p. 166).

After planing one edge, set the table-saw fence to rip-cut (at 30°) the other edge of each board to its finished width (take the measurement from your finished end pieces). Add at least 1/32 in.

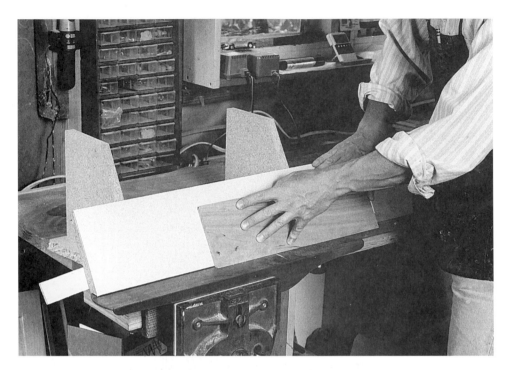

Joint the edge of the side segments at an angle of 30°, using a hand jointer plane held upside-down in a vise (above). An angled fence supports the workpiece at a 30° angle. Photo by Craig Wester.

Wedges hold the end pieces in position as the side and end pieces are assembled (right) to form a hexagonal box. Photo by Craig Wester.

to the width to allow for planing. Use hold-downs to keep the board tight to the rip fence. Then plane the roughsawn edge until the board precisely fits the facet on the end piece. Continue with all six segments.

Cut out the two lid hold-down strips (you can use scrap from the side segment stock), angle-cutting each edge at 30°. Cut the strips to length, that is, the length of the side segments less the thickness of the two hexagonal end pieces. Pick out two side segments and glue and tack the strips flush to one edge. Inset the strip in from the edge by the thickness of the end piece.

Assembling the box

To assemble the segments into a hexagonal box, you'll need to make a jig to hold the end pieces upright and parallel to one another. Note in the photo below left how I used a simple wedge arrangement to lock the end pieces in position on the table of the jig. Using glue and brass escutcheon pins or copper tacks, attach the three fixed side segments to their facets on the end pieces, rotating the assembly in the jig so the board being hammered in place is on top. Apply glue along the edges of the boards also; hold these two joints together while the glue dries with a band clamp. When the glue is dry, remove the clamp and check the fit of the remaining three fold-out lid segments. Plane their edges if necessary to create a tight fit.

Next, cut the lid to cover the bottom well of the box. Cut the side edges of the lid to 30°. Trim the edges with a plane until the lid sits flush to the top edge of the fixed side segments. Cut finger holes with a 1¼-in. drill bit; round over the sharp edges of the hole with a router fitted with a ⅛-in. roundover bit. If you want, glue dividers into the well to create tool compartments. Finally, apply finish to all the wood surfaces. I used a penetrating oil finish.

Attaching the leather strapping

Begin the leather work by cutting strips of leather to hold chisels or other small tools in place under the fold-out lid segments. An effective way to do this is to lay the tools in position under the leather strip as you hammer in the tacks. I use a small cross peen hammer to get in tight between the tools.

To create the pair of closure straps, cut out two 1¼-in. wide by 32-in. long strips of leather. Install the male end of a snap catch to one end of each strip. Beginning 1 in. down from the top edge of one bottom segment, tack the strips across the three bottom segments. Lay out the three fold-out segments side by side next to the box and tack the strips across these as well. Now close the box by folding up these last three segments. Mark the location of the snap catch on each strap (there will be an inch or so of overhang) and install the female part of the catch. All that's left now is for you to install your tools.

Two Tiered Totes

Organ repairman Ray Prince, of Toronto, Ontario, Canada, has come up with an entirely different breed of tote. Rather than building a box that had to be accessed through the opening of a lid, Prince created a tote that is literally all lids. This arrangement is exceptionally efficient for getting at every tool contained within. When Prince fans out the tiers on a waist-height workbench (or on a piece of plywood laid across a pair of sawhorses), the accessibility to his tools is similar to that offered by a typical shop-based standing cabinet.

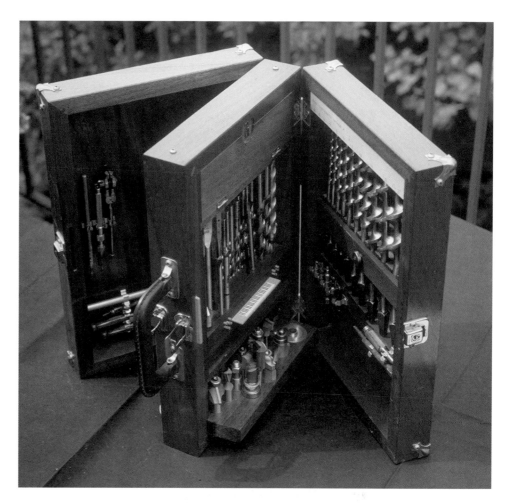

Ray Prince's standing case of Honduras mahogany, basswood and maple carries his pipe-organ repair tools. Designed to stand upright on its three fanned-out tiers, the tote has proven to be exceptionally compact and efficient. Photos by Ray Prince.

In Prince's "organ-ized" tool tote, the auger-bit array resembles the pipes of a wind organ, dowels mimic drawknobs, and a "keyboard" functions as a stop for the tilt-out drill holder. Photo by Ray Prince.

Because it contains fewer tools and a tier's less wood, the two-tiered standing case created by boatbuilder Ellis Rowe, of Bucksport, Maine, is relatively easy to carry and transport. Not only does it display its contents clearly, it is also ultra-accessible—unlike the three-tier tote, you don't have to walk entirely around the case to get at all of the tools. But the lack of the third tier can be a drawback too: Standing on only two tiers (see the photo below), the case is much less stable, especially as you fan it farther out.

Building a Tote with a Coopered Lid

Mark Nels, of Atlanta, Georgia, the maker of the handsome, coopered-lid tote shown in the photos on the facing page, makes his living installing commercial high-end architectural woodwork. Nels decided he needed a new box for his hand tools on the day he realized that either his long-time toolbox was getting larger and heavier or he was getting decidedly less enthusiastic about lugging it around. Also, he noticed that his tools had been changing over the years: His big Yankee screwdriver and pair of bulky panel saws had been replaced by a cordless drill (in its own box) and a single, small Japanese saw. His old toolbox was not only too big, it was obsolete.

DESIGN NOTES

At 24 in. long by 12 in. wide by 18 in. tall, Nels' new box was much lighter and smaller than the old one, and a whole lot prettier, too. Wanting the new box to reflect his growing skills and appreciation for fine woodworking (and, perhaps more important, to discourage his co-worker from sitting on it during lunch), Nels designed the box with a coopered lid. For an additional challenge, Nels added a pair of tackle-box style swing-out stacked trays. The two halves

Ellis Rowe's two-tiered tote holds his boatbuilding tools. Photo by Vincent Laurence.

of the lid lock shut with a shop-made, key-less, spring-loaded brass catch. (You engage the catch by slipping a credit card into the $\frac{1}{16}$-in. gap between a drawer and the end board—a pre-cyberspace "card-lock" system!) A gang-lock system accessed through the top of the box prevents strangers from opening the five drawers.

Other features that contribute to the unique and appealing quality of this box include drawer pulls made from buffalo nickels that have been dish-shaped and sleeved to receive an attachment screw and hand-shaped, inscribed handles (see the photos below). Not feeling confident enough to hand-letter the date and his name on the handle faces, Nels prepared the inscription on a word processor. He stuck a printout to the face of each handle with double-stick tape (which doesn't wrinkle paper, as some glues do),

The drawer pulls were fashioned from buffalo nickels made by a flea-market craftsman for use as belt studs or buttons. Photo by Alec Waters.

This tool tote by Mark Nels features fan veneer on its ends, swing-out trays and drawers for small tools and a well underneath for large tools. A coopered top discourages use of the box as a job-site seat. Photo by Alec Waters.

The inscription on the handle was traced through words generated on a word processor, then carved. Photo by Alec Waters.

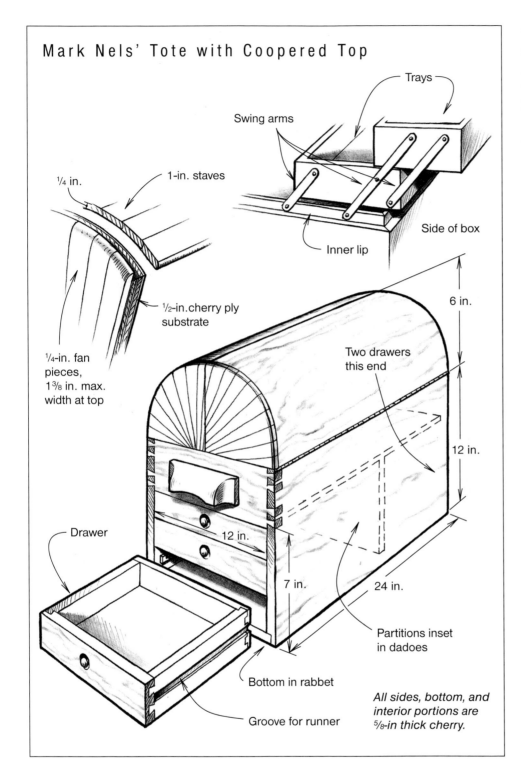

Mark Nels' Tote with Coopered Top

Trays

Swing arms

1-in. staves

¼ in.

Side of box

Inner lip

½-in. cherry ply substrate

¼-in. fan pieces, 1⅜ in. max. width at top

6 in.

Two drawers this end

12 in.

Drawer

12 in.

7 in.

24 in.

Partitions inset in dadoes

Bottom in rabbet

Groove for runner

All sides, bottom, and interior portions are ⅝-in thick cherry.

then scribed through the printout with a sharp razor knife to trace the inscription. After removing the paper, Nels created the relief by tapping between the scribed lines with an awl and hammer.

CONSTRUCTION PROCEDURES

Begin construction of this coopered-lid box by deciding on the overall dimensions. (Nels measured his largest tools, making sure that his new 24½-in. long Japanese-type saw would fit in the main well. Then he studied the rest of his tools to see how they could be arranged in drawers and tray compartments to take up a minimum of room.) Now make up a full-scale drawing of the end view to see how much room you have for the pair of swing-out trays. Lay out the end view of these trays. Also use the drawing to determine the number of staves you'll need to cut. Using ¼-in. thick staves at this radius of curvature, figure on making the staves about 1 in. wide. Finally, the end view should give you an idea of how the box will look with its fan of cherry wedges.

Making the fan-veneered end panels
Begin by cutting out the substrate to which you will glue the fan of cherry wedges: a circle of ½-in. cherry plywood cut to the radius shown in your full-scale end view. (You may have to substitute birch if cherry is unavailable in your area.) Mark the circle on the plywood with a compass scribe, then rough-cut it to the line on the bandsaw. Trim the piece to a clean, perfect circle with a router mounted to a trammel beam. Note in the photo at top left on the facing page that the substrate circle is screwed to a 2x6 clamped upright in a vise.

Trim the circle to the line with a trammel-mounted router. The substrate has been screwed to the 2x6 clamped upright in the vise. Photo by Craig Wester.

Use a carriage jig to cut wedges on the table saw (above). The same jig can be used as a shooting board for planing the wedges smooth (left). The thin cardboard under the wedge shims it slightly higher than the carriage edge. Photos by Craig Wester.

To make the fan, cut out the wedges—three at a time—using a shop-made carriage jig on the table saw (see the photo at top right). Cut the stock for the wedges over-length by ½ in. Set three pieces at a time in the jig and make the first taper cut. Then switch the jig side for side, reinsert the stock and cut the second taper. Using the carriage jig as a shooting board, clean up the sides of the wedges (again three at a time) with a hand plane (see the photo above right). Be sure the edges are square to the face of the wedge and that they come to a sharp point

With the wedges prepared, set up a building board on which to glue up the fan. (Nels used a piece of flat scrap plywood; you can use sound insulation board or a plank of soft wood.) Dry-assemble two half-circles of wedges,

using small finish nails to hold the pieces in place and tightly against one another (see the top photo on p. 172). Trim any irregular-edged fan pieces with a hand plane to a tight, void-free fit. You should end up with two half-circles, each a little greater than 180° to allow for final trimming. When you are happy with the dry run, mark the pieces for location in the fan, remove them from the board,

cover the board with waxed paper, and reassemble the two half-circle fans with glue.

After the fans dry, scrape and sand them smooth. Then remove them from the building board, peel away the waxed paper, and scrape off any remaining glue. Arrange the two fans on the circular piece of substrate, planing the bottom edges of the fans to fit tightly to one another so they form a full circle. Glue

Arrange the wedges in a two semicircles, and pin them to the building board to test the fit before gluing. Photo by Craig Wester.

Glue up the fans on the substrate, then weight the assembly with a block until the glue dries. Photo by Craig Wester.

them together and to the substrate (see the photo below left), placing a scrap of ¾-in. plywood and a cement block on the assembly until the glue dries. Finally, draw the outer circle of the end panel of the tote (again referring to your full-scale rendering for the radius), centering the compass on the focus of the wedges. As before, cut close to this line on the bandsaw and trim the circle cleanly to the line with a router mounted to a trammel beam (see the photo on the facing page). In the last step, lay the circle out into four quarters and cut them out on the bandsaw, trimming them to rejoin perfectly with a hand plane.

Coopering the top

Cut out the staves, leaving them long in length but cutting them to the width indicated on your full-scale end view. Run the edges of the staves by a table-mounted router fitted with a flute and bead set (see the drawing on the facing page), then cut them to finished length. Next, using the type of assembly jig shown in the bottom photo on p. 166, prop up the two quarter-circle ends parallel, plumb and at the exact length required. Then install the staves, running glue along their shaped seams and in the rabbet formed by the fan overhanging the substrate. Draw the staves together with band clamps. When the glue is dry, scrape off any excess and proceed to make up the second quarter-circle unit. With that one dried and out of the jig, trim both to join against one another and to sit on a flat surface. Finally, holding them together in the jig, use a 48-in. long, 100-grit sanding belt turned inside-out to remove the facets and create a smooth, curved surface. After going up to a 120-grit belt, switch to a random-orbit sander for the final sanding.

Building the box

With the two quarter-circle units held together, check the total width of the cover. Because of cutting and trimming the original circle, it is likely you will have to adjust your full-scale rendering of the lower portion of the box.

Using this new width, make up the cut list and cut all the parts to size, including the parts for the drawers and swing-out trays. Now the fun begins: Hand-cut the dovetails at the corner joints and make rabbets and dadoes where necessary to receive the partitions. To support and provide a slide for the drawers, make a guide and groove system similar to that used by David Winter in his machinist's chest (see pp. 38-45).

To figure out how to mount the swing arms to the trays, make up cardboard patterns to represent the ends of the trays and the three swing arms. Find the pivot points by pinning the cardboard arms to the end patterns—first stacking them up on each other and then swinging them out to the open position. When you are satisfied with the range of motion (the upper tray moves as far as it can to one side while still having the lower tray support it), use the final pivot points established on the pattern to mark the actual ends of trays for drilling pilot holes for the lever-arm attachment screws.

Fabricating the gang lock and lid catch

Not finding a commercially made gang lock small enough to suit his box, Nels decided to fabricate his own from a length of brass and some screws and springs. The lock works much like a typical file-drawer lock: When you push the brass arm down, it forces a gang of screws into the locking plates set into the back of the drawer boxes. Instead of a keyed catch, however, this version uses a

A final trim with a trammel-mounted router completes the fan-veneered end panel. Photo by Craig Wester.

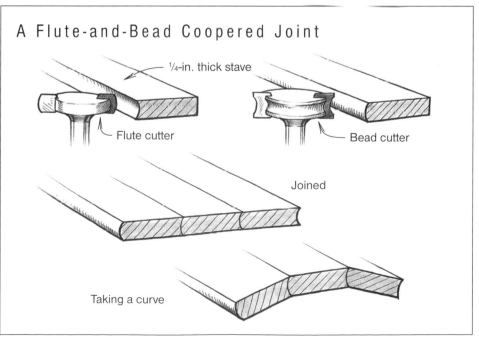

A Flute-and-Bead Coopered Joint

¼-in. thick stave

Flute cutter

Bead cutter

Joined

Taking a curve

Gang-Lock Mechanism

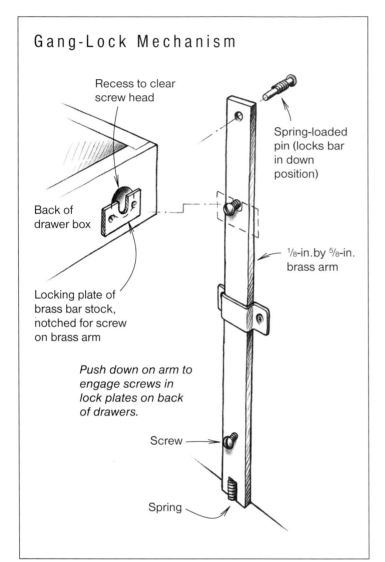

Recess to clear screw head

Back of drawer box

Locking plate of brass bar stock, notched for screw on brass arm

Push down on arm to engage screws in lock plates on back of drawers.

Spring-loaded pin (locks bar in down position)

⅛-in. by ⅝-in. brass arm

Screw

Spring

Credit-Card Locking Catch

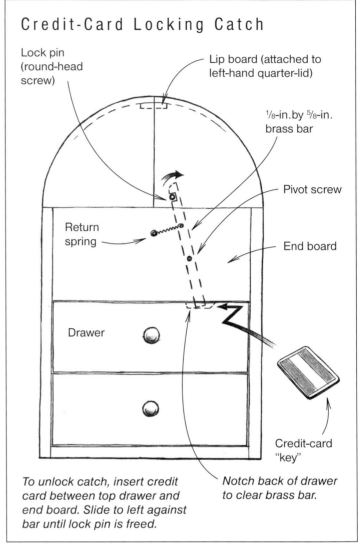

Lock pin (round-head screw)

Lip board (attached to left-hand quarter-lid)

⅛-in. by ⅝-in. brass bar

Pivot screw

Return spring

End board

Drawer

Credit-card "key"

To unlock catch, insert credit card between top drawer and end board. Slide to left against bar until lock pin is freed.

Notch back of drawer to clear brass bar.

spring-loaded pin at the top of the arm to hold the arm in the locked position (see the drawing above left). When you pull back this pin (which can, of course, be accessed only from inside the box), a spring set at the bottom of the arm forces it back up, drawing the screws out of their locking plates.

The drawing above right illustrates the "card-lock" system that Nels designed to secure the lids to the box. To unlock the lid, you slip a credit card between the top drawer and the end board, sliding it to the left until it hits the brass bar. As you exert a little

pressure, the bar pivots and releases the lock pin attached to the inside of the right-hand lid (see the drawing above right). Note that the left-hand lid is captured shut by the lip board. Because of the return spring, this catch automatically locks itself when you shut the right-hand lid. All this action, and not a microchip in sight!

To make the catch, cut a piece of ⅛-in. thick by ⅝-in. wide bar stock long enough to span between the top of the upper drawer and about 1¼ in. up the side of the coopered lid. Cut and file a curve (to guide the lock pin during the closing motion) and a notch (to enclose the lock pin) in the upper end of the bar.

Then drill holes for the pivot screw and the return spring. Install the catch to the back side of the end board, orienting the bar so it just protrudes into the gap between the drawer face and the board. Mark the location of the lock pin on the inside of the lid through the notch in the bar. Install this pin, and then attach the spring. Create just enough spring tension to hold the bar tight against the lock pin. Test the catch. Trim the notch and the curve with a fine file if necessary to ensure a smooth, positive locking action.

Making the carry handles

To make the end-mounted carry handles, start with a long length of stock sized in width and thickness, then use a shaper cutter to create the outside profile. Cut the finger notch with another cutter. If you don't have a shaper, you can rough out both the finger grip undercut and the outside profile on a table saw. Here's how:

Do the undercut first (see the drawing at right). Mark the outline of the notch on two faces of the stock. Then, holding the wood against the miter gauge, run it into the sawblade at the centerline of the notch. Adjust the blade height so that the kerf meets both outlines. Then cut kerfs to either side of the center kerf, being careful to stop the cuts at the outline mark. Do not knock out the waste yet. Instead, set up the saw to cut kerfs in the waste area of the outside profile. Adjust the height of the blade and the rip fence to produce a series of kerfs as shown in the drawing.

With the kerfs cut, remove the waste from both the outside profile and the undercut with a chisel. Smooth the undercut finger grip with the nose of a belt sander. Use the flat of the sander to smooth the outside profile. Finally, cut the handles to length from the shaped stock and again use the nose of the belt sander to form the curved end profiles. Install the handle to the box with screws from the inside of the end boards.

Finally, apply the finish of your choice to all the wood surfaces, inside and out. Install the tilt-out trays and fit out the box with your tools. Then tell your co-workers they are going to have to find another place to sit at lunch time.

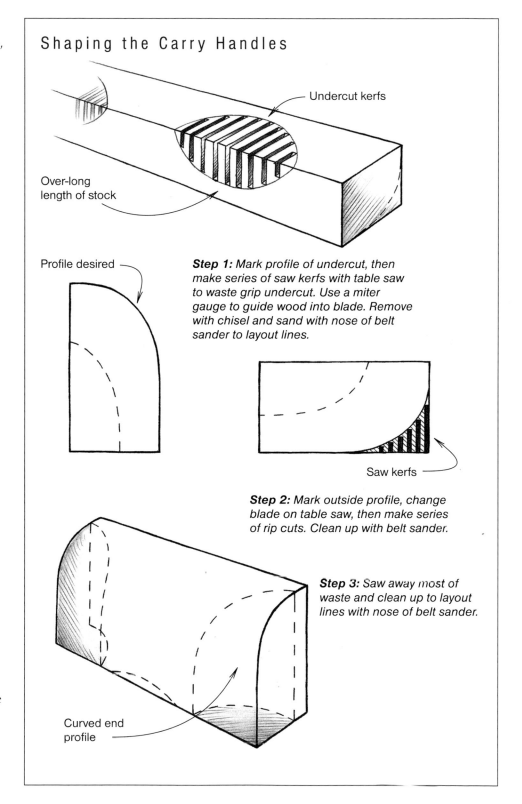

Shaping the Carry Handles

Undercut kerfs

Over-long length of stock

Step 1: Mark profile of undercut, then make series of saw kerfs with table saw to waste grip undercut. Use a miter gauge to guide wood into blade. Remove with chisel and sand with nose of belt sander to layout lines.

Profile desired

Saw kerfs

Step 2: Mark outside profile, change blade on table saw, then make series of rip cuts. Clean up with belt sander.

Step 3: Saw away most of waste and clean up to layout lines with nose of belt sander.

Curved end profile

11
WHEELED SITE BOXES

Almost all the framing and finish carpenters I've known over the years started out with some version of an open shoulder tote to get their tools from home or shop to the job site. As they accumulated more tools, they would build additional boxes to house them. Some took the time and effort to make a more intricate lidded toolbox.

While these assorted toolboxes met the needs of most of my acquaintences, I do remember a few who went considerably further, building a large, enclosed box on wheels to contain nearly every tool and fastener that might be required over the course of a typical workday. On more than one occasion, I learned that the inspiration for this challenging project was a "last straw" day, the day that it was necessary to trudge back out to the truck for the umpteenth time to get a tool or piece of hardware that was in that infamous "other" box.

Cabinetmaker Rodger Reid's wheeled toolbox (shown here with Jim Tolpin) is easily maneuvered into the apartments of his New York City clientele. For more, see p. 178. Photo by Vincent Laurence.

The central partition, which extends through the floor, holds Reid's box upright in the open position. The boxed doors swing out, holding tools close at hand and exposing the interior of the box, which includes a bank of drawers. Photo by Vincent Laurence.

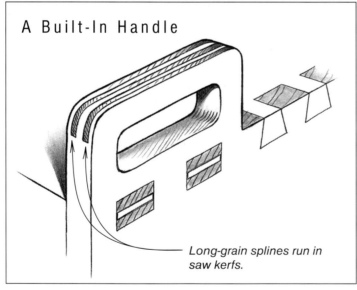

A Built-In Handle

Long-grain splines run in saw kerfs.

A Toolbox that Commutes to the City

For many years, Rodger Reid, of New Preston, Connecticut, worked in the high-end custom cabinet and remodeling business in New York City. As you can imagine, he spent a lot of time and effort carrying his gear from his parked truck into apartment buildings and up elevators. Realizing that a dolly to carry his tools would make life much easier, Reid built a standing toolbox with a built-in dolly system comprised of two 12-in. pneumatic wheels mounted in a well located at the bottom back corner of the box (see the photo on p. 178).

Building the box to move and operate in an upright position turned out to be a good decision. Reid could maneuver the box up tight stairways and into small elevators, and he didn't have to stoop down to get at most of his stored gear. When opened, the boxed-frame doors brought most of his commonly used saws and large layout tools into clear view and to hand height, while the many drawers offered easy access to a wide selection of smaller tools and supplies.

Because Reid most often worked on upscale projects, he felt that his box should represent the high-quality craftsmanship he was offering his clientele. Choosing honey locust for its rich golden hue and black walnut for its beautiful grain and contrasting color, Reid hand-dovetailed and through-mortised the case together. Not wanting to tack on metal hardware for the handles, he extended the side boards to form an integral pair of hand grips (see the drawing above left). To strengthen the handles and to prevent splitting, he made two saw kerfs across the end grain and inserted hardwood splines.

A large, rolling site box can be a daunting project. The design calls for a balancing act between function and size. For while the box must contain a day's worth of tools and supplies, it must also fit through doorways and nestle with the other items you carry in your vehicle. The sheer size of this type of toolbox invites you to load it up with heavy items so you must build for extra strength, yet you must keep the overall weight down to promote maneuverability. Finally, if the box will be exposed to the elements, either on site or in the back of a truck, you must build with weather resistance and watertightness in mind.

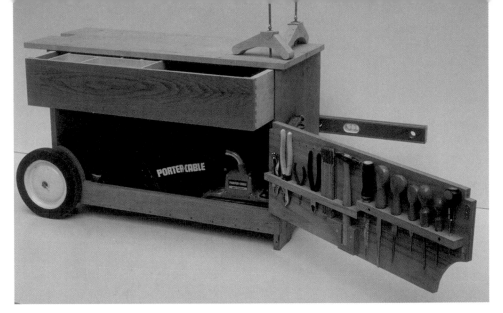

Built for double duty, Bill Baird's rolling box with retractable wheels not only carries most of his tools to and from the job site, but also serves as a work table and door buck. With the pipe clamp/push handles removed, the full-length drawer can be opened to either side of the box. The swing-out side door opens to reveal a tool well. Photos by Bill Baird.

A Rolling Toolbox/Work Table

When finish carpenter Bill Baird, of Pine Bush, New York, set out to design his rolling toolbox, he had in mind a box that would do more than carry most of his basic carpentry tools (which include a 24-in. framing square, a 48-in. level and a selection of hand power tools). He also wanted the box to serve as a portable workbench and door buck. Instead of making a standing box like Rodger Reid's, Baird built his box more like a

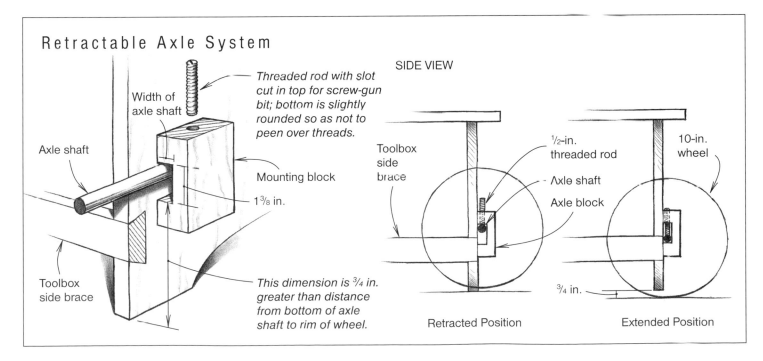

Retractable Axle System

SIDE VIEW

Threaded rod with slot cut in top for screw-gun bit; bottom is slightly rounded so as not to peen over threads.

Width of axle shaft

Axle shaft

Mounting block

1 3/8 in.

Toolbox side brace

This dimension is 3/4 in. greater than distance from bottom of axle shaft to rim of wheel.

Toolbox side brace

1/2-in. threaded rod

Axle shaft

Axle block

Retracted Position

10-in. wheel

3/4 in.

Extended Position

This combination toolbox/workbench by Michael Hayes rolls on a dolly. Note relief carving of hammer on box side, let-in support braces on bench. Photo by Alec Waters.

A Toolbox with a Piggyback Workbench

Like Bill Baird, boatbuilder Michael Hayes of Huntington Beach, California, wanted to build a rolling toolbox that could double as a workbench. Unlike Baird, however, Hayes wanted his toolbox and bench to be independent of one another. But to keep the unit as compact as possible, he also wanted them to roll to the site on one set of wheels. His solution, as you can see in the photo at left, was to make the tool chest nest under the lift-up bench. So the chest and bench could work in conjunction with one another, he built them the same height (with the chest lifted from the dolly).

Hayes built the combination box and bench from solid Honduras mahogany (except for the birch-plywood drawer sides), using frame-and-panel construction to form the large side pieces of the chest. Following boatbuilding techniques, he covered the countersunk screws that attach the sides to the top and bottom of the case with plugs cut from a mahogany offcut ("bungs," in boatbuilding terminology). Once tapped in place and leveled flush with the surrounding surface, these bungs are nearly invisible. Hayes embellished his toolbox with some exceptional relief carvings of hand tools on the sides, and scroll patterns on the drawer faces.

The Rolling Boxes of Louis Plourd

Contractor Louis Plourd, of Edmonton, Alberta, Canada, has a philosophy: "a place for everything and everything in its box." Living and working in a rugged climate, Plourd has learned the hard way

traditional joiner's chest, designing it to sit 24 in. above the floor and to offer a 14-in. by 37-in. work surface.

Though Baird built the main body and the internal lengthwise vertical partition of the box from solid oak (choosing the wood for its strength and beauty), he made the top of the box—the work surface—from pine. The reason: The softness of pine offers a much "tackier" work surface, and things tend to slip less than on dense hardwoods. Baird also added shop-made hold-downs to steady the stock during cutting and shaping and to secure additional power tools and other items for transporting.

To prevent the box from rolling about when used as a work table, Baird made the 10-in. rubber wheels retractable. In the drawing on p. 179 you can see how simple his system is: A threaded rod runs through each of the ash mounting blocks to bear against the axle. When he backs off the rods, the axle raises up and takes the weight of the box off the wheels. This makes the box rigid and level. These mounting blocks also serve as part of a built-in door buck. The notch in the table surface forms the upper portion of this door-holding system. To use the buck to support the door on edge when installing hinges or latches, Baird slides the end of the door between the axle blocks and the table notch and then taps in shims to hold the door rigid.

This rolling toolbox by Louis Plourd tilts on end to open. Plywood panels wrap around an interior frame of steel tubing, forming a strong, weatherproof skin. Photos by Forfar Products.

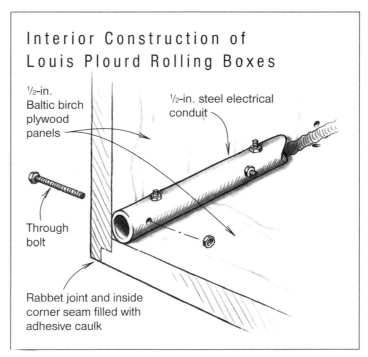

Interior Construction of Louis Plourd Rolling Boxes

½-in. Baltic birch plywood panels

½-in. steel electrical conduit

Through bolt

Rabbet joint and inside corner seam filled with adhesive caulk

Plourd's table-saw box nearly encloses the machine. Photo by Forfar Products.

that construction tools last longest when provided with a secure, weathertight home. That's why, over the years, he has built a box of some kind for nearly every construction tool he owns. Plourd carries these boxes and additional supplies and accessories in larger wheeled boxes. One such box—the one shown in the photo at top right with the table saw— not only serves as a support and extension table for the saw, but also

contains an air compressor with its hoses, nail guns and fasteners.

Plourd builds his larger rolling boxes by bolting joined plywood panels to an interior framework constructed from steel tubing (see the drawing above). He prefers ½-in. Baltic birch plywood for the panels because it is strong and because exterior enamel paints adhere well to it. With the vulnerable edges of the plywood panels buried in either rabbet or dado joints, and with adhesive caulking applied to all the seams, Plourd had found this plywood to be highly resistant to the elements. (Note, however, that this resistance demands an initial high-quality paint job and regularly scheduled maintenance that includes touching up scratches and applying a fresh top coat every few years.) To extend the life of the paint job, Plourd covers the boxes with custom-fitted waterproof canvas covers whenever they sit outside on the truck or on the job site (see the photo at bottom right on p. 131).

Building a Punch-List Carpenter's Toolbox

For carpenter Kevin Skurpski, of East Syracuse, New York, the last straw came the day he had to park his truck several blocks away from the job site. This was the day that it took him seven trips from the truck to the site to assemble everything he needed to take care of his general contractor's punch list. Then his cordless drill ran out of juice, and he realized that even after seven trips his charger was still behind the truck's front seat. The time to build a wheeled toolbox that could carry all Skurpski's tools and supplies onto the site in one shot had come.

DESIGN NOTES
Skurpski felt strongly about not compromising the size of the box—he couldn't stomach another day like that last one. Sitting down to draw the design, he realized that fortunately he would have little problem getting a large box on wheels up to, and through, the entrance of most of his construction sites. Nearly all were commercial buildings, which by law must provide wheelchair access ramps. However, once inside the

Punch-list carpenter Kevin Skurpski built this box so he wouldn't have to make repeated trips back to his van for tools and supplies. The box tilts on end to get through tight spaces. Photo by Photomedia.

building, a box large enough to serve his needs could be troublesome to maneuver into rooms accessed through narrow passageways.

Finding inspiration in a two-wheeled garden cart, Skurpski configured the box as a long (54 in.), low (28 in.) chest narrow enough to fit between most passageway jambs (29 in. in overall width). So that he would be able to maneuver it through restricted places, Skurpski designed the toolbox to tilt up completely on end; he accomplished this by placing the large wheels, and the heaviest tools, at the end opposite the main push handle.

To keep items from shifting during such a radical maneuver, Skurpski designed the interior partitions to run up to the top of the box. Bringing the partitions full height did other good things for the design: It gave support to the lid, allowing it to be made out of thin, lightweight material—¼-in. mahogany plywood. As a happy side effect, these full-height and width partitions created a honeycomb structure, imparting considerable strength to the case (and allowing it, too, to be made from the ¼-in. mahogany plywood, thus lowering the overall weight of the box). As Skurpski put it, "The box can support two people plus lunch."

Interior Tool Layout

Battery charger for
cordless screwdriver

Wood glue and
miscellaneous
items

Finish nail tray
above;
sharpening
stones, Tapcon
driver below

Drill bits, nail sets
and chisels above;
tool wrenches below

Circular saw on
supports above;
hot glue gun,
router, electric
hand plane below

7½ in.

3 in.

3½ in.

6¾ in. by
11½ in.

4¼ in.
by
19½ in.

10¼ in. by
19½ in.

7¼ in. by
19½ in.

3½ in.

6¾ in.

11 in. by
16 in.

10 in.

Belt sander,
jigsaw,
extension
cords above;
reciprocating
saw below

7¾ in.

14 in.

Charger
cords

Battery charger, note
pad, hand plane

Area sized for
eight coffee
cans of nails
and screws

Hand-tool area with
shelf above; hand-tool
tray set on shelf

⅜-in. hammer
drilll, screw gun,
battery-operated
screw gun

Interior partitions as high as the top of
the carl keep the contents of the bins from
shifting and also strengthen the case. Photo
by Photomedia.

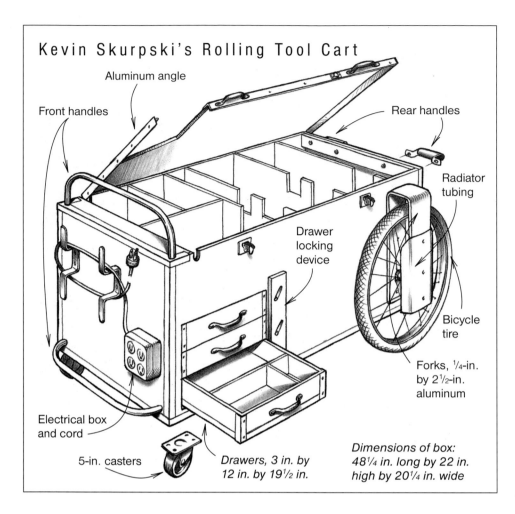

Kevin Skurpski's Rolling Tool Cart

Aluminum angle

Front handles

Rear handles

Radiator tubing

Drawer locking device

Bicycle tire

Forks, ¼-in. by 2½-in. aluminum

Electrical box and cord

5-in. casters

Drawers, 3 in. by 12 in. by 19½ in.

Dimensions of box: 48¼ in. long by 22 in. high by 20¼ in. wide

To get at small supplies without having to rummage through the box—or to even have to open the lid—Skurpski decided to add drawers that would open to the exterior of the box. These drawers open to either side, locking closed for transport with a sliding plate made from a strip of ¼-in. plywood. (There is one on each side of the box). The strip forming the drawer stop is attached to the side of the box with screws running through a pair of slotted holes. Because the slots angle downward, gravity draws the strip into the stop position. Skurpski didn't bother, however, to add a lock to the lid, figuring that anyone wanting in would just rip off the top of the box anyway. Instead, a pair of trunk-style catches holds the lid down.

Skurpski thought long and hard about the kind of wheels that would work best for this box. He knew he didn't want to be stopped by the thick extension cords that snake across most construction sites, or by the ubiquitous 2x4 cutoffs. He settled on a pair of 20-in. bicycle wheels, sacrificing a little shock absorbency by going with solid rubber instead of air-filled. But at least he wouldn't have to deal with flats.

Locating the axle for the large wheels was a design problem. Running it under the box would raise the box considerably, making it difficult to fit under the storage platforms built into Skurpski's van. Running the axle through the box would impinge on the interior space and layout of the tools, especially since Skurpski wanted to locate the heaviest ones directly over the center of the

wheels. He eventually solved the problem by making a fork for each wheel and mounting it on its own short axle to the outside of the box. (The covering over the bottom half of the fork is a piece of radiator tubing installed to protect walls and door jambs from the protruding axle nut.) To allow the box to be moved when sitting flat and level, Skurpski installed a pair of 5-in. full-swivel casters to the end opposite the bike wheels. He made the large push handle and the lower lift handle from ½-in. electrical conduit.

CONSTRUCTION PROCEDURES

Skurpski built most of the box from ¼-in. thick exterior-grade lauan mahogany plywood, joining the sized parts together by riveting them to aluminum angle stock (drop-ceiling wall angle). To ease the finishing process, he prefinished the exterior surfaces before assembly. He also precut most of the notches in the partitions (to accept certain tools) before installing them to the inside walls and floor (again with rivets to the angle stock). To protect the edges of the lid and to give it some rigidity, he attached a perimeter rim of this same aluminum angle stock.

Making the forked axles

Skurpski made the forks for the bike wheels by bending ¼-in. by 2½-in. aluminum bar stock into the appropriate shape; he attached them to the case with carriage bolts running though the fork and into the 1-in. tube stock fixed to the inside of the box (see the top drawing on the facing page). He attached the casters to the floor of the box, through-bolting into a ¾-in. thick piece of plywood fitted to the inside floor. He also attached the lower lift handle—a piece of ½-in.

electrical conduit bent to shape with an electrician's brake—to this same backing block. The upper push handle of conduit is bolted to the inside corner of the box through the angle stock.

Making the drawers

To keep things simple, Skurpski used the same method of construction for the three drawers as he employed to build the box, riveting ¼-in. plywood to an external aluminum-angle framework. To mount the drawers so they would open to either side, he encased them into the corner of the box with two plywood panels, adding horizontal plywood partitions to support the drawers. After rejecting numerous, and invariably complex, solutions to the problem of locking the drawers for transport, he finally settled on a simple stop system (see the bottom drawing at right). A turn of the screw covering the angled slot fixes the lock in either the closed or open position.

Interior and exterior finish

Though he applied stain and varnish to the exterior of the box to enhance the beauty of the lauan plywood (before assembly, to avoid having to apply the finish around the angle stock), Skurpski realized that such a finish would not work well on the interior. Besides becoming quickly scratched as tools went in and out of the box, the varnished wood would be too dark. Instead, Skurpski painted the entire interior of the box with white semigloss latex enamel paint.

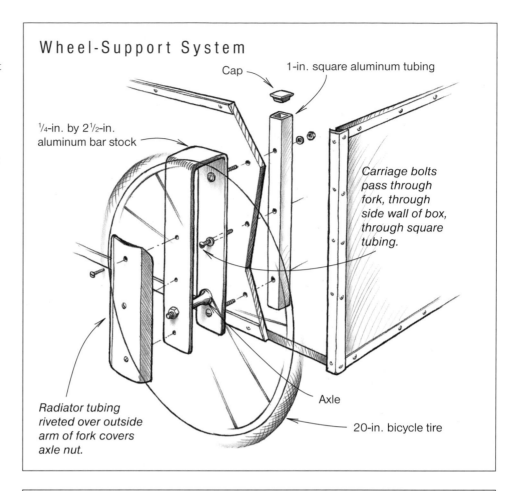

Wheel-Support System

Cap

1-in. square aluminum tubing

¼-in. by 2½-in. aluminum bar stock

Carriage bolts pass through fork, through side wall of box, through square tubing.

Radiator tubing riveted over outside arm of fork covers axle nut.

Axle

20-in. bicycle tire

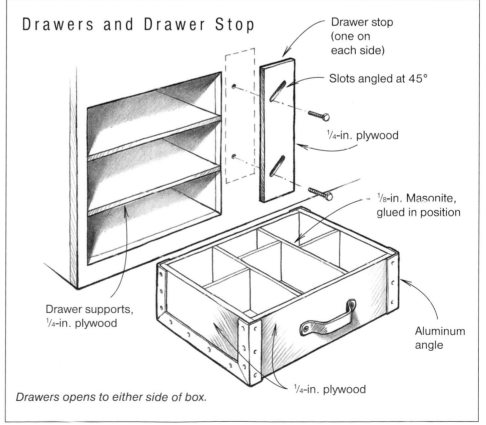

Drawers and Drawer Stop

Drawer stop (one on each side)

Slots angled at 45°

¼-in. plywood

⅛-in. Masonite, glued in position

Drawer supports, ¼-in. plywood

Aluminum angle

¼-in. plywood

Drawers opens to either side of box.

The ultimate rolling toolbox: Jerry Hillenburg's van and the tools it carries. All photos in this chapter are by Spectrum Professional Photography.

12

A TOOLBOX
FOR THE ROAD

When cabinetmaker Jerry Hillenburg, of Martinsville, Indiana, set out to make a toolbox to carry his tools and supplies to the job site, he didn't fool around. Instead, he built the utimate rolling tool tote—one with a motor in it. Hillenburg's tool box is a 1992 ¾-ton Ford van carefully fitted out to hold an astonishing array of tools, totes and accessories—everything, in fact, that Hillenburg's four-man crew needs to run architectural moldings, hang doors and install his custom cabinets and built-in furniture. Yet looking into the doors of the van, I was amazed to see the large amount of open space. There is plenty of room to get around, browse through boxes and occassionaly haul materials or a cabinet in need of repair back to the shop. (Hillenburg hauls cabinetry and most materials in an enclosed cargo trailer.)

Hillenburg arranged the storage systems around the perimeter of the van, building shelving along the two sides and a bank of lift-out

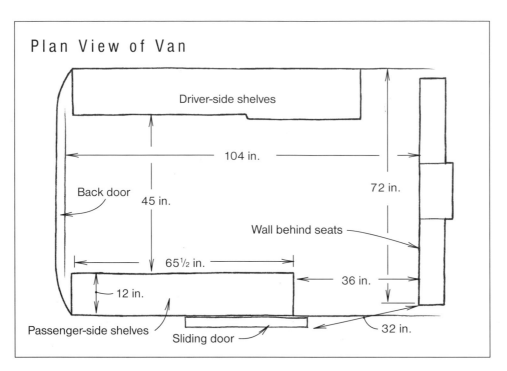

Plan View of Van

Driver-side shelves

104 in.

72 in.

Back door

45 in.

Wall behind seats

65½ in.

36 in.

12 in.

Passenger-side shelves

Sliding door

32 in.

Lining the perimeter of the van's cargo space are shelving and removable, dual-purpose carry totes/storage bins, leaving an ample amount of open space to facilitate access.

extending it up the walls for soundproofing and insulation. To make the carpet in the bed area easy to clean (and to replace in the event of wear or a permanent stain), Hillenburg attached it to removable ¼-in. plywood panels. Scrap carpet glued to the underside of the plywood panels further cushions the workers' knees. A replaceable oak board in front of the back doors absorbs most of the wear and tear of people going in and out and the loading and offloading of equipment.

In daily use, Hillenburg minimizes traffic in and out of the van by having the workers unload all the removable totes and other loose items at the beginning of each workday. Each morning, one person stationed in the van feeds items to people coming to the doors—mostly the large sliding side door. At the end of the day, the totes and other items are blown clean with compressed air on site and then returned en masse to the van. The van is equipped with an alarm system, which activates a beeper on Hillenburg's belt in the event of any suspicious activity during the day.

Storage Walls on the Sides of the Van

Most of the dual-purpose totes are stored on shelving installed on the driver's side of the van. All the totes but one are secured with a loop of bungee cord running between an eye in the van's wall and around a cleat mounted beneath the floor of the tote. Hillenburg installed a second cleat opposite the first on the underside of the tote. This gives him a tie-down point for the bungee cord no matter which way the tote faces when set onto its storage shelf. Another neat trick for the sake of efficiency—you don't have to check the orientation of the tote each time you go to stow it.

storage bins and drawers between the driver's compartment and the van's bed. Custom-made spring-loaded clips hold levels to the upper walls, while bungee cords hold loose items like a stepladder and some of the totes. Even the back doors are fitted for storage, with reels of extension cords and air hoses, and pockets for clamps and jumper cables.

To keep the weight down, Hillenburg built the casework, shelving and most of

the totes almost entirely of oak-veneered plywood. He used solid oak sparingly for trim, drawer faces and some smaller totes. The parts are joined together with glue and 2½-in. long #8 wood screws, countersunk and plugged with walnut bungs.

For comfort when "knee walking" and to prevent dropped items from rolling about, Hillenburg installed indoor/outdoor carpet in the cargo bed area,

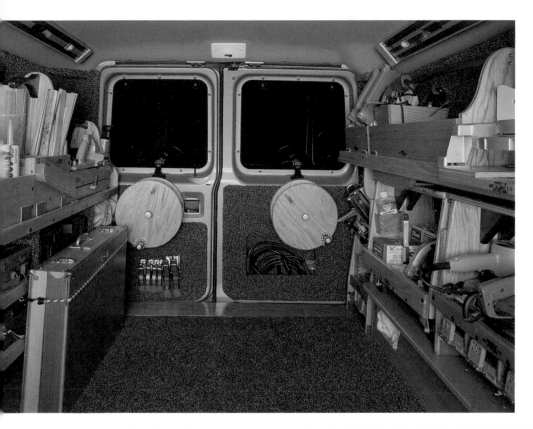

Bungee cords batten down loose items and totes, like the sanding stool/tote shown in the photo below. Indoor/outdoor carpeting on the floor of the van (left) makes it easier for people to kneel. It also dampens noise.

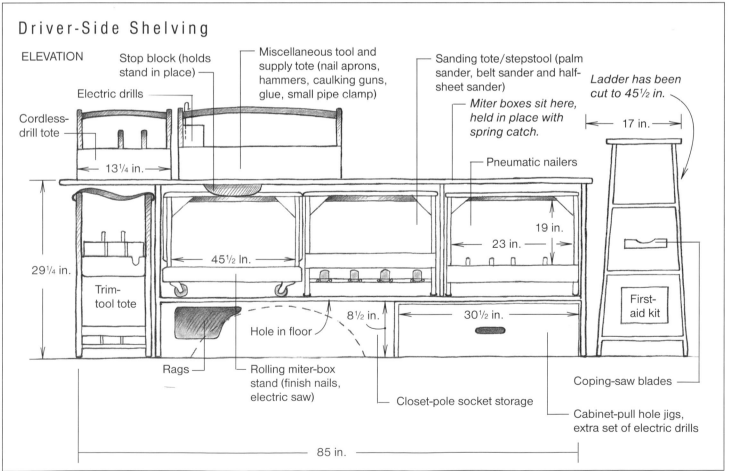

Driver-Side Shelving

ELEVATION

Cordless-drill tote

Stop block (holds stand in place)

Electric drills

Miscellaneous tool and supply tote (nail aprons, hammers, caulking guns, glue, small pipe clamp)

Sanding tote/stepstool (palm sander, belt sander and half-sheet sander)

Miter boxes sit here, held in place with spring catch.

Ladder has been cut to 45½ in.

17 in.

Pneumatic nailers

13¼ in.

19 in.

23 in.

29¼ in.

45½ in.

Trim-tool tote

Hole in floor

8½ in.

30½ in.

First-aid kit

Rags

Rolling miter-box stand (finish nails, electric saw)

Closet-pole socket storage

Coping-saw blades

Cabinet-pull hole jigs, extra set of electric drills

85 in.

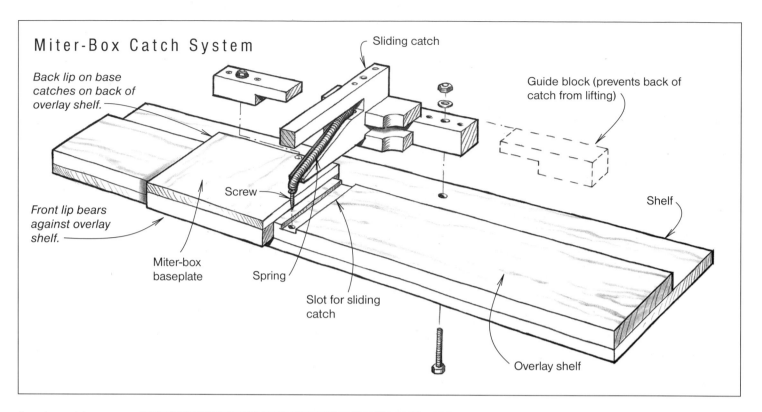

Miter-Box Catch System

Sliding catch

Back lip on base catches on back of overlay shelf.

Guide block (prevents back of catch from lifting)

Screw

Front lip bears against overlay shelf.

Miter-box baseplate

Spring

Shelf

Slot for sliding catch

Overlay shelf

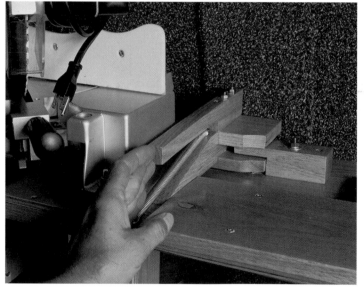

A spring catch closes over the baseplate of the miter saw. When the catch is pushed open, the saw is released.

Again with efficiency in mind, the rolling miter box stand/supplies tote set to the far left of the lower shelf does not need a bungee cord at all to be secured in place. Instead, it is locked in place by a wood block mounted to the underside front edge of the overlying shelf and by the presence of the sanding tote/stepstool to its right.

To secure the two miter boxes to the upper shelves, Hillenburg devised a spring-loaded wooden catch mechanism. Working in conjunction with a baseplate fitted to the bottom of the saws, the mechanism is self-activating: You place the miter box on the shelf and push it back against the catch until it allows the back runner of the baseplate to drop into a receiving notch on the shelf. The catch

then springs forward, locking down the baseplate. To remove the tool, you push back on the catch's lever arm and lift the baseplate up and off the shelf.

Hillenburg also designed a self-activating catch to hold and lock the 78-in. level in place against the curved part of the roof of the van (see the top photo on the facing page). To engage the catch, you push the level against the spring-loaded capture pocket until the far end of the level clears and then enters its holding pocket. To remove the level, you again push against the spring in the capture pocket until you can swing the far end clear of its holder.

On the passenger side of the van, Hillenburg uses the shelving to store supplies, a couple of power tools in their metal cases and two removable totes. One of the totes carries a selection of shim stock while the other carries a variety of hand power tools. Mounted above the shelves are a fire extinguisher, another spring-loaded level holder (for a 48-in. level) and a handsaw.

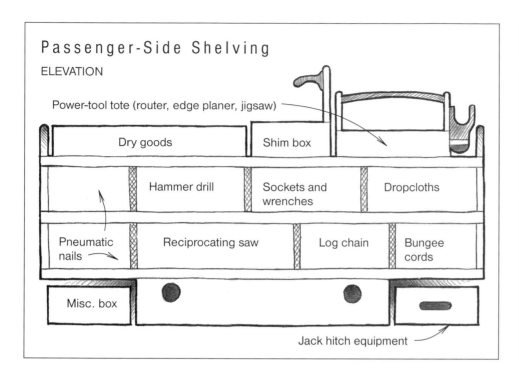

Passenger-Side Shelving
ELEVATION

Power-tool tote (router, edge planer, jigsaw)

Dry goods	Shim box

	Hammer drill	Sockets and wrenches	Dropcloths

Pneumatic nails	Reciprocating saw	Log chain	Bungee cords

Misc. box			

Jack hitch equipment

Task-Specific Totes

At the heart of Hillenburg's rolling toolbox is the assortment of multi-purpose totes stored on the sides of the van. Hillenburg designed each of these totes with four criteria in mind: First, each tote would have to organize and contain a certain logical grouping of tools or supplies. Second, the totes had to be easy to carry. Third, whenever possible, the totes needed to be multi-functional, serving as a tool stand, stepstool or a rolling seat when not being used as a toolbox. And finally, every tote would have to be sized and shaped to fit snugly into a specific compartment or shelf unit along the van's walls—when all the totes were set in their niches, they would hold each other tightly in place while consuming a minimum of room.

SANDING TOTE/ STEPSTOOL

The combination sanding tote/stepstool carries three power sanders: a ¼-sheet palm sander, a half-sheet sander, and a 3-in. by 21-in. belt sander. Built in

essentially the same way as the rolling miter-box stand, this tote also has pigeonholes to hold sandpaper. Blocks attached to the shelf edge with self-closing cabinet hinges and inscribed with the sandpaper's grit number hold precut sheets or sanding belts in place. To make sure that the tote would support a carpenter fully loaded with tools, Hillenburg doubled the angle braces supporting the top, just as he did

on the miter-box stand. A hand hole provides a carry point. Finally, notice the leather strips wrapped over the tote's feet—they help keep the tote from slipping on or damaging finished floors.

ROLLING MITER-BOX STAND

Hillenburg built his rolling stand (and all the other totes shown here) of ¾-in. oak plywood, joining the pieces with glue

The sanding tote (left) holds three sanders and does double duty as a stepstool.

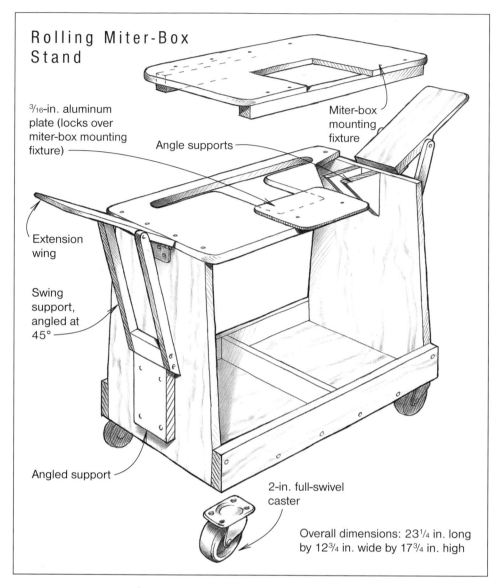

Rolling Miter-Box Stand

3/16-in. aluminum plate (locks over miter-box mounting fixture)

Angle supports

Miter-box mounting fixture

Extension wing

Swing support, angled at 45°

Angled support

2-in. full-swivel caster

Overall dimensions: 23¼ in. long by 12¾ in. wide by 17¾ in. high

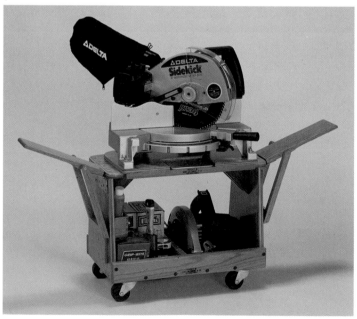

The rolling miter-box stand also carries a trim saw and finish materials.

and square-drive screws. It was designed to transport a miter box from room to room for cutting finish work. Hillenburg added fold-away extension wings (which support boards extending off either end of the miter-saw table) and a special lock-down system to capture the saw's mounting plate. A double pair of angle supports makes the stool rigid and keeps the top from flexing under the saw during use. Hillenburg uses the floor of the tote to carry another trim saw and a selection of finish materials. He chose these items for this tote because, like the miter saw, they are often needed to install finish work.

CORDLESS-DRILL TOTE

The curved-handle cordless-drill tote (see the photo at top left on the facing page) carries two cordless drills, along with their battery charger and several extra batteries. The handles of the drills are stored upright for easy access. Notice how the charger's cord feeds through a hole in the divider into the adjoining open compartment—a quick place to stuff the cord at the end of the day. Leather strips attached to the bottom of the tote (as on all the other non-wheeled totes) prevent it from scratching a finished floor or counter surface.

TRIM-TOOL TOTE

Hillenburg designed the trim-tool tote (see the photo at top right on the facing page) to accommodate most of the tools and supplies needed to install casing stock. Along with a pair of pneumatic nailers to punch in the casing fasteners, the tote carries the following items: pneumatic nails, a block plane to trim the joints, sandpaper to smooth them, adhesives and caulk, a removable tote for cans of putty, and a putty knife. Notice

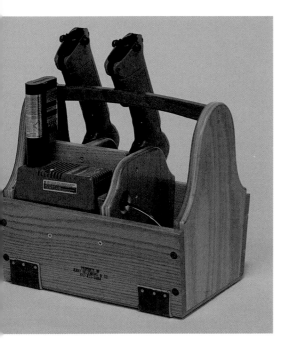

The cordless-drill tote (above) holds two drills, a battery charger and extra batteries.

The trim-tool tote carries tools and supplies needed to install casings. It is shown here in the working position, with the compartment holding the nailers extended upwards. When the tote is stored in the van, the compartment slides down to the bottom of the slots.

The shim box (below) contains materials used for hanging doors.

the finger-jointed box next to the putty tote on the bottom shelf—its only function is to catch the ooze-out from the caulking gun.

Hillenburg wanted to make the stand tall enough so he wouldn't have to crouch when removing or replacing the heavy nail guns, but he soon discovered this height would make the tote hard to fit in the van. His solution was to make the compartment supporting the guns collapse into the stand on a simple pin and slot system. This not only reduced the height of the tote so it would fit under the storage shelf, but also lowered the unit's center of gravity, making it more stable. Hillenburg carries the stand onto the site in the collapsed mode, slinging the leather carry strap over his shoulder.

SHIM BOX

The shim box (see the photo at right) contains a selection of shim materials used specifically in the hanging of entry and interior doors. The front two compartments contain plywood blocking squares while the two in back hold tapered shim stock. The comfortable carry handle is shaped from walnut, and the side compartment holds the long pneumatic nails used for setting the door jambs to the studs through the shims or blocking.

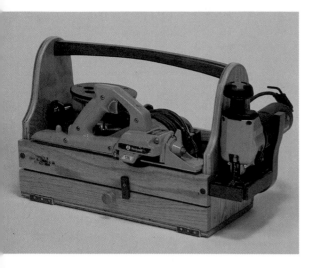

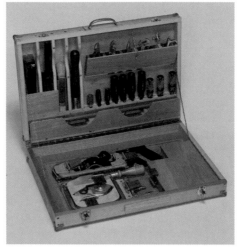

The power-tool tote carries a router, an edge planer and a jigsaw.

The briefcase holds small hand tools, along with drill bits and drivers.

POWER-TOOL TOTE

The curved-handle, open shoulder power-tool tote (see the photo at far left) was designed to carry what are probably the three most frequently used power tools in Hillenburg's repertoire: a router, an edge planer and a jigsaw. In the drawer, which is secured with a walnut turn knob, are router bits, jigsaw blades and wrenches for all three tools. Though the tote looks unbalanced with the outboard-mounted jigsaw, the heavy router brings the balance point near to the center of the handle's curve.

HAND-TOOL BRIEFCASE

Hillenburg built a briefcase-like tool tote (see the photo at left) to carry hand tools and small accessories, such as twist drills and screwdriver bits. Instead of the ¾-in. oak plywood used in all the other totes, he chose instead to use solid poplar and ½-in. plywood on the outside, and poplar and ¼-in. birch plywood on the interior of this tote. These materials are lighter in weight than the oak plywood, and because they are thinner they allow more room in the case for storage. The tote is joined with glue and screws. Self-closing cabinet-door hinges hold several hand tools in place and provide a catch for a lid that covers an interior storage compartment. In the van, the case is strapped against the passenger side shelves, and is among the first items to be taken out at the site.

The Partition Wall

Separating the driver's compartment from the cargo area is a set of modular shelving units filled from top to bottom with solid-oak finger-jointed storage bins. On the oak lipping that prevents the bins from sliding out, brass labels identify the contents of each bin. Though securely anchored to the framework of the van's

Partition-Wall Elevation

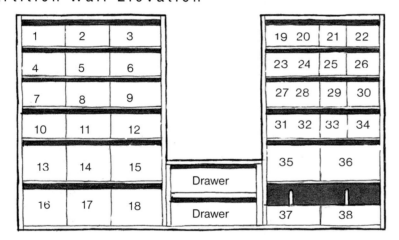

1. 8d box nails
2. 12d box nails
3. 12d finish nails
4. Plastic concrete anchors
5. Brads
6. Field-joint bolts
7. 1½-in. ring-shank nails
8. Miscellaneous cabinet hinges
9. Hinge jigs
10. Electrical repair equipment
11. Miscellaneous tools
12. First-aid kit
13. Bypass-door guides
14. Outside corners (for toe-kick ends)
15. Tissue rollers
16. Miscellaneous hardware
17. Closet sockets
18. Strike plates
19. Hinge screws
20. Piano-hinge screws, ¾-in. pan-head screws

21. Miscellaneous flat-head screws
22. Finishing washers, 1-in. flat-head screws
23. Pilaster clips
24. Shelf supports, clips
25. Felt pads, safety chain
26. Magnetic catches, name tags
27. Oak plugs
28. Birch plugs
29. Miscellaneous 8/32 screws
30. 1-in. 8/32 screws
31. 1¼-in. 8/32 screws
32. 1½-in. 8/32 screws
33. 1¾-in. 8/32 screws
34. Drills and bits
35. Plungers
36. Door stops
37. Phillips screws
38. ½-in. Quadrex screws

body frame, the modules can be removed from the van for ease of initial installation and to allow eventual modification or repair work. Handled totes filled with commonly used installation and assembly screws are stored on the lowest shelf; these are usually taken onto the site with the rest of the tools at the beginning of the workday. The center drawers open to either side—one holds CDs while the other serves as a catch-all junk drawer. Above the modules, a pipe clamp is mounted on a pair of blocks, and the handle of a floor broom is inserted behind the modules' bottom support.

The Driver's Compartment

As Hillenburg got into designing and building these storage systems, he saw little reason to stop with the cargo area of the van—so he continued on into the driver's compartment. Using the same materials and construction techniques as he used on the totes, he built a center console (see the photo above right), fitting it with small drawers and bins to contain writing supplies and CDs as well as holders for cups and his cellular phone. Under the console lurks the speaker system for his 400-watt stereo system, as well as a removable waste basket (hidden under the cooler). To the roof of the cabin he attached a shallow cabinet for holding notebooks and other paperwork (a snap-on strap holds them in place), and a paper-towel holder that can be reached from either the front or the back of the van.

Though some storage capacity in the partition wall was sacrificed to the opening for the console, two significant benefits more than make up for the loss: First, the opening allows the driver to see

The central console, shown here removed from the vehicle, holds writing supplies, CDs and other amenities.

The driver's compartment has been as painstakingly fitted for storage with as much care as the rear of the van.

directly behind the vehicle using the interior rear-view mirror—a big plus for safety. And second, with the console removed, molding stock up to 12 ft. long can be carried completely within the vehicle.

Hillenburg has used the van/toolbox for literally hundreds of trips to job sites, yet he never ceases to be amazed and delighted by how well it works for him. I'm not surprised—I too would quickly grow to love any toolbox that carried my tools with such good care and

organization—and featured a built-in 400-watt stereo system. My only question for Jerry Hillenburg is this: How can you tear yourself away from your toolbox long enough to get any work done?

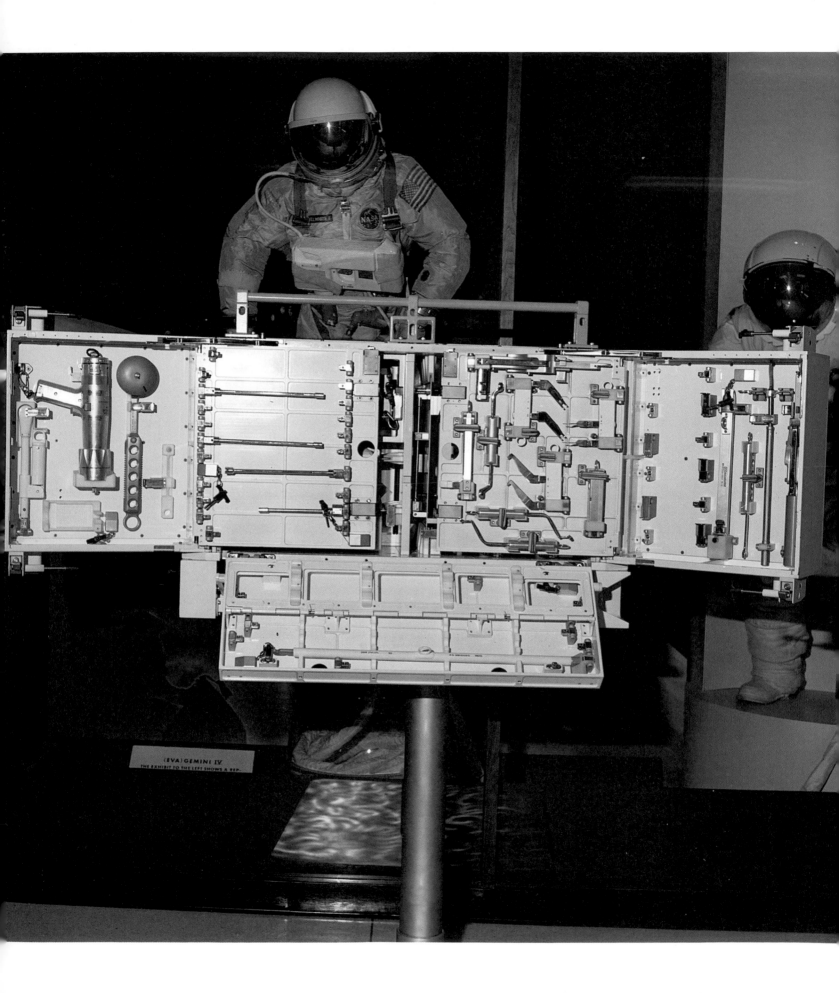

(EVA) GEMINI Ⅳ
THE EXHIBIT TO THE LEFT SHOWS A REP.

EPILOG

As toolboxes leave the bonds of earth in company with the space-tradespeople who will work out of them, perhaps a new golden age of tool chests will dawn. For once again there may arise a group of workers who will find themselves totally dependent on a precious collection of hand tools. Indeed, a misplaced tool might all too easily be lost to the void of space, not only risking the success of a mission but possibly endangering a space worker's life.

This may be reaching a bit, but perhaps the tradespeople of our extraterrestrial future will once again come to cherish their tools enough to find the motivation to build magnificent—as well as technically advanced—toolboxes in which to house and protect them. If they build them with exceptional workmanship and a joyful expression of beauty, a new golden age of the toolbox may yet find its place among the stars. After all, a toolbox can contain much more than just a collection of tools. It can carry into the future the honor of those people who, throughout history, have won their daily bread through the good works of their hands.

This highly sophisticated aluminum tool box carried into space the tools used to repair the Hubble Space Telescope. Lacking the help of gravity, each tool was held to the box in at least two places, or captured by a single powerful snap catch. The box itself was secured shut by a four-point latching system, engineered to withstand the high G-forces of an orbital launch. The three full-length handles (two hidden behind the doors) were installed not so much to help the astronauts carry the box (which weighs nothing in space) but to provide grips for pulling themselves over to where the tools are.

INDEX

EDITOR: Laura Tringali

DESIGNER/LAYOUT ARTIST: Jodie Delohery

ILLUSTRATOR: Michael Gellatly

COPY EDITOR: Ruth Dobsevage

ART ASSISTANT: Amy L. Bernard

TYPEFACE: Berling

PAPER: Warren Patina Matte, 80 lb., neutral pH

PRINTER: Quebecor Printing, Kingsport, Tennessee